Empathy Beyond US Borders

How do middle-class Americans become aware of distant social problems and act against them? US colleges, congregations, and seminaries increasingly promote immersion travel as a way to bridge global distance, produce empathy, and increase global awareness. But does it? Drawing from a mixed methods study of a progressive, religious immersion travel organization at the US-Mexico border, *Empathy Beyond US Borders* provides a broad sociological context for the rise of immersion travel as a form of transnational civic engagement. Gary J. Adler, Jr. follows alongside immersion travelers as they meet undocumented immigrants, walk desert trails, and witness deportations. His close observations combine with interviews and surveys to evaluate the potential of this civic action, while developing theory about culture, empathy, and progressive religion in transnational civic life. This timely book describes the moralization of travel, the organizational challenges of transnational engagement, and the difficulty of feeling transformed but not knowing how to help.

GARY J. ADLER, JR. is Assistant Professor of Sociology at The Pennsylvania State University. His research on culture, organizations, and religion has been published in numerous journals, including *Social Problems*, *Social Science and Medicine*, and *Journal for the Scientific Study of Religion*. He was the founding Director of Research for the Institute for Advanced Catholic Studies at the University of Southern California. He is the editor of *Secularism, Catholicism, and the Future of Public Life* (2015) and coeditor of a volume on Catholic parishes: *American Parishes: Remaking Local Catholicism*, which will be published in 2019.

Cambridge Studies in Social Theory, Religion, and Politics

Editors

David E. Campbell, University of Notre Dame
Anna M. Grzymala-Busse, Stanford University
Kenneth D. Wald, University of Florida
Richard L. Wood, University of New Mexico

Founding Editor

David C. Leege, University of Notre Dame

In societies around the world, dynamic changes are occurring at the intersection of religion and politics. In some settings, these changes are driven by internal shifts within religions; in others, by shifting political structures, institutional contexts, or by war or other upheavals. Cambridge Studies in Social Theory, Religion, and Politics publishes books that seek to understand and explain these changes to a wide audience, drawing on insight from social theory and original empirical analysis. We welcome work built on strong theoretical framing, careful research design, and rigorous methods using any social scientific method(s) appropriate to the study. The series examines the relationship of religion and politics broadly understood, including directly political behavior, action in civil society and in the mediating institutions that undergird politics, and the ways religion shapes the cultural dynamics underlying political and civil society.

Mikhail A. Alexseev and Sufian N. Zhemukhov, *Mass Religious Ritual and Intergroup Tolerance: The Muslim Pilgrims' Paradox*

Luke Bretherton, *Resurrecting Democracy: Faith, Citizenship, and the Politics of a Common Life*

David E. Campbell, John C. Green, and J. Quin Monson, *Seeking the Promised Land: Mormons and American Politics*

Ryan L. Claassen, *Godless Democrats and Pious Republicans? Party Activists, Party Capture, and the "God Gap"*

Darren W. Davis and Donald Pope-Davis, *Perseverance in the Parish?: Religious Attitudes from a Black Catholic Perspective.*

Paul A. Djupe and Christopher P. Gilbert, *The Political Influence of Churches*

Joel S. Fetzer and J. Christopher Soper, *Muslims and the State in Britain, France, and Germany*

François Foret, *Religion and Politics in the European Union: The Secular Canopy*

Jonathan Fox, *A World Survey of Religion and the State*

Jonathan Fox, *Political Secularism, Religion, and the State: A Time Series Analysis of Worldwide Data*

Anthony Gill, *The Political Origins of Religious Liberty*

Brian J. Grim and Roger Finke, *The Price of Freedom Denied: Religious Persecution and Conflict in the Twenty-First Century*

Kees van Kersbergen and Philip Manow, editors, *Religion, Class Coalitions, and Welfare States*

Mirjam Kunkler, John Madeley, and Shylashri Shankar, *A Secular Age beyond the West: Religion, Law and the State in Asia, the Middle East and North Africa*

Karrie J. Koesel, *Religion and Authoritarianism: Cooperation, Conflict, and the Consequences*

(continues after index...)

Empathy Beyond US Borders

The Challenges of Transnational Civic Engagement

GARY J. ADLER, JR.

The Pennsylvania State University

CAMBRIDGE
UNIVERSITY PRESS

University Printing House, Cambridge CB2 8BS, United Kingdom

One Liberty Plaza, 20th Floor, New York, NY 10006, USA

477 Williamstown Road, Port Melbourne, VIC 3207, Australia

314–321, 3rd Floor, Plot 3, Splendor Forum, Jasola District Centre, New Delhi – 110025, India

79 Anson Road, #06–04/06, Singapore 079906

Cambridge University Press is part of the University of Cambridge.

It furthers the University's mission by disseminating knowledge in the pursuit of education, learning, and research at the highest international levels of excellence.

www.cambridge.org
Information on this title: www.cambridge.org/9781108474566
DOI: 10.1017/9781108605571

© Gary J. Adler, Jr. 2019

First published 2019

Printed and bound in Great Britain by Clays Ltd, Elcograf S.p.A.

A catalogue record for this publication is available from the British Library.

Library of Congress Cataloging-in-Publication Data
NAMES: Adler, Gary, 1975– author.
TITLE: Empathy beyond US borders : the challenges of transnational civic engagement / Gary Adler, Pennsylvania State University.
OTHER TITLES: Empathy beyiond United States borders
DESCRIPTION: Cambridge, United Kingdom ; New York, NY, USA : Cambridge University Press, [2019] | Series: Cambridge studies in social theory, religion, and politics | Includes bibliographical references and index.
IDENTIFIERS: LCCN 2018051441 | ISBN 9781108474566 (hardback : alk. paper) | ISBN 9781108464987 (pbk. : alk. paper)
SUBJECTS: LCSH: Volunteer tourism. | Foreign study. | International travel–Social aspects. | Americans–Foreign countries. | Volunteer workers in social services. | BorderLinks (Program)
CLASSIFICATION: LCC G156.5.V64 A45 2019 | DDC 361.3/7–dc23
LC record available at https://lccn.loc.gov/2018051441

ISBN 978-1-108-47456-6 Hardback

For Selena and Samuel,
my two brightest "California stars."

Contents

Figures

Tables

Preface: Are You Ready to Be Transformed?

I recently had the chance to see Bruce Springsteen and the E Street Band in concert. That night, he walked onto the stage, said "Hello," then growled, with a sly grin: "Are you ready to be transformed?" Across the crowd, thousands yelled – screamed – "Yes!" Three and a half hours later many of us seemed to feel transformed from this musical immersion. Despite how impossibly naive this sounds, my life felt focused and reenergized. I promised myself that I would carry the feeling and authenticity beyond the moment. I suspect thousands of fellow hip-shakers felt similarly. I suspect, too, that you, the reader, may have had a similar experience; perhaps not Springsteen, but rather with Alicia Keys, Lady Antebellum, Drake, U2, a Broadway show, or the latest K-Pop band instead. But what do I – you – have to show for our moments of feeling transformed? I would be hard-pressed to point to anything that was different about my beliefs, behaviors, or commitments as a result of that concert. It was only a concert, after all, so who cares?

But what if, instead of a concert, the transformative experience was a trip to meet with distant others suffering from living amid extreme inequality, economic instability, structural violence, or political failure? How, if at all, might you or I be changed? What could we do with our new awareness? What if our lives had nothing to show for it?

These are the questions that are confronted by an increasing number of people in the United States as they travel abroad to broaden their horizons, meet distant others, and become global citizens. Relatively unnoticed beside the large presence of professionalized humanitarian organizations that operate around the globe, an array of small nongovernmental organizations (NGOs) produce transnational engagement and personalize global civic life for millions of travelers each year. The names for these organized attempts at global civic engagement have proliferated in recent decades: short-term mission trips, alternative spring breaks, solidarity trips, short-term study abroad, alternative tourism, justice tourism, volunteer vacations, and more. I call them all immersion trips.

Immersion trips are a pragmatic way for congregations, colleges, and other civic organizations in the Unites States to activate ideals of being involved, being aware, and doing good. The same sort of organizations that fostered increased *domestic* civic engagement in the 1990s now promote a wave of direct, civic engagement by Americans with "the globe." Make no mistake: traveling to engage with suffering *somewhere* in the globe has become a mark of cosmopolitan concern and civic character.

Immersion travel is posed as a means to an ideal civic end, but, as this book will explore, it is a complicated means to unclear, hoped-for ends. Along the way, we will uncover the invisible organizational work that enables transnational civic engagement, pull apart the cultural processes that structure travel, catalogue the emotions that emerge, trace the influence of progressive religion in global engagement, and observe earnest but problematic attempts by travelers to produce personal connections with suffering others.

Maybe you have been on an immersion trip. Or, maybe you had a travel experience like this and came back wondering why others made such a big deal of their own experience. Maybe you have wondered about the bubbling group of excited travelers with matching T-shirts proclaiming "Mission to Mexico" that you once passed in the airport. Or, maybe you have worried whether your school, congregation, or college should spend so much time and money to send privileged people so far away when they could just as easily learn about global problems at home, sending the monetary savings abroad as donations. Or, maybe you have wondered whether this phenomenon is "good" for international communities, for individual travelers, or for global justice writ large. I invite all of these potential readers. For all, this book looks at immersion travel as the latest imperfect practice in a centuries-long attempt by people and organizations in privileged, Western countries to understand and address distant suffering.

Acknowledgments

The research behind this book would have been impossible without the advice and encouragement of my dissertation committee at the University of Arizona. I tried out the idea for this research as part of a graduate course with Jeff Sallaz and my familiarity with civic action at the US-Mexico border grew from research work with Kraig Beyerlein. Joseph Galaskiewicz encouraged me to see the distinct organizational processes involved. Ronald Breiger indulged my initial attempts to make sense of my extensive data, pointing me toward the fundamental cultural processes at play.

BorderLinks, the thirty-year-old immersion trip producer located in Tucson, Arizona, which this book revolves around, was gracious in providing access to its space, participants, staff, and immersion trips. The director of BorderLinks at the time, Delle McCormick, was extremely helpful in supporting the project. The staff, who remain anonymous throughout, were patient with my intrusion into their lives. I was welcomed and treated with respect by the groups and travelers on the six immersion trips that I joined. Some travelers have provided comments that have strengthened my thinking. One traveler who spent seven days with me – and joined me in scrounging for coffee at every turn on the trip – gave me what I consider the highest compliment. In saying goodbye, he said, "I now know what motivates sociologists: conscience and caffeine." The latter has certainly motivated my writing; I can only hope my contribution to his self-understanding and the sociological understanding of transnational civic engagement reflects the former.

For a portion of my research time, I lived 500 miles away from Tucson. Many people supported my return trips for fieldwork. Thanks are due to

Dan Martinez, Jessica Hamar Martinez, Garrett Schneider, A. Joseph West, Lorenzo Gamboa, and Sister/Dr. Katie Hoegeman for the assistance they provided in this regard. Throughout the project, I received invaluable feedback about how to sharpen my questions, to understand my data, and to tell the story of immersion travel in a way that captured the feel of participants but also revealed underlying social mechanisms. Those who have provided helpful comments at various stages include Nancy Ammerman, Mary Jo Bane, Kelly Bergstrand, Kelly Bohrer, Tricia Bruce, Matt Carnes, S.J., Nina Eliasoph, John Evans, Michael Evans, Roger Finke, Richard Flory, Kim Greenwell, Janet "Lucie" Luce, Donald Miller, Brad Nabors, Steven Offutt, Susan Fitzpatrick-Behrens, Brady Potts, Joel Robbins, Rebecca Sager, and Grace Yukich. Jerome Baggett, Caroline Lee, Paul Lichterman, John McCarthy, and three anonymous reviewers read and provided feedback on large portions of the manuscript. Richard Wood, an early pioneer in tracing religious processes in progressive social action, provided invaluable encouragement and advice for my ideas. I thank him, his fellow series editors, and Sarah Doskow at Cambridge University Press for seeing a place for this book.

A special thanks to Ignacio Evangelista and Murphy Woodhouse, whose photos of Nogales and the Sonoran Desert illuminate this book.

This project was greatly enhanced by a dissertation fellowship from the Louisville Institute. Additional research funding came from the Society for the Scientific Study of Religion, the Association for the Sociology of Religion, the University of Arizona Social and Behavioral Science Research Institute, the Institute for Advanced Catholic Studies at the University of Southern California, and my home department of Sociology and Criminology at the The Pennsylvania State University (PSU). I greatly benefitted from a writing fellowship given by the Rock Ethics Institute at PSU, as well as the insight into empathy provided by Daryl Cameron as part of that fellowship. Portions of this work received feedback from presentations at the American Sociological Association, the Society for the Scientific Study of Religion, the Association for the Sociology of Religion, UC-San Diego, Loyola Marymount University, Saint Alban's College, the Catholic University of Leuven, Belgium, and the Louisville Institute. Some of Chapter 3 previously appeared as "'Neutral' Talk, Conscience, and Political Legitimacy" in *Religion and Progressive Activism: New Stories about Faith and Politics*, edited by Todd N. Fuist, Ruth Braunstein, and Rhys H. Williams (New York University Press, 2017).

Living in Arizona during the mid-2000s, less than seventy miles from the US-Mexico border, exposed me to the inhumanity of failing political policies, the brute power of economic forces, the din of nativism, and the inspiring work of many for the just treatment of immigrants and the descendants of immigrants. Immigration continues to be a symbolic battleground with real costs in US history. One of the puzzles I have tried to understand through this project is what people with resources, voice, and conscience do once they are aware. This research was part of my answer to that puzzle. I dedicate this to all those who refuse to turn their eyes, bodies, and imaginations away from suffering but struggle with knowing what to do. A model in my life for how to do this with integrity has been my fabulous wife, Selena E. Ortiz, PhD. The challenging conversations with her and the personal experiences she has shared with me have sustained my work, my curiosity, and my hope.

I

From Distance to Concern

> When confronted with suffering all moral demands converge on the single imperative of action. . . . But what form can this commitment take when those called upon to act are thousands of miles away from the person suffering?[1]

When the travelers from Eastern College landed at the Tucson International Airport in 2009, seventy miles north of the US-Mexico border, months of meetings and fundraising drives had finally come to fruition. These eight students and two professors had traveled two thousand miles to begin a weeklong immersion trip focused on undocumented immigration.

Immigration, especially undocumented immigration, had once again become a prominent public topic. In the previous year, more than 150 dead bodies of immigrants were found in this section of the US-Mexico border.[2] Drug-related violence in border cities was increasingly in the news. One student's first question to me as I introduced myself at the luggage carousel to join the group was, "Have you heard of the beheadings?," a reference to the mysterious, violent deaths of women in Juarez, Mexico.

[1] Luc Boltanksi, *Distant Suffering: Morality, Media, and Politics*, trans. Graham Burchell (New York: Cambridge University Press, 1999 [1993]), p. xv.
[2] Daniel E. Martinez et al., "Structural Violence and Migrant Deaths in Southern Arizona: Data from the Pima County Office of the Medical Examiner, 1990–2013," *Journal on Migration and Human Security* 2, 4 (2014).

This small group had come to Tucson to travel through BorderLinks, a faith-inspired organization with roots to the 1980s Sanctuary movement. Over twenty-five years, BorderLinks had become well known to colleges, universities, churches, and seminaries for producing a progressive, religious form of immersion travel. In a nonpartisan, nondogmatic tone, BorderLinks' goal was to "raise awareness" and "inspire action" about undocumented immigration for about a thousand such travelers a year. In the week I spent with Eastern College, I rode for hours with travelers crammed into the back of a van on the way to meetings with local clergy, discussions with US border protection officials, and visits with undocumented migrants. One night, we divided into pairs to eat, talk, and stay with a Mexican family in a border town. On another day, we walked in the remote desert along trails where immigrants crossed the forbidding desert. In formal reflections and informal conversations, the group discussed the discomfort of hearing immigrants' problems that they could not immediately resolve; their admiration for the activists they met; their opinions of federal agencies that arrested immigrants; and the urgent sense of wanting to "do something" when they returned home, far from the borderlands.

Six months later, I spoke with the travelers, now returned to their normal lives. During an interview with the group's leader, she told me that she "never expected it [the trip] to be so transformative" for her or the students. One of her students explained to me that the trip was "emotionally wrenching" and gave her "a new level of personal experience with the [immigration] issue." Another student recounted his "haunting experience" of walking in the desert and being "in the tracks of people" trying to cross into the United States. He commented,

I really felt like I had been through a very transformative experience. . . . I think it was transformative in the fact that I feel like I went through a significant experience in my week there. I felt like my eyes were opened to a lot of different things that I had never really been exposed to before.

To the ears of civil society organizations like BorderLinks that organize immersion travel and those that send travelers to be immersed, these sentiments are evidence of the power of using travel to generate moral concern for distant injustice. They suggest that encounters with distant suffering can lead to empathy, that Americans' circles of moral concern can expand to be cosmopolitan in their reach, and that spiritually meaningful experiences can lead to new social commitments.

But alongside these feelings of connection and transformation, my travel with BorderLinks revealed other pieces of evidence that call into question comfortable assumptions about what this type of transnational engagement accomplishes. Many BorderLinks travelers had been progressive and proimmigrant to begin with, making it unclear what such travel was meant to achieve. Direct interactions with immigrants often went poorly, challenging an ideal of personalized connection. Upon returning home, travelers struggled – sometimes intensely – with not knowing how to turn their sense of transformation into action back at their churches and colleges. As Kate, a seminary student, explained with an air of frustration many months after her immersion trip,

[I'm] trying to see how all this knowledge is going to work into my ministry and what God is calling me to do. I don't know what that looks like. . . . [I've been] asking God to show me how my concern for the border and for Hispanic immigrants can work. . . . It's been hard to live up to how I felt like I needed to change my life.

These problematic interactions, confusing feelings, and unclear futures are the other side of immersion travel. But far from being unique to immersion travel, they evoke the ethical and theoretical quandaries that have long characterized a prominent problem of modernity: awareness of suffering at a distance and the difficulty of addressing it by residents of the "developed" West and the Global North. Immersion travel like that offered by BorderLinks has provided the opportunity for many travelers to be firsthand witnesses to what Luc Boltanski calls "distant suffering": the social problems and circumstances of people separated by physical, social, and cultural distance.[3] For much of the twentieth century, middle-class Americans addressed distant suffering primarily through supporting large, specialized organizations that did work "over there." Today, through immersion travel, an expanding portion of middle-class America personally witnesses and directly engages distant social problems and suffering. The face-to-face relationship pattern so often associated with the *absence* of distance in social relations is increasingly promoted as an effective way to motivate concern *across* great distance. This is a striking

---

[3] Boltanski, *Distant Suffering*. Western modernity has tended to treat suffering as a social fact, something that is morally repulsive, caused by nondivine forces, and able to be changed. See Iain Wilkinson and Arthur Kleinman, *A Passion for Society: How We Think about Human Suffering* (Berkeley: University of California Press, 2016).

historical shift in the way Americans can engage with humanitarian and social problems outside the United States.

But, as the epigraph that begins this chapter suggests, discovering distant suffering and acting against it are not one and the same. The space between concern and action involves complex social processes of interaction, interpretation, and evaluation. The moral resonance of distant suffering, as well as the willingness to act, are social accomplishments, not inevitable outcomes. This book illuminates these organizational, cultural, and religious aspects of transnational civic engagement by investigating the assumed possibilities and invisible problems of a new way to enact distant concern: immersion travel.

THE REACH OF IMMERSION TRAVEL

If your college promotes "alternative spring breaks" to foreign countries, if your congregation sponsors short-term mission trips, if your university has doubled down on short-term study abroad, or if you know someone who was changed by a similar trip, then you have witnessed the wide-ranging emergence of immersion travel.[4] Travel organized by small groups, often outside the structures of international nongovernmental organizations (INGOs), is used as a way to discover distant social suffering and to accomplish civic and political ends. Diverse immersion travelers distribute charitable aid, create transnational political identity, support distant advocacy campaigns, provide medical care, share religious faith, and support alternative trade networks. While the exact scope of immersion travel is difficult to pin down given its heterogeneity, a few statistics help to show the embrace of immersion travel by mainstream civic organizations in the United States, as well as

---

[4] Brian Howell, *Short-Term Mission: An Ethnography of Christian Travel Narrative and Experience* (Downers Grove, IL: IVP Academic, 2012); Shaul Kelner, *Tours That Bind: Diaspora, Pilgrimage, and Israeli Birthright Tourism* (New York: New York University Press, 2010); Sally Brown and Alastair M. Morrison, "Expanding Volunteer Vacation Participation: An Exploratory Study on the Mini-Mission Concept," *Tourism Recreation Research* 28, 3 (2003); Nancy Gard McGehee, "Alternative Tourism and Social Movements," *Annals of Tourism Research* 29, 1 (2002); Robert J. Priest and Joseph Paul Priest, "'They See Everything, and Understand Nothing' Short-Term Mission and Service Learning," *Missiology: An International Review* 36, 1 (2008); Jill Piacitelli et al., "Alternative Break Programs: From Isolated Enthusiasm to Best Practices: The Haiti Compact," *Journal of Higher Education Outreach and Engagement* 17, 2 (2013); Kevin J. Sykes, "Short-Term Medical Service Trips: A Systematic Review of the Evidence," *American Journal of Public Health* 104, 7 (2014).

the number of people with the opportunity to directly engage foreign communities through such travel.

In 2012, more than one-quarter (27 percent) of all religious congregations in the United States reported organizing an international trip in the previous year to provide aid to those in need.[5] That translates to roughly 100,000 congregations *a year*. Over the last three decades, the popularity of these short-term mission trips among religious organizations drastically increased.[6] By the mid-2000s, more than 1.5 million US church-going adults were traveling overseas each year with their religious congregations.[7]

Immersion travel has also increased in popularity among US-based civic organizations more generally. Allison Schnable reports that "the number of new American aid organizations registering annually with the IRS quadrupled from 2000 to 2010, compared with only 19 percent growth for other 501(c)3s."[8] Many of these organizations use travel to facilitate direct connections between people in the United States and foreign communities, thereby supporting work-camps, educational projects, and other forms of short-term civic service.[9] According to the Current Population Survey, a monthly survey of households conducted by the United States Census Bureau, about half a million "individuals in the United States reported volunteering each year internationally from 2004 to 2014" for time periods of less than a month.[10] Scholars of tourism have documented a similar trend over the last twenty years, with greatly increased interest in "volunteer tourism" among global travelers, leading to a rise in tourism organizations that facilitate volunteer

---

[5] Gary J. Adler Jr. and Andrea L. Ruiz, "The Immigrant Effect: Short-Term Mission Travel as Transnational Civic Remittance," *Sociology of Religion* 79, 3 (2018).

[6] LiErin Probasco, "Giving Time, Not Money: Long-Term Impacts of Short-Term Mission Trips," *Missiology: An International Review* 41, 2 (2013); Priest and Priest, "'They See Everything, and Understand Nothing' Short-Term Mission and Service Learning."

[7] Robert Wuthnow, *Boundless Faith: The Global Outreach of American Churches* (Berkeley: University of California Press, 2009).

[8] Allison Schnable, "New American Relief and Development Organizations: Voluntarizing Global Aid," *Social Problems* 62, 2 (2015), p. 311.

[9] Amanda Moore McBride et al., "Civic Service Worldwide: Defining a Field, Building a Knowledge Base," *Nonprofit and Voluntary Sector Quarterly* 33, 4 Supplemental (2004); Margaret Sherrard Sherraden et al., "The Forms and Structure of International Voluntary Service," *Voluntas: International Journal of Voluntary and Nonprofit Organizations* 17, 2 (2006).

[10] Benjamin J. Lough, "A Decade of International Volunteering from the United States, 2004 to 2014," (Saint Louis, MO: Center for Social Development, Washington University, 2015), p. 1.

experiences, environmental projects, and cultural exchange.[11] As these examples show, many organizations promote short-term, face-to-face, pragmatic involvement beyond the United States, leading to a large, but decentralized, mobilization of transnational civic engagement.

This form of engagement has been accompanied by new visions of service and citizenship. One root of these visions came from the rapid embrace of experiential and transformative learning theory among US higher education institutions since the 1980s.[12] As theorists connected a processual understanding of learning with a humanistic vision of learners' social obligations, educators increasingly promoted new pedagogies beyond the traditional curricula, such as service-learning and community-based learning.[13] With roots to William James, John Dewey, and Maria Montessori, experiential learning advocated for using new experience as an input into "a process of learning that questions preconceptions of direct experience ... and extracts the correct lessons from the consequences of action."[14]

The rise in experiential learning dovetailed with the 1990s lionization of civil society and voluntary participation in the wake of the Soviet Union's collapse.[15] That historical moment saw reawakened philosophical interest in cosmopolitanism and social interest in global connectivity.[16] The curricular and cocurricular offerings of secondary and tertiary

[11] Stephen Wearing, *Volunteer Tourism: Experiences that Make a Difference* (New York: CABI Publishing, 2001); Mary Mostafanezhad, *Volunteer Tourism: Popular Humanitarianism in Neoliberal Times* (New York: Routledge, 2016).

[12] David A. Kolb, *Experiential Learning: Experience as the Source of Learning and Development* (Upper Saddle River, NJ: Pearson Education, 2014 [1983]); Jack Mezirow, "Understanding Transformation Theory," *Adult Education Quarterly* 44, 4 (1994); Thomas E. Smith and Clifford E. Knapp, *Sourcebook of Experiential Education: Key Thinkers and Their Contributions* (New York: Routledge, 2011).

[13] Sam Marullo and Bob Edwards, "Editors' Introduction: Service-Learning Pedagogy as Universities' Response to Troubled Times," *American Behavioral Scientist* 43, 5 (2000).

[14] Kolb, *Experiential Learning: Experience as the Source of Learning and Development*, p. xxi.

[15] Sara M. Evans and Harry C. Boyte, *Free Spaces: The Sources of Democratic Change in America* (Chicago: University of Chicago Press, 1992); Robert D. Putnam, *Bowling Alone: The Collapse and Revival of American Community* (New York: Simon & Schuster, 2001); Eric Hartmann and Richard Kiely, "Pushing Boundaries: Introduction to the Global Service-Learning Special Section," *Michigan Journal of Community Service Learning* 21, 1 (2014).

[16] Ulf Hannerz, *Transnational Connections: Culture, People, Places* (New York: Routledge, 1996); Steven Vertovec and Robin Cohen, "Introduction: Conceiving Cosmopolitanism," in *Conceiving Cosmopolitanism: Theory, Context, and Practice*, ed. Steven Vertovec and Robin Cohen (New York: Oxford University Press, 2002).

educational organizations showed a dramatic embrace of global citizenship and engagement ideals. In 1997, only thirty-two secondary programs in the United States had global engagement curricula; by 2012, 4,400 did.[17] In a 2015 Campus Compact survey of higher education institutions, 64 percent reported tracking outcomes related to "global learning" and "social justice orientation," while even higher percentages reported tracking outcomes related to civic engagement.[18]

These developments yoked together an organizational commitment to engagement with a widened field of moral vision (the globe), finding a visible and popular vehicle in the form of immersion travel. In higher education, immersion travel has been used in many ways: for alternative spring breaks, as part of study abroad, and as part of global service-learning.[19] In 2010, more than 150,000 students from American higher education institutions enrolled in short-term study abroad trips, engaging with international communities and social issues.[20] In 2016, nearly one-quarter of all study abroad by college students was for a period of less than four weeks, with volunteer work often a component of the experience.[21] Immersion travel has long since reached the institutionalized acclaim of a "best practice" for civic engagement.[22]

In each of these different streams, in congregations or colleges, immersion travel tends to reflect patterns of civic action in American life more generally. The group basis of immersion travel evokes an American

[17] Jeffrey S. Dill, *The Longings and Limits of Global Citizenship Education: The Moral Pedagogy of Schooling in a Cosmopolitan Age* (New York: Routledge, 2013).

[18] Campus Compact, "2015 Annual Member Survey," (Campus Compact, 2016).

[19] Hartmann and Kiely, "Pushing Boundaries: Introduction to the Global Service-Learning Special Section."; Catherine Fobes and Tera Hefferan, "Educating Students for the Twenty-First Century: Using Praxis Projects to Teach about Global Learning in Mid-Michigan," *Michigan Sociological Review* 23 (2009); Piacitelli et al., "Alternative Break Programs."

[20] Patricia Chow and Rajika Bhandari, "Open Doors 2011 Report on International Educational Change," (New York: Institute of International Education, 2011), as cited in Matthew J. Stone and James F. Petrick, "The Educational Benefits of Travel Experiences: A Literature Review," *Journal of Travel Research* 52, 6 (2013).

[21] Institute of International Education, "Detailed Duration of U.S. Study Abroad, 2005/6–2015/16," in *Open Doors Report on International Education Exchange* (New York, 2017); Mostafanezhad, *Volunteer Tourism*.

[22] Ken Crane, Lachelle Norris, and Kevin Barry, "Mobilizing Communities through International Study Tours: Project Mexico Immersion and New Immigrants in the Midwest," *Human Organization* 69, 4 (2010).

cultural and religious preference for small groups to achieve civic goals.[23] The brief duration of immersion travel incorporates the short-term packaging of civic engagement that has become common in the United States, a trend that has accelerated in the past twenty years as nonprofit organizations provide "drop-in" opportunities for people to achieve a tangible end in a short amount of time.[24] The nonspecialized skills required of travelers encourages participation by an expansive pool of participants, bypassing the time- and resource-intensive commitments associated with traditional transnational roles, such as missionary or Peace Corps volunteer. The emphasis on face-to-face interaction with foreign locals and immersion into their life contexts ties together an American civic preference for relational social assistance with a valuing of "authentic" cross-cultural experience.[25] And the mixing of personal growth with civic action continues a long history of intertwining personal and social reform in American life.[26]

Immersion travel's widespread popularity suggests exciting newness and uniqueness for those that embrace it. But, to understand immersion travel requires seeing it as a practice whose processes, meanings, and appeal are rooted in, respond to, and illuminate central tensions in global civic life.[27]

[23] Paul Lichterman, *Elusive Togetherness: Church Groups Trying to Bridge America's Divisions* (Princeton, NJ: Princeton University Press, 2005); Robert Wuthnow, *Sharing the Journey: Support Groups and America's New Quest for Community* (New York: Free Press, 1994).

[24] Nina Eliasoph, *Making Volunteers: Civic Life after Welfare's End* (Princeton, NJ: Princeton University Press, 2011); Erica Bornstein, "Volunteer Experience," in *What Matters? Ethnographies of Value in a Not So Secular Age*, ed. Courtney Bender and Ann Taves (New York: Columbia University Press, 2012).

[25] Robert Wuthnow, *Acts of Compassion: Caring for Others and Helping Ourselves* (Princeton, NJ: Princeton University Press, 1991); Nina Eliasoph, *The Politics of Volunteering* (Malden, MA: Polity Press, 2013); Howell, *Short-Term Mission: An Ethnography of Christian Travel Narrative and Experience*; Wuthnow, *Boundless Faith*; Daniel Immerwahr, *Thinking Small: The United States and the Lure of Community Development* (Cambridge, MA: Harvard University Press, 2015).

[26] Wuthnow, *Acts of Compassion*; Rebecca Anne Allahyari, *Visions of Charity: Volunteer Workers and Moral Community* (Berkeley: University of California Press, 2000); Paul Lichterman, "Beyond the Seesaw Model: Public Commitment in a Culture of Self-Fulfillment," *Sociological Theory* 13, 3 (1995); Eliasoph, *The Politics of Volunteering*; Michael P. Young, *Bearing Witness against Sin: The Evangelical Birth of the American Social Movement* (Chicago: The University of Chicago Press, 2006).

[27] For debates about the origins, measurement, and theory of global civil society, see Gordon Laxer and Sandra Halperin, *Global Civil Society and Its Limits* (New York: Palgrave MacMillan, 2003); Mary Kaldor, Sabine Selchow, and Henrietta L. Moore, *Global Civil Society 2012: Ten Years of Critical Reflection* (New York: Palgrave

DISTANT SUFFERING AND ITS ENCOUNTER

Historically speaking, immersion travel is best understood as an emerging practice for producing and managing a relationship between humans in the global core (e.g., the United States and Europe) and humans in the global periphery (e.g., Third World countries, developing nations, or the Global South). This relationship has been a central religious, political, and sociological question in the course of the past three centuries as the sufferings and social injustices of people living in other countries became a relevant concern for Westerners.[28]

The very idea of "the social" as a category of people with shared characteristics and reasons for suffering developed at the beginning of the modern period, gaining steam in the late eighteenth century.[29] In tandem, "human" became a moral category, rooted in assumptions of universal rationality, the common ability to feel pain, and the experience of personal subjectivity.[30] This turn in cultural life, which socialized the causes and consequences of suffering while emphasizing the experience of individual persons, was pushed along by a range of institutional developments that expanded Western contact and knowledge beyond the borders of Europe.[31] For example, Norbert Elias showed how increasing cross-national interaction and interdependence among European elites transformed social life in a widening "civilizing" ripple, restraining violence and fostering sympathy toward a wider circle of people.[32] Similarly, historian Thomas Haskell has shown how capitalist expansion widened

Macmillan, 2012); Helmut K. Anheier, "Reflections on the Concept and Measurement of Global Civil Society," *Voluntas* 18, 1 (2007); Manuel Castells, "The New Public Sphere: Global Civil Society, Communication Networks, and Global Governance," *The Annals of the American Academy of Political and Social Science* 616, 1 (2008); John Keane, *Global Civil Society?* (New York: Cambridge University Press, 2003).

[28] Wilkinson and Kleinman, *A Passion for Society.*

[29] Wilkinson and Kleinman, *A Passion for Society.*

[30] Lynn Avery Hunt, *Inventing Human Rights: A History* (New York: W.W. Norton & Company, 2007); Hans Joas, *The Sacredness of the Person: A New Genealogy of Human Rights* (Washington, DC: Georgetown University Press, 2013); Thomas W. Laquer, "Mourning, Pity, and the Work of Narrative in the Making of 'Humanity'," in *Humanitarianism and Suffering: The Mobilization of Empathy*, ed. Richard Ashby Wilson and Richard D. Brown (New York: Cambridge University Press, 2009).

[31] Peter Stamatov, *The Origins of Global Humanitarianism: Religion, Empires, and Advocacy* (New York: Cambridge University Press, 2013).

[32] Norbert Elias, *On the Process of Civilisation* (Dublin, Ireland: University College Dublin Press, 2012).

the circle of Western sympathy, a development pushed along as readers of new mass-market novels encountered suffering fictional characters with whom they could emotionally identify.[33]

Even if the suffering of distant others was becoming known to Westerners, however, the conclusion that there was a moral obligation to do something about it was not yet widely shared. Adam Smith, writing in the late eighteenth century, argued that sympathy tended to arise primarily and most intensely for those who were near and dear.[34] Long-distance sympathy might arise through imagining the feeling of distant suffering, Smith argued, but he was suspicious about the moral implications of such awareness given that people were unable to do anything about it. He famously wrote in the late 1700s that, if we learned of humans suffering at a removed distance, "to give ourselves any anxiety upon that account, seems to be no part of our duty."[35] As Fonna Forman-Barzilai explains, Smith "found it absurd and cynical to extend duty to actions that were better suited to saints and beyond the capacities of ordinary eighteenth-century people" who were oriented toward local, personal attachments.[36]

One of the ironies of history is that, at the moment Smith was writing, the first organized attempts to address distant social suffering by ordinary Westerners were already well underway.[37] Peter Stamatov has shown that, by the seventeenth century, religious activists within European colonial powers created long-distance advocacy networks to critique and address the social conditions of colonized places and persons.[38] During Smith's own time and within his geographic orbit, the slavery abolition movement was already in motion.[39] Describing the 1790s British sugar boycott and its use of narrative to publicize the scourge of slavery to a

---

[33] Thomas L. Haskell, "Capitalism and the Origins of the Humanitarian Sensibility, Part 1," *The American Historical Review* 90, 2 (1985); Hunt, *Inventing Human Rights: A History.*

[34] Fonna Forman-Barzilai, "Sympathy in Space(s) Adam Smith on Proximity," *Political Theory* 33, 2 (2005).

[35] Adam Smith, *The Theory of Moral Sentiments* (Cambridge University Press, 2002 [1759]), p. 161.

[36] Forman-Barzilai, "Sympathy in Space(s)," p. 202.

[37] Peter Stamatov, "Activist Religion, Empire, and the Emergence of Modern Long-Distance Advocacy Networks," *American Sociological Review* 75, 4 (2010); Fonna Forman-Barzilai, "And Thus Spoke the Spectator: Adam Smith for Humanitarians," *The Adam Smith Review* 1 (2004).

[38] Stamatov, "Activist Religion."

[39] Adam Hochschild, *Bury the Chains: Prophets and Rebels in the Fight to Free an Empire's Slaves* (New York: Houghton Mifflin Harcourt, 2005).

Western public, Thomas Lacquer noted that it promoted the "causal" linking of distant bodily pain to a listener's obligation to act.[40] By the late nineteenth century, both transnational humanitarian organizations and social movements emerged as forms of distant political engagement.[41] And, fifty years further on, just after World War II, numerous organized ways of connecting first-world citizens to distant social problems existed, embedded in divergent international networks and moral visions.[42] All of these transnational civic practices tried to constitute objects of distant suffering to mobilize aid. But, given Adam Smith's doubts and the pragmatic reality of massive disengagement by first-world audiences, how did these processes of constituting distant suffering actually work to produce concern, obligation, and action by individuals?

In his examination of how distant suffering was made into a morally obliging problem in the Western public sphere, Boltanski argues that the representation of suffering across social and global distance is intimately related to the possibility of action against that suffering.[43] Boltanski notes the constitutive divide between spectators and sufferers, a divide that prevents spectators' close familiarity with the conditions of sufferers. Echoing Smith, Boltanski suggests that proximity to suffering produces a familiarity that can be easily translated into action, either through an individualized, compassionate response or by politics-based justice. Drawing from Hannah Arendt, Boltanski contrasts that familiarity with the "spectacle of suffering" created by distance.[44] In the spectacle of suffering, individual sufferers become an undifferentiated mass. Instead of easily producing action, the distant spectacle produces a "politics of pity" in which suffering victims are represented instead of engaged, actors are at a distance instead of nearby, and tools for redress are unclear instead of easily deployed. In the politics of pity, Boltanski writes, "the instruments which can convey a representation [of suffering] and those which can convey an action are not the same."[45] In this situation,

[40] Laquer, "Mourning, Pity, and the Work of Narrative in the Making of 'Humanity'."

[41] Charles Tilly, *From Mobilization to Revolution* (Reading, MA: Addison Wesley, 1978); Michael Barnett, *Empire of Humanity: A History of Humanitarianism* (Ithaca, NY: Cornell University Press, 2011).

[42] Margaret E. Keck and Kathryn Sikkink, *Activists beyond Borders: Advocacy Networks in International Politics* (Ithaca, NY: Cornell University Press, 1998); Barnett, *Empire of Humanity*; John Boli and George M. Thomas, *Constructing World Culture: International Non-Governmental Organizations since 1875* (Redwood City, CA: Stanford University Press, 1999).

[43] Boltanksi, *Distant Suffering.*   [44] Ibid., p. 3.   [45] Ibid., p. 17.

Westerners are challenged with how to produce a response whose scale and efficacy supersedes the limits of face-to-face compassionate response while at the same time avoiding abstract commitments that fail to pragmatically address the causes of suffering.

Before the question of action can be addressed, Boltanski suggests more attention be given to the ways that the "spectacle of suffering" is communicated, since the success of this mediation determines whether obligation arises. The communication of distant suffering has been produced by distinct historical forms of representation that shaped knowledge and emotion about that suffering.[46] Boltanski traces three historical forms and their logics: the form of denunciation that shows suffering to be unjust, the form of sentiment that shows suffering to be touching, and the form of aesthetics that shows suffering to be sublime. Whatever the form of representation, a recurring problem has been the dependence of distant audiences on mediating spectators; those who relay knowledge of suffering.

Despite these intermediaries' best efforts, the material conditions of suffering remain unfamiliar to the removed audience. An intermediary must inform and inspire, but this is a tough balance to get right. Boltanski proposes that an intermediary must become like Smith's "idealized spectator." For Smith, the idealized spectator was a conscience "inside the breast" that balanced emotional response and rational consideration.[47] What happens when this conscience exits the breast and becomes public in the form of a real mediating spectator with firsthand knowledge? Out of concern for accuracy and the avoidance of hyperbole, witnesses should attempt to display some impartiality about the suffering they report. These spectators do not purport to be sufferers but display enough involvement with the conditions of suffering to relay information accurately. And yet, such witnesses must not be cool in their objectivity because that would reduce the emotional effect of the suffering they are representing to audiences back home. Having witnessed suffering, they must relay emotional investment, articulating the obligating character of suffering by showing what witnessing it has done to them. The challenge for witnesses is that they "must bring together particular situations and thereby convey them, that is to say cross a distance, while retaining as far as possible the qualities conferred on them by a face to face encounter."[48] Thus, the

---

[46] Robin Wagner-Pacifici, "Pity and a Politics of the Present," *Theory & Event* 5, 4 (2001).
[47] Forman-Barzilai, "Sympathy in Space(s)."   [48] Boltanksi, *Distant Suffering*, p. 2.

representation of suffering to distant audiences must constantly navigate the tension of demonstrating the personal, emotional experience of suffering while connecting that suffering to social conditions that can be addressed. The unintended problems that arise from this process of representing suffering to audiences are legion.[49]

But what if the role of firsthand witness could be multiplied exponentially? Smith and Boltanski, as well as today's cosmopolitans and promoters of global citizenship, all suggest that direct, face-to-face engagement is the preferred way to understand and empathize with the sufferings of others. It is in this light that immersion travel appears as a new development in global civic life. Immersion travel could, conceivably, increase the density of direct contact with distant suffering while avoiding the problems of representation that can impede the "swing to commitment"[50]; the moment when spectators become actors. Immersion travel might, by bridging distance among the multitudes, bridge the separation between awareness and action.

Considering immersion travel this way, not merely as a civic or political action but as a motivational tool for other types of civil and political action, connects this practice to the familiar concept of awareness raising. Awareness raising is a broad term for the motivational process that occurs within individuals as a precursor to new social commitments and actions.[51] In its pure form, awareness raising implies a simple formula: information + critical thinking = personal change and involvement.[52] The term has cognitivist roots, emphasizing processes that increase the supply of information and provide new frames for understanding.[53] But there are substantial problems with thinking about awareness raising in this way.

---

[49] Lilie Chouliaraki, *The Ironic Spectator: Solidarity in the Age of Post-Humanitarianism* (Malden MA: Polity Press, 2013); Eagleton, *The Trouble with Strangers: A Study of Ethics*; Michael Barnett and Thomas G. Weiss, *Humanitarianism in Question: Politics, Power, Ethics* (Ithaca, NY: Cornell University Press, 2008).

[50] Boltanksi, *Distant Suffering*, p. 30.

[51] Bert Klandermans and Dirk Oegema, "Potentials, Networks, Motivations, and Barriers: Steps towards Participation in Social Movements," *American Sociological Review* 52, 4 (1987); Aldon Morris and Naomi Braine, "Social Movements and Oppositional Consciousness," in *Oppositional Consciousness: The Subjective Roots of Social Protest*, ed. Jane Mansbridge and Aldon Morris (Chicago: Univeristy of Chicago Press, 2001).

[52] Randall Collins, "Social Movements and the Focus of Emotional Attention," in *Passionate Politics*, ed. Jeff Goodwin, James M. Jasper, and Francesca Polletta (Chicago: University of Chicago Press, 2001).

[53] Robert D. Benford and David A. Snow, "Framing Processes and Social Movements: An Overview and Assessment," *Annual Review of Sociology* 26 (2000).

One is that awareness raising can seem like an information contest to grab attention from a mass public. Highly publicized examples, like the 2012 social media campaign against Ugandan warlord Joseph Kony, reinforce this perception.[54] In these cases, there is lots of awareness, but it is thin and quickly disregarded. A second problem is that the motivational power of awareness is easily depleted. As an example, the mediatization of distant suffering since the 1970s has dramatically widened the reach of global awareness but may have weakened its effect, turning viewers into "ironic spectator[s] of vulnerable others."[55] A third problem is that awareness raising is rarely sufficient to produce new action. Its harvest depends on much more.

There are other examples of awareness raising, though, that suggest a continuum from simple informational awareness to an enveloping, experiential awareness. Indeed, the goal of awareness raising among successful civic and social movement organizations has often been comprehensive: to go beyond information attainment in order to transform individuals.[56] Awareness raising in this sense, and in historical examples ranging from antislavery abolitionists to women's movement liberationists, refers to a process of motivation that involves the purposeful manipulation of information, identity, emotions, and body to overcome the divide between private self and public life.[57]

---

[54] Clifford Bob, "The Market for Human Rights," in *Advocacy Organizations and Collective Action*, ed. Aseem Prakash and Mary Kay Gugerty (Cambridge: Cambridge University Press, 2010); Antonia Kanczula, "Kony 2012 in Numbers," *The Guardian*, April 20 2012.

[55] Chouliaraki, *The Ironic Spectator*, p. 2.

[56] Verta Taylor and Nancy E. Whittier, "Collective Identity in Social Movement Communities: Lesbian Feminist Mobilization," in *Frontiers in Social Movement Theory*, ed. Aldon D. Morris and Carol M. Mueller (New Haven, CT: Yale University Press, 1992); Michael Young, "A Revolution of the Soul: Transformative Experiences and Immediate Abolition," in *Passionate Politics: Emotions and Social Movements*, ed. Jeff Goodwin, James M. Jasper, and Francesca Polletta (Chicago: The University of Chicago Press, 2001); Doug McAdam, "Recruitment to High-Risk Activism: The Case of Freedom Summer," *The American Journal of Sociology* 92, 1 (1986).

[57] Emma F. Thomas, Craig McGarty, and Kenneth I. Mavor, "Transforming 'Apathy into Movement': The Role of Prosocial Emotions in Motivating Action for Social Change," *Personality and Social Psychology Review* 13, 4 (2009); Arne Johan Vetlesen, *Perception, Empathy, and Judgement: An Inquiry into the Preconditions of Moral Performance* (University Park, PA: The Pennsylvania State University Press, 1994); Hochschild, *Bury the Chains: Prophets and Rebels in the Fight to Free an Empire's Slaves*; Young, "A Revolution of the Soul."; C. Wright Mills, *The Sociological Imagination* (New York: Oxford University Press, 2000 [1959]).

Immersion travel is a technique where this deeper ideal of awareness raising is harnessed to travel. The interactions of travel provide a first-hand experience of discovery that may create intimacy and familiarity. The immersion traveler is put into the context of suffering in the moment, an experience that may spur a sense of commitment unconstrained by theoretical arguments over the causes of suffering or the justifications for confronting it.[58] Travel may produce an evocative, personal story for travelers, one that shapes identity and choices going forward.[59] Immersion travelers might even become representatives of distant suffering, Boltanski's idealized spectators that can motivate listeners back home. These are all possibilities, but just possibilities. To account for travel as a form of awareness raising, and to determine whether it enables a relationship with distant suffering, requires a sense of what travel is and what travel does.

The Faces of Global Travel

International travel by "ordinary" Westerners has been highly visible for more than a century, closely tied with the development of the modern imaginary.[60] The possibilities of international travel have often been articulated through reference to two institutionalized forms: pilgrimage and tourism. Both exist through a material structure of international transportation, depend on a system of diplomatic relations that enable free movement, and are made possible by mechanisms of currency exchange. Both are temporary, transporting daily routines into new space and place, but both encode different purposes and different claims about what happens through travel.[61] By briefly examining the meanings and practices of travel generated by pilgrimage and tourism, we can anticipate

---

[58] Wagner-Pacifici, "Pity and a Politics of the Present."; Young, "A Revolution of the Soul: Transformative Experiences and Immediate Abolition."

[59] Hans Joas, *The Genesis of Values* (Chicago: University of Chicago Press, 2000).

[60] Travel by anthropologists and Christian missionaries contributed to the production of a modern global imaginary, as they used travel to encounter, understand, and transform foreign others. Edward W. Said, *Orientalism* (Pantheon Books, 1978); David A. Hollinger, *Protestants Abroad: How Missionaries Tried to Change the World but Changed America* (Princeton, NJ: Princeton University Press, 2017). They are protagonists in the encounter of the West with "the globe," but not the central focus of this story as they traveled for long periods as part of centralized projects with well-demarcated ideological orientations and the support of national powers.

[61] Edward M. Bruner, *Culture on Tour: Ethnographies of Travel* (Chicago: University of Chicago Press, 2005).

how immersion travel incorporates elements of both into a distinct travel form. The resulting bricolage of meanings and practices within immersion travel increases the possible ways that it "works" to raise awareness.

Using Arnold van Gennep's work on social ritual, Victor Turner presented pilgrimage as a unique moment of social life during which participants entered a state he termed "anti-structure," a space devoid of the constraining structures and behaviors of normal society.[62] In place of structure, *comunitas* emerged. According to Turner, this phase of social life generated ideals of equality, creativity, and individuality in contrast to hierarchy, routine, and conformity.[63] There was a directionality to pilgrimage, such that the pilgrim's movement toward a sacred geographic location indexed movement toward personal transformation. As an anthropologist working within the Durkheimian tradition, Turner's work posed this type of travel as a social release valve in which individuals could regenerate themselves and society.[64] While ensuing studies of pilgrimage have questioned the representativeness of this model, pilgrimages today still provide time and space for moral transformation that is otherwise difficult or impossible to acheive.[65]

During the post–World War II decades, leisure tourism became a massive economic structure whose imprint was increasingly recognizable across the globe. Given the relative absence of overt religiosity – in motivation or institutional structure – within mass tourism and the central roles of leisure time and money, the meaning of travel diverged sharply from pilgrimage. Dean MacCannell's classic, *The Tourist*, portrayed tourism as the shared cultural activity of a particular class.[66] MacCannell linked the motivating force of tourism to the alienation of modern citizens of industrial nations. Tourism (like religion in classic

---

[62] Victor Turner and Edith Turner, *Image and Pilgrimage in Christian Culture: Anthropological Perspectives* (New York: Columbia University Press, 1978); Victor Turner, *The Ritual Process: Structure and Anti-Structure* (Piscataway, NJ: Aldine Transaction, 1995).

[63] John Eade, "Introduction to the Illinois Paperback," in *Contesting the Sacred: The Anthropology of Pilgrimage*, ed. John Eade and Michael Sallnow (Urbana: University of Illinois Press, 2000).

[64] Neil J. Smelser, *The Odyssey Experience: Physical, Social, Psychological, and Spiritual Journeys* (Berkeley: University of California Press, 2009).

[65] Vikash Singh, *Uprising of the Fools: Pilgrimage as Moral Protest in Contemporary India* (Redwood City, CA: Stanford University Press, 2017).

[66] Dean MacCannell, *The Tourist: A New Theory of the Leisure Class* (New York: Schocken Books Inc, 1989).

Marxist theory) was partially a response of escape, a secularized pilgrimage in which travelers sought authentic experience. MacCannell showed how cultural sites became commodified by this new force and how tourism purveyors produced authentic culture for the easy consumption of tourists, who remained unaware of its invisible production. In the ensuing decades, numerous studies showed the production, packaging, and consumption of authentic experience in tourist destinations.[67] Some scholars further emphasized the consumptive, disembedding nature of tourism found in the "tourist gaze," which sees the foreign world as a set of expected sights and symbols that reconfirm what a traveler already knows.[68] A tourist is attracted to the difference of the places he or she visits, but the structure of tourism protects the traveler "from any consequences of failure to understand the difference that attracted them" in the first place.[69] According to this line of research, tourists see much, fail to understand most of it on its terms, reinforce global inequality, and leave without being implicated in the moral complicity or the moral complexity of the places they have visited.[70]

Pilgrimage and tourism serve as orienting poles of scholarship on travel, the former emphasizing the generic, transformative character of travel, the latter emphasizing the place-specific and consumptive character of travel. Today, the empirical reality is that a variety of hybrid travel forms exist that intertwine the expectations for transformation in pilgrimage and the expectation for encountering authentic foreign people and places found in tourism. What this diversity suggests is that travel can incorporate many meanings and purposes.

What travel can achieve, then, is a function of the institutions that organize travel. For example, as Shaul Kelner observes, "by the latter half

---

[67] Erik Cohen, "The Changing Faces of Contemporary Tourism," *Society* 45 no. 4 (2008); Erik Cohen, "The Sociology of Tourism: Approaches, Issues, and Findings," *Annual Review of Sociology* 10 (1984); Yaniv Belhassen, Kellee Caton, and William P. Stewart, "The Search for Authenticity in the Pilgrim Experience," *Annals of Tourism Research* 35, 3 (2008); Kevin Fox Gotham, "Tourism and Culture," in *Handbook of Cultural Sociology*, ed. John R. Hall, Laura Grindstaff, and Ming-Cheng Lo (New York: Routledge, 2010).

[68] John Urry and Jonas Larsen, *The Tourist Gaze 3.0*, 3rd ed. (Thousand Oaks, CA: Sage Publications, Ltd., 2011).

[69] Dean MacCannell, *The Ethics of Sightseeing* (Berkeley: University of California Press, 2011), p. 228.

[70] Edward M. Bruner, "Transformation of Self in Tourism," *Annals of tourism Research* 18, 2 (1991).

of the 20th century, nation-states and nongovernmental organizations had discovered that they could systematically deploy this novel cultural form [e.g., tourist travel] to influence political identities."[71] An enormous number of "alternative" tourism formats have sprung up, partially driven by the international spread of nongovernmental organizations promoting global engagement, partially by the "Peace Corps effect" that encourages self-development through encounter, and partially through the opening of heretofore off-limit destinations seeking resources to address poverty and disease.[72] Scholarship in the last fifteen years has especially coalesced around "volunteer tourism," a form of alternative tourism that "is seen as having the potential to bridge the spatial distance between the giver and receiver of moral concern and altruistic intent associated with ethical consumption."[73]

IMMERSION TRAVEL AS TRANSNATIONAL CIVIC PRACTICE

When populated with new meanings and behaviors, travel can be turned into a technique for accomplishing new ends across global distance. Immersion travel is a *modus operandi* for awareness raising, incorporating pieces of pilgrimage and tourism toward religious, civic, and/or political ends. As we move toward understanding and evaluating immersion travel, it is helpful to keep in mind four characteristics that distinguish it as a transnational civic practice in global civic life.

First, immersion travel facilitates direct, personal engagement across a great distance.[74] Distance refers to physical (usually geographic) separation that inhibits regular social interaction, reifies distinct cultural identities of salient difference (nationhood, race, ethnicity), and makes the coordination of shared action more difficult. Immersion trips target places that seem to be the antithesis of the tourist ideal: locations of poverty,

---

[71] Kelner, *Tours That Bind*, p. 191.

[72] Ann Swidler and Susan Cotts Watkins, *A Fraught Embrace: The Romance and Reality of AIDS Altruism in Africa* (Princeton, NJ: Princeton University Press, 2017); Mostafanezhad, *Volunteer Tourism*; Bianca Freire-Medeiros, *Touring Poverty* (New York: Routledge, 2014).

[73] Peter Smith, "International Volunteer Tourism as (De) Commodified Moral Consumption," in *Moral Encounters in Tourism* (New York: Routledge, 2016), p. 33.

[74] The adjective implied by "distance" in this book is "international," from one country to another. Immersion trips do occur solely within nations, but that brings up a different set of salient questions about social difference, national identity, and civic imagination.

inequality, and violence.[75] No *one* place is defined as *the* place to travel to encounter suffering.[76] Instead, the open travel networks of globalization, along with the concentrations of poverty abetted by neoliberalism, have made potential travel destinations innumerable.[77] Immersion travel transfers the spiritual directionality found in pilgrimage onto international distance, sometimes imbuing foreign places with an attraction based on what they are perceived to lack. As immersion travelers move across boundaries, they approach the goal of face-to-face engagement. As Ann Swidler and Susan Watkins explain in their analysis of "butterfly altruists" providing AIDS relief in Africa, the desire for transnational connection is strong due to the assumption that, "face-to-face altruism can create a powerful emotional connection between individual donors and those whom they want to help."[78]

Second, the organizational structure of immersion travel is characterized by coordination between three nodes: a group of travelers constituted by shared membership in a domestic organization (e.g., college, congregation, school), a brokering organization (e.g., binational NGO; INGO), and a group of people in a foreign community (e.g., a congregation, local NGO, a village).[79] Travelers are usually sent as a group from domestic organizations, which I refer to as *feeder organizations*. Meanwhile, travelers often have their travel arranged by a broker, which I refer to as *immersion travel producers*. Immersion travel producers help feeder organizations connect to distant persons and places.[80]

[75] Freire-Medeiros, *Touring Poverty*; Howell, *Short-Term Mission.*

[76] Robert J. Priest et al., "Researching the Short-Term Mission Movement," *Missiology: An International Review* 34, 4 (2006).

[77] Mike Davis, *Planet of Slums* (New York: Verson, 2006); Stephen Offutt, *New Centers of Global Evangelicalism in Latin America and Africa* (New York: Cambridge University Press, 2015).

[78] Swidler and Watkins, *A Fraught Embrace: The Romance and Reality of AIDS Altruism in Africa*, p. x.

[79] Nancy Tatom Ammerman, *Pillars of Faith: American Congregations and Their Partners* (Berkeley: University of California Press, 2005); Nancy T. Kinney, "Structure, Context, and Ideological Dissonance in Transnational Religious Networks," *Voluntas* 26, 1 (2015); McBride et al., "Civic Service."; Allison Schnable, "What Religion Affords Grassroots NGOs: Frames, Networks, Modes of Action," *Journal for the Scientific Study of Religion* 55, 2 (2016); Swidler and Watkins, *A Fraught Embrace: The Romance and Reality of AIDS Altruism in Africa.*

[80] Erica Bornstein, "Child Sponsorship, Evangelism, and Belonging in the World of World Vision Zimbabwe," *American Ethnologist* 28, 3 (2001); Judith N. Lasker, *Hoping to Help: The Promises and Pitfalls of Global Health Volunteering* (Ithaca, NY: Cornell University Press, 2016).

Third, immersion travelers eschew tourist practices and discursively define themselves against problematic images of tourism.[81] Immersion travelers tend to articulate their activity as an overt combination of self-development *and* social engagement, not merely leisure or consumption.[82] Since a large swath of, if not most, immersion trips go to destinations off the beaten tourist path, travelers are away from usual tourist locales and services related to food, lodging, and entertainment. In the tradition of early adopters of the tool of travel, like anthropologists and missionaries, immersion travelers aim to "immerse" themselves in the lifeworld of a distant place as a way of generating a more authentic understanding of people and place.[83] Kelner notes that the ability of travel to be "a medium of socialization rests to a large extent in the fact that it is an embodied practice that fully engages people as actors in an immersive environment."[84]

Finally, immersion travel takes advantage of the cultural structure of group-based, time-delimited travel.[85] Like with pilgrimage, the liminal structure of immersion travel is characterized, for travelers, by changed role expectations and unsettledness in time and space. Since travel involves contingency, immersion travel can take advantage of this as a way to increase the creative feel.[86] Travelers are meant to have a phenomenological experience of authenticity, of "being true to one's self."[87]

---

[81] Robert J. Priest, *Effective Engagement in Short-Term Missions: Doing It Right!* (Pasadena, CA: William Carey Library Publishers, 2008); Howell, *Short-Term Mission*; David L. Gladstone, *From Pilgrimage to Package Tour: Travel and Tourism in the Third World* (New York: Routledge, 2013); Wanda Vrasti, *Volunteer Tourism in the Global South: Giving Back in Neoliberal Times* (New York: Routledge, 2012).

[82] Brian Howell and Rachel Dorr, "Evangelical Pilgrimage: The Language of Short-Term Missions," *Journal of Communication and Religion* 30, 2 (2007); Helene Snee, "Framing the Other: Cosmopolitanism and the Representation of Difference in Overseas Gap Year Narratives," *The British Journal of Sociology* 64, 1 (2013); Bornstein, "Volunteer Experience."

[83] Hollinger, *Protestants Abroad.*   [84] Shaul Kelner, *Tours That Bind*, p. 182.

[85] Karen Stein, "Time Off: The Social Experience of Time on Vacation," *Qualitative Sociology* 35, 3 (2012).

[86] Kelner, *Tours That Bind.*

[87] Phillip Vannini and Alexis Franzese, "The Authenticity of Self: Conceptualization, Personal Experience, and Practice," *Sociology Compass* 2, 5 (2008); Smelser, *The Odyssey Experience*; Thomas DeGloma, *Seeing the Light: The Social Logic of Personal Discovery* (Chicago: The University of Chicago Press, 2014); Stein, "Time Off: The Social Experience of Time on Vacation."; Chaim Noy, "This Trip Really Changed Me: Backpackers' Narratives of Self-Change," *Annals of Tourism Research* 31, 1 (2004); Belhassen Caton, and Stewart, "The Search for Authenticity in the Pilgrim Experience."

According to Kelner, this is an "instrumentalization of culture," as immersion travel organizations depend on the force of the travel pattern to produce *something* in travelers.[88] This something is usually meant to have moral dimensions. As the organizations that use immersion travel sense, such an experience of "self-formation and self-transcendence" can be put to use to shape individuals.[89]

These four characteristics provide a generic outline of what immersion travel entails. But what makes immersion travel a window for understanding global civic engagement is that it is a practice that can be linked to a range of institutions, motivations, meanings, and vocabularies about what distant suffering is and what it requires of first-world audiences. As evidence of this diversity to which immersion travel can be put to use, Kelner notes that, "the fact-finding and fundraising missions of any number of nonprofit organizations attest to its [travel's] ability to be placed in the service of a variety of humanitarian, environmental, and other causes."[90] Take, for example, the immersion trips by American churchgoers to war-torn Central American countries in the 1980s. According to Sharon Erickson Nepstad, these became experiences of discovery and bonding, solidifying moral opinions and activist identities against US-sponsored militarism.[91] Or, for example, note how travelers from a Midwestern evangelical church supported educational and religious projects in the Dominican Republic, returning home with refreshed religious identities.[92] Or, in another of many such examples, observe how travelers from medical schools brought medical supplies and services to foreign countries while picking up inspiration for their future careers.[93]

Lest immersion travel be seen as a mechanism only for progressive purposes or humanitarian concerns, we can point to its use by other institutions for other purposes. Before making war against Poland, nationalist and Nazi groups protested the shape of Germany's borders with short trips to the "bleeding border" during which travelers met with borderland residents to hear grievances and consolidate national

---

[88] Kelner, *Tours That Bind.*   [89] Joas, *The Genesis of Values,* p. 164.

[90] Shaul Kelner, *Tours That Bind,* p. 8.

[91] Sharon Erickson Nepstad, *Convictions of the Soul: Religion, Culture, and Agency in the Central America Solidarity Movement* (New York: Oxford University Press, 2004).

[92] Howell, *Short-Term Mission.*   [93] Lasker, *Hoping to Help.*

identity.[94] More relevant to the United States and the topic of this book, the Minuteman Project invited people from across the United States to come to the US-Mexico border. The group used the gatherings to tell stories about their work and to surveil the border to stop immigration.[95] According to Harel Shapira's account, "what the Minutemen [were] fundamentally after [was] an experience" in which they could associate with other veterans to act as defenders of America's frontier.[96]

While the ideological visions, concerns, and actions of these examples differ drastically, they all suggest an enticing hope among those concerned with distant injustice: that travel can connect travelers with it, transforming the former in service of the latter.

The Promise and Paradox of Immersion Travel

We have seen that immersion travel is a new transnational civic practice to raise awareness about distant suffering and that it has been put to use for a wide array of civic and political purposes. But this genealogy reveals little about how immersion travel works in practice, what it achieves, or how it might come up short. Perhaps more importantly, our description of immersion travel has so far neglected the aura that surrounds it: the assumptions among those who idealize immersion travel and what it can do.

In the eyes of the feeder organizations that promote immersion travel, travelers should return home changed by what they experienced. Colleges hope for increased global commitment, congregations hope for new spiritual understanding, and all hope that travelers' circles of moral concern will expand. Immersion travel is seen as fostering a disposition at the core of cosmopolitanism, what Ulf Hannerz has described as "a willingness to engage with the Other."[97] In the eyes of supporters, immersion travel is an ideal vehicle for producing the perspective-taking, other-directed feeling, and prosocial orientations of empathy on a global

[94] Elizabeth Harvey, "Pilgrimages to the Bleeding Border: Gender and Rituals of Nationalist Protest in Germany, 1919–39," *Women's History Review* 9, 2 (2000).

[95] April Lee Dove, "Framing Illegal Immigration at the U.S.-Mexican Border: Anti-Illegal Immigration Groups and the Importance of Place in Framing," *Research in Social Movements, Conflicts and Change* 30 (2010).

[96] Harel Shapira, *Waiting for José: The Minuteman's Pursuit of America* (Princeton, NJ: Princeton University Press, 2013), p. 120.

[97] Hannerz, *Transnational Connections*, p. 103.

scale. To advocates of global engagement, empathy is an ideal, symbolizing the potential to create authentic relationships across distance as part of a new era of global relations.[98]

Immersion travel is expected to produce equitable relationships, substituting in localized, personalized partnerships for the foreign donor- or state-driven development that critics of neoliberalism denounce.[99] Instead of engaging a foreign place through the gaze of "poverty pornography," immersion travel advertises a personal relationality that leads to authentic understanding.[100] In a study of "twinning" relationships between US and Haitian religious congregations that was conducted through immersion travel, Tara Heffernan argued that organizers assumed that through "a first-hand understanding of one another's 'culture, customs, and needs,' the distance between the parties [was] thought to be mediated, maybe even eliminated."[101] In theory, immersion travel makes possible a style of global neighborliness.

An array of research on immersion travel does suggest that it can produce *some* of these results. For example, immersion travelers that have volunteered abroad display more international awareness, envision more global connections, and feel effective in what they did during travel.[102] Among American youth, immersion travel leads to increased religious activity, stronger religious beliefs, increased volunteering, greater donations to charitable causes, and more political awareness.[103] In some cases, the transnational civic connections of immersion travel

[98] Jeremy Rifkin, *The Empathic Civilization: The Race to Global Consciousness in a World in Crisis* (New York: Penguin, 2009).

[99] Erica Bornstein, *Disquieting Gifts: Humanitarianism in New Delhi* (Redwood City, CAStanford University Press, 2012); Tara Hefferan, *Twinning Faith and Development: Catholic Parish Partnering in the U.S. and Haiti* (Bloomfield, CT: Kumarian Press, 2007).

[100] Fabian Frenzel, Ko Koens, and Malte Steinbrink, *Slum Tourism: Poverty, Power and Ethics* (New York: Routledge, 2012).

[101] Hefferan, *Twinning Faith and Development: Catholic Parish Partnering in the U.S. And Haiti*, p. 11.

[102] Amanda Moore McBride, Benjamin J. Lough, and Margaret Sherrard Sherraden, "International Service and the Perceived Impacts on Volunteers," *Nonprofit and Voluntary Sector Quarterly* 41, 6 (2012); Benjamin J. Lough et al., "The Impact of International Service on the Development of Volunteers' Intercultural Relations," *Social Science Research* 46, July (2014).

[103] Kraig Beyerlein, Gary Adler, and Jennifer Trinitapoli, "The Effect of Religious Mission Trips on Youth Civic Participation," *Journal for the Scientific Study of Religion* 50, 4 (2011); Probasco, "Giving Time, Not Money: Long-Term Impacts of Short-Term Mission Trips."; Jenny Trinitapoli and Stephen Vaisey, "The Transformative Role of Religious Experience: The Case of Short Term Missions," *Social Forces* 88, 1 (2009).

are experienced as beneficial partnerships.[104] Resource transfer does happen, enabling small-scale construction, medical, educational, or religious projects.[105] Robert Wuthnow has suggested that US religious organizations' use of immersion travel turns attention toward the misery generated by unequal globalization, helping to "channel resources from the rich to the poor."[106]

Yet, there are reasons to be circumspect about what immersion travel represents and what it achieves. The power of immersion travel groups from the United States to come and go as they please suggests an underlying inequality. Even the central element of immersion travel – interaction with foreign persons in their communities – can serve as the site where global inequality is reproduced.[107] The few studies that report the experiences of foreign hosts reveal perceptions of serious problems related to incivility, paternalism, status competition, and wasted resources.[108]

Other studies have shown that the changes one might want to see among travelers either do not occur or only occur for a short time.[109] Most immersion travelers do not change much in their basic understanding of foreign social realities, resorting to paternalistic interpretations that merely reproduce difference, generating a limited cosmopolitanism that fails to grasp new information and new relationships.[110] Travelers may convert differences in economic inequality into intangible spiritual

---

[104] Gary J. Adler Jr. and Stephen Offutt, "The Gift Economy of Direct Transnational Civic Action: How Reciprocity and Inequality Are Managed in Religious 'Partnerships'," *Journal for the Scientific Study of Religion* 56, 3 (2017); Swidler and Watkins, *A Fraught Embrace: The Romance and Reality of AIDS Altruism in Africa*.

[105] Offutt, *New Centers of Global Evangelicalism in Latin America and Africa*; Swidler and Watkins, *A Fraught Embrace: The Romance and Reality of AIDS Altruism in Africa*; Adler Jr. and Ruiz, "The Immigrant Effect."

[106] Wuthnow, *Boundless Faith*, p. 89.

[107] Joe Bandy, "Paradoxes of Transnational Civil Societies under Neoliberalism: The Coalition for Justice in the Maquiladoras," *Social Problems* 51, 3 (2004); Hefferan, *Twinning Faith and Development*; Adler Jr. and Offutt, "The Gift Economy of Direct Transnational Civic Action."

[108] Vrasti, *Volunteer Tourism in the Global South*; Adler Jr. and Offutt, "The Gift Economy of Direct Transnational Civic Action."; Lasker, *Hoping to Help*.

[109] Kurt Alan Ver Beek, "Lessing from the Sapling: Review of Quantitative Research on Short-Term Missions," in *Effective Engagement in Short-Term Missions:Doing It Right!*, ed. Robert J. Priest (Pasadena, CA: William Carey Library Publishers, 2008).

[110] Snee, "Framing the Other."; Bruner, "Transformation of Self in Tourism."

growth that makes power invisible.[111] A "good" foreign experience can become a product for personal identity construction instead of further social commitment. One of the most dependable outcomes of immersion travel is a personal narrative of transformation, but the line of causality between self-reports of transformation and social change is tenuous at best.[112]

Given these high ideals and evident tensions, the increasing popularity of immersion travel has been met by arguments, from scholars and practitioners alike, about its utility as a form of transnational civic engagement. Critical voices against transnational civic engagement emerged in the decades after World War II, as Western and specifically American influence in aid relationships prompted anticolonial campaigns and political reform movements.[113] One of the most provocative voices in this critique came from Ivan Illich, a Catholic priest tasked with setting up intercultural training for religious volunteers that were increasingly traveling to Mexico and Central America. In 1968, in a stunning reversal of the work he had fostered for years, Illich argued that North Americans should stop traveling; should stop directly engaging and supporting aid, development, and reform projects. Illich addressed his comments to a professional audience dedicated to supporting just such direct, personalized, localized engagement, saying,

To hell with good intentions. . . . You cannot help being ultimately vacationing salesmen for the middleclass 'American way of life,' since that is really the only life you know. . . . All you will do in a Mexican village is create disorder. . . . There is no way for you to really meet with the underprivileged since there is no common ground whatsoever for you to meet on.[114]

Having argued that immersion travelers were emissaries of destructive globalization who could not overcome an unbridgeable gulf to aid foreign others usefully, Illich addressed the humanistic assumption that, at the very least, travelers could be changed by new awareness. Illich continued,

---

[111] Adler Jr. and Offutt, "The Gift Economy of Direct Transnational Civic Action."; Vrasti, *Volunteer Tourism in the Global South.*

[112] Vrasti, *Volunteer Tourism in the Global South*; Kelner, *Tours That Bind.*

[113] Christian Smith, *The Emergence of Liberation Theology: Radical Religion and Social Movement Theory* (Chicago: University of Chicago Press, 1991); Barnett and Weiss, *Humanitarianism in Question*; Hefferan, *Twinning Faith and Development.*

[114] Ivan Illich, "To Hell with Good Intentions" (paper presented at the The Conference on Interamerican Student Projects, St. Mary's Lake of the Woods Seminary, 1968).

There exists the argument that some returned volunteers have gained insight into the damage they have done to others and have become maturer [*sic*] people. . . . I do not agree with this argument. The damage which volunteers do willy-nilly is too high a price for the belated insight that they shouldn't have been volunteers in the first place.

This mixed evidence – to put it lightly – about what immersion travel is and does reveals that this practice, like other civic practices, brings together a complex mix of idealism and pragmatism. In transnational civic work, the volume of idealism can mute inconvenient realities. For example, as Monika Krause has recently demonstrated, international humanitarian aid is not the product of rational planning that equitably distributes aid to those most in need.[115] Instead, humanitarian aid is fundamentally about organizing "good projects": initiatives that serve the expectations of first-world supporters, doing "good" by shaping donors and recipients into something "good." Similarly, immersion travel carries serious baggage about what international civic engagement is supposed to do socially and personally, for travelers and foreign communities alike.

The remainder of this book unpacks this baggage by showing why immersion travel is valued as a good way to engage the world, how immersion trips attempt to moralize distant social problems, and what becomes of immersion travelers.

A CASE AT THE BORDER

To probe these questions and paradoxes, the analysis in this book revolves around an immersion travel producer, the organization Border-Links. Each year, tens of thousands of Americans cross the US-Mexico border southward to engage – firsthand – with people and communities in Mexico.[116] Over three decades, BorderLinks has been a high-profile binational organization facilitating travel from its headquarters in Tucson, Arizona. Founded in 1988 during the Sanctuary movement, BorderLinks organizes weeklong immersion trips along the US-Mexico border and into the state of Sonora, Mexico.[117]

---

[115] Monika Krause, *The Good Project: Humanitarian Relief NGOs and the Fragmentation of Reason* (Chicago: The University of Chicago Press, 2014).

[116] Priest et al., "Researching the Short-Term Mission Movement."

[117] Christian Smith, *Resisting Reagan: The U.S. Central America Peace Movement* (Chicago: University of Chicago, 1996); Hilary Cunningham, "Transnational Social Movements and Sovereignties in Transition: Charting New Interfaces of Power at the U.S.-Mexico Border," *Anthropologica* 44, 2 (2002).

Day One

	Arrive at Tucson International Airport
	Van ride to BorderLinks' Tucson office
6:00pm	Dinner at BorderLinks
7:00	General Orientation
8:00	Viewing of *Crossing Arizona* documentary film
9:00	Overnight stay in dorm at BorderLinks' Tucson office

Day Two

7:30am	Breakfast
8:30	Pack van
9:00	Leave for Nogales, MX
10:30	Visit No More Deaths humanitarian aid station at the U.S.-Mexico border
12:00pm	Lunch and talk with community leader in Nogales
1:30	Industrial park and *colonia* Kennedy van tour
2:15	Market basket survey exercise
4:00	Reflection and free time at the *Casa de la Misericordia* (BorderLinks Mexico)
6:00	Dinner on a *maquila* worker's wage
8:00	Overnight stay in dorm at the *Casa de la Misericordia*

Day Three

8:00am	Breakfast
9:00	Pack van
9:30	Visit to immigrant shelter in Nogales, MX
11:00	Visit with border artist in Nogales, MX
12:00pm	Lunch with immigrants at immigrant shelter in Nogales, MX
2:00	Visit to border wall in Nogales, MX
3:00	Free time in downtown Nogales, MX
4:00	Visit with microloan agency in Nogales, MX
6:00	Dinner at homestays

Overnight homestays

FIGURE 1 A sample itinerary of the first three days of a weeklong immersion trip.

In any given week, BorderLinks travelers would ride for hours wedged into the back of a van on the way to meetings with clergy activists, a question-and-answer session with Immigration and Customs Enforcement (ICE) officials, a visit to a Fair Trade coffee roaster in Mexico, and an overnight stay in the home of a family in Nogales, Mexico (see Figure 1). Travelers talked with recently deported immigrants, observed mass deportation proceedings at the Federal Courthouse, and snapped pictures of the infamous "border wall." Travelers slept at night on the floor of church fellowship halls or immigrant shelters, visiting with care-givers who provided food, simple first aid, or consolation to migrants. They even slowly walked the desert trails during the day that migrants hurriedly crossed at night. To understand this experience, I traveled with six different groups, interviewed dozens of travelers and staffers, and surveyed more than two hundred travelers at multiple points in time.[118]

BorderLinks represents one version of immersion travel while serv-ing as a theoretically illuminating case for mechanisms shared across different types of immersion travel. Like most immersion travel producers, BorderLinks eschews the behaviors and ideas associated with tourism, prioritizes direct interactions with foreign persons, expects transformation to occur through the experience, guides small groups from feeder organizations, and works with foreign commu-nities. Like much of global civil society, BorderLinks is religious and draws many of its participants from religious organizations. And, like for a substantial minority of immersion trips, BorderLinks brings trav-elers to Mexico.[119] For many if not most Americans, Mexico is a geographically distant place, with unfamiliar settings, in which differ-ences of nationality, race, language, ethnicity, and religion can be salient. The US-Mexico border itself is a topic of intense public debate and pronounced suffering, as tens of thousands of immigrants cross through it each year.

BorderLinks contrasts with other immersion travel producers in ways that heighten its theoretical utility as a case. First, BorderLinks is a binational organization, incorporated with offices in two countries, with a binational staff, and with nearly-equal amounts of time spent by travel-ers on both sides of the border. This transnational status and the length of the organization's life suggest it has deep local roots and is not merely a producer of gazes on Mexico. Scholarship suggests that the most respon-sible immersion travel producers are those with strong local ties, a con-tinuing relationship with local partners, and mutual leadership – all characteristics of BorderLinks.[120]

---

[118] For a description of the multiple research methods involved and their design, see the Methodological Appendix.
[119] Priest et al., "Researching the Short-Term Mission Movement."
[120] Lasker, *Hoping to Help.*

Another way that BorderLinks contrasts with most immersion trip producers is its resistance to providing any aid to immigrants or Mexicans. Indeed, the organization claimed to "do nothing" for immigrants and Mexicans. While most immersion trips appear to provide charitable service, medical care, educational expertise, or religious teaching, BorderLinks focused on the generation of understanding instead of the transformation of locals' lives. This organizational orientation makes the organization less susceptible to critiques by scholars and activists about the charitable, neo-colonialist projects of first-world travelers.[121]

What the organization *does* do is provide a type of experiential education and discovery that is focused on moralization without being heavy-handed or didactic. This makes it similar in spirit to the broader experiential education movement. The style of this approach, which is detailed in the pages ahead, is similar to what Kelner discovered in his study of "homeland tourism" by Birthright Israel. Kelner described how the guides on those trips incorporated "multiple perspectives into their representations, to avoid creating the impression that they [were] attempting to compel adherence to a party line."[122] BorderLinks incorporates multiple perspectives into its work and is relatively open-ended in the conclusions to be drawn. This orientation also means that BorderLinks fills time and space with the sort of face-to-face, discursive activities that are said to be crucial to the moral projects of global cosmopolitanism and global citizenship.[123]

A final reason for the utility of BorderLinks as a case is that it has been studied in different eras by sociologists and anthropologists.[124] This

---

[121] Hefferan, *Twinning Faith and Development* Mostafanezhad, *Volunteer Tourism.*

[122] Kelner, *Tours That Bind*, p. 76.

[123] Dill, *The Longings and Limits of Global Citizenship Education: The Moral Pedagogy of Schooling in a Cosmopolitan Age*; Kwame Anthony Appiah, *Cosmopolitanism: Ethics in a World of Strangers* (New York: W.W. Norton & Company, 2006).

[124] Cecilia Menjivar, "Serving Christ in the Borderlands: Faith Workers Respond to Border Violence," in *Religion and Social Justice for Immigrants*, ed. Pierrette Hondagneu-Sotelo (New Brunswick, NJ: Rutgers University Press, 2007); Jessica Piekielek, "Visiting Views of the U.S.-Mexico Border: Reflections of Participants in Experiential Travel Seminars" MA Thesis, University of Arizona, Tucson (2003); Jodi Rae Perin, "Educational Travel for Societal Change: An Exploration of Popular Education along the Mexico-U.S. Border" MA Thesis, University of Arizona, Tucson (2003); Hilary Cunningham, "Transnational Politics at the Edges of Sovereignty: Social Movements, Crossings and the State at the U.S.-Mexico Border," *Global Networks* 1, 4 (2001).

familiarity to scholars suggests that the organization has been seen as an important place to identify and analyze processes related to transnationalism, religion, and experiential education. The existence of past research on BorderLinks also makes it possible to trace change over time and to compare eras.

Together, these differences from the modal immersion trip are what makes BorderLinks a potential model for improving immersion travel and transnational civic engagement more generally. The awareness-focused, dialogical, and equitable structure of BorderLinks might provide a template for improving immersion travel produced by other organizations. But this is a question left for a destination at which we have not yet arrived.

THEORIZING THROUGH IMMERSION TRAVEL

In the following pages, I build the analysis around four questions. These questions highlight how transnational civic organizations work, how empathy through transnational engagement develops or not, how culture influences civic engagement, and how progressive religion facilitates transnational engagement.

Organizations and Transnational Civic Engagement

My first orienting question is, "how and why do civic organizations prioritize experiential knowledge as a crucial element for fostering transnational civic engagement?" The topic of immersion travel orients us toward civic engagement that occurs on the margins of institutionalized global civil society and existing scholarship, outside the well-documented, publicized domains of humanitarian INGOs and transnational social activism.[125] In the US context, scholars have advocated for observing a more heterogeneous set of civic organizations and their modes of

---

[125] Keck and Sikkink, *Activists beyond Borders*; Jackie Smith, "Transnational Processes and Movements," in *The Blackwell Companion to Social Movements*, ed. David A. Snow, Sarah A. Soule, and Hanspeter Kriesi (Malden, MA: Blackwell Publishing Ltd., 2004); Donatella Della Porta and Sidney Tarrow, "Transnational Processes and Social Activism: An Introduction," in *Transnational Protest and Global Activism: People, Passions, and Power*, ed. Donatella Della Porta and Sidney Tarrow (Lanham, MD: Rowman & Littlefield, 2005).

action.[126] A similar expansion of analytic vision is needed for the transnational context. To this end, one of the questions posed by Krause at the conclusion of her study of international humanitarianism provides a useful call: "What are all the different kinds of linkage to distant suffering we can observe once we pay attention to organizational and field dynamics?"[127] Immersion travel is one such linkage.

The linkage to distant suffering provided through transnational immersion travel is the result of brokering work by an immersion travel producer like BorderLinks. To those familiar with nonprofit organizations, immersion travel producers are curious beasts. They tend to be small, without a membership constituency or a long-serving professional staff. The existence of this organizational niche space reveals that immersion travel producers offer a service that addresses problems that feeder organizations (e.g., colleges and churches) are unable to address. In this way, immersion travel producers are like the "movement halfway houses" of the civil rights movement, venues that coalesce a pool of individuals in order to motivate them toward actions that address social injustice.[128] Niche organizations like these are intriguing because they are often hybrids, combining resources, logics, meanings, and activities from distinct institutional fields.[129] The immersion travel producer analyzed in this book shows how hybridity enables a new form of transnational civic action and perpetuates organizational survival.

But why is immersion travel attractive, and why are immersion travel producers useful, to feeder organizations in the United States? After all, feeder organizations have means other than high-cost travel to produce concern for distant social problems. They could raise awareness through educational materials, like classes, books, movies, or speakers, or other tactics of distance-focused civic action, like letter campaigns and boycotts. It seems that the feeder organizations that hire immersion travel

---

[126] Kenneth T. Andrews and Bob Edwards, "Advocacy Organizations in the U.S. Political Process," *Annual Review of Sociology* 30 (2004); Paul Lichterman and Nina Eliasoph, "Civic Action," *American Journal of Sociology* 120, 3 (2014).

[127] Krause, *The Good Project*, p. 175

[128] Aldon D. Morris, *Origins of the Civil Rights Movement: Black Communities Organizing for Change* (New York: The Free Press, 1986).

[129] Debra C. Minkoff, "The Emergence of Hybrid Organizational Forms: Combining Identity-Based Service Provision and Political Action," *Nonprofit and Voluntary Sector Quarterly* 31, 3 (2002).

producers trust the capacity of travel to affect their members uniquely, in a way they could not themselves achieve. For feeder organizations, immersion travel is a "cultural resource," a tool used to promote the predetermined, if vague and difficult to realize, ends related to distant suffering.[130]

The expectation, shared by both feeder organizations and immersion travel producers, is that immersion travel will produce an experiential, embodied awareness that is connective, meaningful, authentic, and transformative. The moral nature of this goal is central to understanding the "pull" of immersion travel. In a formal sense, immersion travel enables the possibility of new personal relationships, a moral good in itself. But the deeper moral good sought is the development of a specific, felt obligation found through interaction with others, which should subsequently move travelers toward some new form of personal understanding and altruistic response. This moral good has been especially supported and legitimated in recent decades through the rise of experiential education. Occasions of new experience – especially experiences that are emotionally intensive, disruptive, disorienting, and relational – are sought out for their transformative effects. As Richard Kiely, a practitioner and scholar of global service-learning, writes: "The ideal end result of transformational learning is that one is empowered by learning to be more socially responsible, self-directed, and less dependent on false assumption."[131] This is the ideal.

Immersion travel producers are expected to turn this ideal into a reality. Thus, the work of an immersion travel producer addresses a perennial concern in sociology: how ideas get translated into practice. The civic sphere, in which immersion travel occurs, is often considered to be *the* social sphere in which the link between ideal and practice is rather straightforward.[132] For example, isn't it obvious that civic volunteers do good things for nonprivileged people, or that deliberation processes make democracy accountable? Actually, no. Volunteers do many things for

---

[130] Corey M. Abramson, "From "Either-or" to "When and How": A Context-Dependent Model of Culture in Action," *Journal for the Theory of Social Behaviour* 42, 2 (2012).

[131] Richard Kiely, "A Transformative Learning Model for Service-Learning: A Longitudinal Case Study," *Michigan Journal of Community Service Learning* 12, 1 (2005), p. 7.

[132] Eliasoph, *The Politics of Volunteering*; Paul Dekker, "Civicness: From Civil Society to Civic Services?," *Voluntas: International Journal of Voluntary and Nonprofit Organizations* 20, 3 (2009); Jeffrey Alexander, *The Civil Sphere* (New York: Oxford University Press, 2006).

themselves, while stage-managed deliberation can curtail democracy.[133] Similarly, much of the story in this book will be about the difficulties for immersion travel producers of bringing ideals into reality. What immersion travel producers say they are doing is not the same as what actually occurs, usually through no intentional fault of their own. This loose coupling between means and ends is common among civic organizations.[134] To understand what happens in immersion travel requires observing the way that ideals translate into organizational activity. This book furthers this pragmatic, critical purpose by showing how an immersion travel producer's "deep story" of facilitating transformation becomes fractured as it turns into practice.[135] The resulting transformative experience is often still powerful for travelers but is of a different kind than originally planned.

Empathy and the Production of Social Concern

A second orienting question takes us deeper into transnational processes, asking, "How are empathy and emotion aroused in transnational engagement and to what effect?" In the emic folk theory of immersion travel among its supporters, travelers easily discover suffering firsthand through contact and interaction. But, as we will see, this is an incredible accomplishment that requires extensive organizational work that is invisible, involves compromises, and is never seamlessly achieved. Immersion travel producers come to rely on specific strategies to produce a species of awareness about distant suffering, again and again, in traveler after traveler.

These strategies are discursive, emotional, and imaginative, suggesting the relevance of a cultural approach to understanding motivation in collective action.[136] In this tradition, emotions, bodily experience, and interpretive creativity are all useful mechanisms that can problematize

---

[133] Eliasoph, *Making Volunteers*; Caroline W. Lee, *Do-It-Yourself Democracy: The Rise of the Public Engagement Industry* (New York: Oxford University Press, 2015).

[134] Jerome P. Baggett, *Building Private Homes, Building Public Religion: Habitat for Humanity* (Philadelphia: Temple University Press, 2005); Francesca Polletta, "How Participatory Democracy Became White: Culture and Organizational Choice," *Mobilization: An International Quarterly* 10, 2 (2005).

[135] Arlie Russell Hochschild, *Strangers in Their Own Land: Anger and Mourning on the American Right* (New York: The New Press, 2016).

[136] James M. Jasper, *The Art of Moral Protest: Culture, Biography, and Creativity in Social Movements* (Chicago: University of Chicago Press, 1997).

and moralize social suffering. Immersion travel appears to simultaneously saturate traveler experience with lots of motivational components, including perspective-taking activities, interactions with suffering people, testimonials of suffering, and discursive framings.[137] To make sense of this diversity that occurs to travelers in one experience, I incorporate the concept of empathy.[138] By doing so, my argument helps to specify elements of the persuasion process that Keck and Sikkink identified as crucial for actualizing the "beyond borders" power of transnational advocacy networks.[139]

As a conceptual base for understanding the complex emotional and moral connections between humans, empathy has in recent years received booming research attention and criticism.[140] The core of empathy, what Daniel Batson calls empathic concern, is defined as "other-oriented emotions elicited and congruent with the perceived welfare of someone else."[141] Empathy is a synthetic concept, helping us to see multiple processes occurring together, coming close to how actual people experience them as a whole.

As I follow travelers through a panoply of activities, I pay attention to how and whether empathy develops. I draw on insights from dual-process cognition models, which have become increasingly common in sociology as a way to model behaviors connected to basic processes of motivation.[142] Since the data used in this book are across a span of time, I can provide an evaluation of how different activities work toward the goals of awareness raising, empathic concern, and commitment. Both discursive and embodied processes play a role in moralization, similar to that seen in recent research on religious and ethical self-making.[143]

---

[137] Kiely, "A Transformative Learning Model for Service-Learning."

[138] C. Daniel Batson and Adam A. Powell, "Altruism and Prosocial Behavior," in *Handbook of Psychology* ed. Theodore Millon and Melvin J. Lerner. Hoboken (Hoboken, NJ: John Wiley & Sons, Inc., 2003); Mark H. Davis, "Empathy," in *Handbook of the Sociology of Emotions*, ed. Jan E. Stets and Jonathan H. Turner (New York: Springer, 2006).

[139] Keck and Sikkink, *Activists beyond Borders*.

[140] Paul Bloom, *Against Empathy: The Case for Rational Compassion* (New York: Random House, 2017).

[141] C. Daniel Batson, *Altruism in Humans* (New York: Oxford University Press, 2011), p. 11.

[142] Omar Lizardo et al., "What Are Dual Process Models? Implications for Cultural Analysis in Sociology," *Sociological Theory* 34, 4 (2016).

[143] Daniel Winchester, "A Hunger for God: Embodied Metaphor as Cultural Cognition in Action," *Social Forces* 95, 2 (2016).

These processes are complementary in the flow of immersion travel, but some immersion trip activities work better than others. Of particular interest in the pages ahead are my data about what happens when immersion travelers and immigrants meet face to face. This moment of personal interaction is the paragon of intercultural contact theorists, global cosmopolitanism advocates, and immersion travel champions. But the unexpected difficulties and unintended results of this key activity suggest the outer limit of transnational civic engagement.

Culture and Action

A third orienting question of this book is, "what processes develop or diminish, strengthen or weaken the meanings of immersion travel?" This particular theme takes us into a roiling discussion in sociology: how culture works. Two problems that cultural sociology has been focused on in recent years involve theorizing how "unsettledness" influences social action and how group culture shapes experience.

While most research on unsettledness is focused on objective conditions of social collapse or drastic social change, immersion travel represents a type of unsettledness relatively common in social life: voluntary, temporary, and subjectively induced.[144] Think of a work retreat, a gap year, or a road trip. The characteristics of unsettledness in these activities – and immersion travel – include contingency, separation, liminality, and reintegration, all of which provide material for the project of transformation.[145] As a cultural form, unsettling experiences like immersion travel create and enact expectations of transformation, providing a new experience for individuals to work with to accomplish something new.[146] Is this generic power of the cultural form the most critical element of unsettling experiences? The answer provided here is a soft "no."

One problem with focusing solely on the cultural form of immersion travel is that it neglects the content. Scholars of other forms of civic

[144] Ann Swidler, *Talk of Love: How Culture Matters* (Chicago: University of Chicago Press, 2001); Omar Lizardo and Michael Strand, "Skills, Toolkits, Contexts and Institutions: Clarifying the Relationship between Different Approaches to Cognition in Cultural Sociology," *Poetics* 38, 2 (2010).

[145] Kelner, *Tours That Bind*; Turner, *The Ritual Process: Structure and Anti-Structure*; Smelser, *The Odyssey Experience*; Georg Simmel, *On Individuality and Social Forms* (Chicago: University of Chicago Press, 1971).

[146] DeGloma, *Seeing the Light*.

engagement, like high school activity clubs, have suggested that, while such forms may have generic effects, it is only by analyzing the variations within the form that we understand how they socialize participants.[147] A goal of my analysis is to disentangle the effects of immersion travel as cultural form from the specific content that occurs within it. By focusing on distinct activities of immersion travel, I make visible the intentional work that immersion travel producers, and transnational civic organizations in general, do to produce the felt outcomes of transformation and how that work shapes travelers' experiences.

If we were to focus only on the form of immersion travel, we would also miss how group processes structure unsettling experiences. Since immersion travelers usually come from feeder organizations, like colleges and churches, there are salient elements of social life that preexist and postexist immersion travel. Drawing from the line of "group style" research, my analysis illustrates how small groups influence the most basic feel of immersion travel.[148] The condition of unsettledness induced by the cultural form of immersion travel brings forth group styles as the content of immersion travel. Group styles mediate between the institutional roots of feeder organizations and the new experience that individual travelers encounter, bringing forth preexisting ways of seeing, feeling, and thinking. The tacit presence of group styles during immersion travel lays bare one characterization of immersion travel: that it is a relatively conservative mode of civic engagement and awareness raising, one that is stabilized through the familiarity of group processes.

But the unsettledness of immersion travel, theoretically, should also provide an opportune moment for creative ideological work, for meaning-making that problematizes reality.[149] It is this moment of reflexivity that many scholars of international travel seriously doubt occurs, but that many supporters of immersion travel hope arises. As we will see, this creative aspect of culture does not arise naturally, only among some groups and only through the intellectual leadership of some group

---

[147] Daniel A. McFarland and Reuben J. Thomas, "Bowling Young: How Youth Voluntary Associations Influence Adult Political Participation," *American Sociological Review* 71, 3 (2006); Lichterman and Eliasoph, "Civic Action."

[148] Nina Eliasoph and Paul Lichterman, "Culture in Interaction," *American Journal of Sociology* 108, 4 (2003).

[149] Bennett M. Berger, *The Survival of a Counterculture: Ideological Work and Everyday Life among Rural Communards* (New York: Transaction Publishers, 2004 [1981]); Lizardo and Strand, "Skills, Toolkits."

leaders. For the groups that meet this ideal condition of reflexivity, it is crucial for the long-term effects of immersion travel on individuals.

Progressive Religion and Social Action

A final orienting question is, "how does progressive religion shape transnational engagement in distinct ways?" After decades of scholarly disinterest, and despite demographic changes that challenge the size of its membership base, progressive religion is back in the spotlight. A notoriously difficult field to define, progressive religion includes those persons, groups, organizations, and efforts that produce progressive action, express progressive values, promote progressive identities, and/ or create progressive theology.[150] The organization in this book covers most of those categories: it focuses on the inequalities and violence of undocumented immigration, it espouses social justice values, it promotes social change, and it identifies with progressive religious thinkers and groups. But the case also shows aspects of progressive religion that are not well understood by scholars interested in civic engagement: how a progressive religious group distinguishes its practices against similar ones used by conservative religious groups and how progressive religion engages beyond US borders in a nonmissionizing way.

Progressive religious groups often worry about their image and engage in distinction work against other forms of religious engagement that they see as problematic or even heretical. In a national context where religious action is so often assumed to be conservative, this distinction work is crucial for both the internal and external identity of religious groups.[151] Richard Madsen has argued that practices that are distributed throughout the American religious landscape, like immersion travel, are done in ways that enable distinctive religious meanings and relationships to evolve.[152] How this happens brings insight to the way variations in a religious

[150] Todd N. Fuist, Ruth Braunstein, and Rhys H. Williams, "Religion and Progressive Activism–Introducing and Mapping the Field," in *Religion and Progresssive Activism: New Stories about Faith and Politics*, ed. Ruth Braunstein, Todd N. Fuist, and Rhys H. Williams (2017).

[151] Grace Yukich, *One Family under God: Immigration Politics and Progressive Religion in America* (New York: Oxford University Press, 2013).

[152] Richard Madsen, "The Archipelago of Faith: Religious Individualism and Faith Community in America Today," *American Journal of Sociology* 114, 5 (2009).

practice emerge through positioning against other organizations that deploy a similar practice.[153]

Most immersion travel produced by American religious organizations is known as "short-term mission" travel, a moniker that echoes a history of evangelicalism that progressive religious groups now reject.[154] A progressive, religious immersion trip producer like BorderLinks must work to portray its distinct identity and distinct use of travel. The case here shows that the way this happens is more conflictual and less straight-forward than might be expected for the organization, even though oppos-ing religious groups or audiences are not physically present. This is the case for two reasons. First, progressive religious groups often constrain their theological language as they attempt to display inclusivity.[155] So, a progressive, religious organization is not likely to assert dogmatic beliefs as part of its identity work. Second, many progressive religious groups shy away from social certainty and political partisanship.[156] So, a progres-sive, religious organization is not likely to make authoritative claims to truth.

Given these cultural limits to progressive religion, the case in this book shows three avenues for solving this problem. First, a progressive, reli-gious organization can plot itself in a narrative of progressive, religious history. BorderLinks continually recounts its connections to a history of

[153] John Levi Martin, "What Is Field Theory?," *American Journal of Sociology* 109, 1 (2003); Mustafa Emirbayer and Victoria Johnson, "Bourdieu and Organizational Analysis," *Theory and Society* 37, no. 1 (2008); Roger Friedland, "God, Love and Other Good Reasons for Practice: Thinking through Institutional Logics," *Institutional Logics in Action: Research in the Sociology of Organizations* 39 (2013); Tina Fetner, *How the Religious Right Shaped Lesbian and Gay Activism* (Minneapolis, MN: Univer-sity of Minnesota Press, 2008).

[154] Adler Jr. and Offutt, "The Gift Economy of Direct Transnational Civic Action."; Stephen Offutt, "The Role of Short-Term Mission Teams in the New Centers of Global Christianity," *Journal for the Scientific Study of Religion* 50, 4 (2011).

[155] Richard L. Wood, *Faith in Action: Religion, Race, and Democratic Organizing in America* (Chicago: University of Chicago Press, 2002); Paul Lichterman and Rhys H. Williams, "Cultural Challenges for Mainline Protestant Political Progressives," in *Religion and Progressive Activism: New Stories about Faith and Politics*, ed. Ruth Braunstein, Todd N. Fuist, and Rhys H. Williams (New York: New York University Press, 2017).

[156] Wood, *Faith in Action: Religion, Race, and Democratic Organizing in America*; Rhys H. Williams, "What Progressive Efforts Tell Us about Faith and Politics," in *Religion and Progressive Activism: New Stories about Faith and Politics*, ed. Ruth Braunstein, Todd N. Fuist, and Rhys H. Williams (New York: New York University Press, 2017); Laura Desfor Edles, "Contemporary Progressive Christianity and Its Symbolic Ramifi-cations," *Cultural Sociology* 7, 1 (2013).

people and groups that interwove faith and social analysis. It introduces the ideas of Paulo Freire and liberation theology from the 1960s; it recounts its founding moment in a progressive, religious movement community of the 1980s; it even brings in "living legends" from the local religious activist community to meet travelers. Its reference points of historical persons and movements are not widely known to most travelers, implicitly creating a progressive, religious tradition for them to latch onto.

Second, a progressive organization can change the meanings of a practice by making a direct contrast to conservative religious behavior. In this case, BorderLinks tells travelers it does not "do" short-term mission travel. Even though its version of immersion travel retains the basic elements it shares with other versions – interpersonal contact, unsettledness, transformative expectations – the organization changes the practice by regulating the type of relationship that forms between travelers and hosts. Travelers are told not to give money to people they meet or to provide any help. This removes immediate charitable and philanthropic response, framing foreign "others" as conversation partners and teachers of human experience.

Third, a progressive, religious organization can foster new behaviors that construct a different way of being religious.[157] The organization presented here has developed a way of producing spiritual experience and moral truth, but not primarily through prayer, scriptural study, or theological argument. Similar to the collaborative activist spaces discovered by Ann Mische in Brazil, BorderLinks produces a way of doing religion that is "elaborative" for all people, focused on expanding understanding of social reality before acting on it.[158] The organization prioritizes the authority of suffering, encouraging discursive engagement, bodily experience, and emotional processing around the goal of knowing others' suffering. It interlaces stories of suffering with travelers' personal stories to promote a bigger story that ties together personal and social transformation. Theoretically, anyone can join in this "religious" process, religious or not.

[157] Courtney Bender, *Heaven's Kitchen: Living Religion at God's Love We Deliver* (Chicago: University of Chicago Press, 2003).
[158] Ann Mische, *Partisan Publics: Communication and Contention across Brazilian Youth Activist Networks* (Princeton, NJ: Princeton University Press, 2007).

What this results in is evidence of how US-based religious groups can engage global communities and issues in a way that is fundamentally different from the stereotyped images of their missionary forbears. Some observers still mistakenly see "missionary" whenever US religious groups engage beyond US borders. The prominence of this lens is partially due to the high visibility of evangelical groups, which catch the eyes of social scientists. This sort of lens misrepresents a wide range of transnational engagement and misconceptualizes the structure of transnational religion.[159]

Ironically, as historian David Hollinger has recently shown, an accurate understanding of the twentieth-century US missionary enterprise would reveal its *usefulness* as a reference point for what progressive, religious organizations like BorderLinks do for transnational engagement.[160] Hollinger recounts that Christian missionaries usually left the United States with condescending, harmful ideas, but often returned transformed by their foreign experience. As he narrates, "An enterprise formidably driven by ethnocentrism and cultural imperialism … generated dialectically a counterreaction that was enabled by the religious ideology of its origin."[161] In his recounting, this led to an unexpected "missionary cosmopolitanism" in US foreign affairs, higher education, and religious life in the twentieth century. Immersion travel in general and the case in this book should be understood against this historical background. Having inherited healthy skepticism of the ideology and practice of missionary activity, progressive, religious organizations are nonetheless still transnationally engaged.[162] Progressive, religious immersion travel producers do not primarily seek change in foreign others, but instead seek the dialectic effects of immersion travel, hoping to rectify the global effects of the United States' economic and political power.

---

[159] Ryan Dunch, "Beyond Cultural Imperialism: Cultural Theory, Christian Missions, and Global Modernity," *History and Theory* 41, 3 (2002); Adler Jr. and Ruiz, "The Immigrant Effect."; Wuthnow, *Boundless Faith*; Evelyn L. Bush, "Measuring Religion in Global Civil Society," *Social Forces* 85, 4 (2007).

[160] Hollinger, *Protestants Abroad.*   [161] Ibid., p. 2.

[162] Amy Reynolds, *Free Trade and Faithful Globalization: Saving the Market* (New York: Cambridge University Press, 2014); Rachel M. McCleary and Robert J. Barro, "Private Voluntary Organizations Engaged in International Assistance, 1939–2004," *Nonprofit and Voluntary Sector Quarterly* 37, 3 (2008); Wuthnow, *Boundless Faith*.

WHAT COMES OF IMMERSION TRAVEL

Many readers, perhaps influenced by the spread and ubiquitous presence of similar trips in their organizations, will be most interested in one question I have not yet highlighted: Are immersion trips effective, and should they be supported? This book addresses this question primarily from the viewpoint of US organizations and travelers, an avowedly one-sided and problematic approach. The data presented here add to the growing pile of evidence that immersion travel does *something* to travelers. However, most travelers and organizations alike are unclear about what the exact effects of immersion travel should be. Given this puzzle, my approach is to treat immersion travel as a process to be *explained*, temporarily suspending interest in what immersion travel itself explains. This means treating the question of "whether immersion trips are effective" as itself an outcome of what immersion travel is. The ideals, transformational expectations, and emotions of immersion travel are so dominant that they make it difficult to disentangle how trips work and how they work differently for some travelers.

To highlight these difficulties, it is helpful to hear from immersion travelers themselves. Here, I briefly introduce three travelers whose biographies reveal the challenge of understanding what changes in immersion travel and why.

Jonathan, whose voice we heard at the beginning, was a white, male, upper-class student I met while traveling with Eastern College. He was almost finished with his degree at Eastern College, a top-tier liberal arts college. Like many of his classmates, he could converse in Spanish and was fluent in analyzing the political economy of immigration and the symbolic violence of discrimination against Hispanics. He had grown up religious in a conservative, Christian family, participating in Young Life as a teenager. During the trip I accompanied him on, he was struck by the many religious activists he met who were dedicated to immigrants. Six months after the trip, as I interviewed him about his life thereafter, Jonathan explained that his progressive opinions about immigration had become more public. He felt increasingly divided from the anti-immigrant religiosity of his parents, but also felt spiritually called in his life's purpose as he looked forward to working with immigrants after graduation. Looking back, he said, "the trip was another subversive act from my family" as he became an adult. Jonathan's story is an exemplar for fans of immersion travel: a traveler whose experience led in a tangible direction related to what he encountered during travel.

Roland's story, by contrast, exemplifies how immersion travel can produce a sense of dramatic impact, but for unclear ends. Roland was a white, middle-aged, well-educated engineer for a major multinational corporation who traveled with his church, St. Michael's. Roland had been on numerous short-term mission trips before, including to New Orleans after Hurricane Katrina. On the second day of the BorderLinks trip, Roland sheepishly explained that he had brought work boots and a Leatherman tool in expectation of doing volunteer work in Mexico alongside his fellow churchgoers. Through conversations with immigrants and visits to immigrant aid stations, Roland became increasingly upset about what he saw. By the end of the trip, he promised to "raise awareness" in his corporation about the labor conditions in *maquila* factories similar to those where his corporation off-shored jobs. Six months after the trip, when I spoke with him, Roland's commitment and motivation seemed diminished. He expressed exasperation about his inability to change his corporation's international activities or even his church's nonchalant attitude toward immigration. He even admitted that he had "rationalized" his inactivity to himself as his life returned to normal.

If Jonathan is held up as an exemplar of how immersion travel can influence a person and Roland is an example of how the motivational potential of the experience can evaporate, Kate's story is altogether different. Kate, whom we heard from in the opening pages, was a white, female, young adult who traveled with her seminary class from the South. She knew little about undocumented immigration, was from a working class background, and was unsure of her life plans. The trip was supposed to help prepare her for social justice work as part of her future ministry. But the trip and its implications were complicated and confusing. During a hike in the desert along migrant trails, she had a panic attack. Later in the trip, she was shocked at the lack of respect for shackled immigrants in a federal deportation courtroom. Six months later, when we talked, she seemed to be disturbed by the trip and confused about what it meant for her life. She had not figured out a way to "take action" and was unsure that she ever would. Near the end of the interview, she explained: "It's been hard to live up to how I felt like I needed to change my life."

These vignettes make clear the confusion around what immersion travel does to travelers. Is Jonathan an example of immersion travel success if he was *already* concerned about and connected to the immigrant rights movement? Or is Roland a better sign of success, as someone ensconced in a career who could now see moral connections where none had existed before? Or is Kate an even better example of success, as she felt changed in her life, even if struggling to find the direction? The pages ahead will help us to evaluate such puzzles.

The journey of the book continues in Chapter 2, which introduces BorderLinks' history, deep story, and experiential education pedagogy. For the organization's founders and its feeder organizations from across the nation, BorderLinks was an organizational answer to a boundary problem: the line between education and action. Begun in the 1980s, the organization formed around ideas of liberation theology and Paulo Freire's popular education pedagogy, framing travel as an opportunity for unexpected transformation through interaction with foreign others. For three decades, it has bridged meanings of education and religion, bringing travelers closer to action on behalf of people south of the US border, with renewed focus as immigrant deaths skyrocketed in the 2000s. BorderLinks continually works to distinguish itself against both traditional classroom pedagogy and religious short-term mission trips, creating a space for moral discovery and progressive religious action. The bridging work of the organization illustrates a unique role for awareness-raising organizations and immersion travel in the ecology of advocacy and social movement organizations.

Chapter 3 observes how BorderLinks' ideals of experiential education and personal transformation get transformed into practice through the "See-Judge-Act" model of social analysis, long familiar to religious activists and experiential educators alike. This approach to immersion travel reflects a faith in the power of encounter with suffering to reveal reality. I uncover a surprising local culture of *formal neutrality* in which the organization's staff members downplay their expertise, create discursive complexity instead of clarity, and are nondirective about what travelers could do in the future. I describe three unintentional practices that emerge to balance this internal culture: "whack-a-mole," the "testimonial economy of 'real people'" and the "heart-knowledge processor." These practices fracture the organization's explicit ideals, but are critical for organizational survival. Travelers are given little direction about what to do after travel beyond "sharing the story," but the context is set for other pieces of travel experience to shape travelers.

Part II examines the activities of immersion travel. Chapter 4 begins with an overview of the many activities that occur on an immersion trip, before analyzing how travelers respond emotionally to the activities. This analysis disentangles the generic effect of the cultural form of "travel experience" from the effect of specific activities that occur during travel. I demonstrate the payoff of investigating this content. Travelers' time is taken up with three types of activities that represent undocumented immigration in different ways: talks, visits, and simulations. Not surprisingly, travelers liked doing activities they could not do from afar. Using a unique measure of two emotions – anger and sorrow – I show that different trip activities produced distinctly different types of emotions. Outside activists that talked with groups helped anger develop, while interactions with immigrants generated sorrow. The viewing of federal deportation proceedings generated both. The progressive immersion travel of BorderLinks thus appears to produce a complex emotional palette as a way of connecting to suffering.

Chapter 5 turns toward a close ethnographic analysis of two core activities that aim to produce personal connection with immigrants. I term these two types, which rely on different cognitive processes, *empathy strategies*. Empathy strategies are the formal ways that an organization attempts to produce empathic concern for social suffering. At BorderLinks, a relational empathy strategy involves face-to-face inter-action with undocumented immigrants while a mimetic empathy strategy simulates the conditions of immigration crossing through a desert hike. As my observations show, face-to-face engagement, which is idealized in cosmopolitanism and contact theory, is laced with interactive problems, producing weak empathic concern. By contrast, the simulation of a desert hike generates a deeply felt, longer-lasting, and symbolically evocative sense of empathy. I use this unexpected contrast to argue two points. First, empathy is an important concept that can be used to systematically compare organizational activities; and, second, direct human interaction is more symbolically than practically important for accomplishing the goals of transnational engagement.

Part III turns from immersion travel activities to understanding travel-ers' responses to those activities. Chapter 6 analyzes how culture works in immersion travel. I use the concept of group styles to clarify a paradox suggested early in the book: if travel is so transformative, why do feeder organizations trust it instead of fear it? Using recent cultural theory, I argue that immersion travel should be seen as a subjectively induced form of cultural unsettledness, what I term guided unsettledness. Groups seek unsettledness, but are implicitly guided through it by group styles tied to their feeder organizations. I contrast the *sleuthing* style of groups from nonreligious institutions with the *story-building* style of groups from religious institutions. The former groups doubt immigrant accounts as never-quite-true and are wary of emotions, while the latter groups accept individual immigrant stories as archetypes of larger truths and embrace emotions. Both styles stabilize the experience of immersion travel and guide travelers in distinct ways. Feeder organizations (and travelers) know that immersion travel will be unsettling, and count on it being so, but all can trust its effect because of the invisible structure of group membership that guides travelers.

Chapter 7 investigates what happens after immersion travel is done. This question is anything but easy to answer, since the organizers, supporters, and travelers of immersion travel *know* that change will occur and often expect transformation. I revisit the three travelers introduced in Chapter 1 to show how the immersion travel experience sticks with them, making the return back home difficult. I overview evidence of change in travelers' emotions, attitudes, and consumption and political behaviors. I then review three motifs travelers use to talk about their experience and show how these are loosely coupled with change documented by a survey. The chapter ends by examining *critical reflexivity*, an intense process of ideological questioning that deepens the moral salience of immersion travel. Importantly, this aspect of immersion travel is *not* generated by the immersion travel producer and is not experienced by most immersion travel groups. Overall, the chapter demonstrates the complex answer to whether immersion travel "works," showing evidence for travel's effects as well as its limited scope.

In the final chapter, I consider what this evidence about immersion travel says about transnational civic engagement. I revisit some of the surprises of the research, especially the form/content distinction, the difficulties of face-to-face empathy strategies, the role of intentional unsettledness, and the unequal emergence of critical reflexivity. I conclude with suggestions for deploying immersion travel in a way that deals with the problems of distance, inequality, and interaction.

PART I

ORGANIZATIONAL ROOTS AND DILEMMAS

2

At the Border between Education and Action

In the year I first came into contact with BorderLinks, its mission was to be "an international leader in experiential education that raises awareness and inspires action." Written on pamphlets, web pages, and application forms, the organizational vision continued:

As a bi-national organization, BorderLinks brings people together to build bridges of solidarity across North and Latin American borders and promote intercultural understanding and respect.

There are many ways the bridging of the southern border of the United States could be done. For example, BorderLinks could have organized groups to build homes and churches in Mexican border cities. Or, it could have organized volunteers to provide aid – food, shelter, legal help – to undocumented migrants in southern Arizona. Instead, BorderLinks supported a specific way of transnational relationship building, using travel to cross boundaries, both geographic and moral. Why did BorderLinks do immersion travel this way and why was this style so appealing to feeder organizations and travelers?

BorderLinks, it turns out, was an organizational answer to a boundary problem faced by many feeder organizations: how to traverse the distance between formal education (making people aware) and action (motivating people to act).[1] The founding of BorderLinks was an attempt to bridge institutional and organizational boundaries in order

---

[1] Michele Lamont and Virag Molnar, "The Study of Boundaries in the Social Sciences," *Annual Review of Sociology* 28 (2002).

to move Americans toward civic action that would be responsive and effective across national boundaries.

This chapter begins with the organization's founding history, telling the mythology of its "deep story" and describing its pedagogy of social transformation. From these roots, over the course of three decades, the organization has promoted a distinctive style of experiential education and globally engaged religion, while dealing with the challenges of historical change. This bridging history reveals BorderLinks as a hybrid organization, one that helps feeder organizations challenge dominant forms of education and religion.

THE FOUNDING

BorderLinks was created in 1988 by activists connected to the Central American peace and Sanctuary social movements. According to John Fife, a charismatic minister and well-known founding figure of the Sanctuary movement in southern Arizona, BorderLinks was designed to become the "educational arm" of the Sanctuary movement. In 1982, Fife and his Tucson church declared a sanctuary for Central American refugee immigrants. A few years later, Fife and other activists were charged with federal crimes and went to trial, though most only served probation as a result. During an interview with me, Fife explained that, after that high-profile trial, the leaders of the movement were thinking,

'What's the new strategy? What do we need to do?' And one of the things we decided was we need[ed] an education component. So that's kind of where the idea emerged. We needed something for the Sanctuary movement here in Tucson to give people experiential education on the border, about border issues, particularly around refugees in Central America at that point. . . . Essentially [we decided] we need[ed] to reach churches, and colleges, and universities. That was our original understanding, that those are the constituencies that we need[ed] to reach.

In the late 1980s, the Sanctuary movement was increasingly fielding interest from religious and educational organizations that sought ways to assist the movement from afar. BorderLinks' role was to motivate and mobilize "conscience constituents" from organizations *not* located at the border to support the work of the Sanctuary movement.[2]

BorderLinks' marks of identity came from the progressive, religious backgrounds of its early founders and a network of social movement

---

[2] John D. McCarthy and Mayer N. Zald, "Resource Mobilization and Social Movements: A Partial Theory," *The American Journal of Sociology* 82, 6 (1977).

organizations.[3] As the organization coalesced, it selected Rick Ufford-Chase as its first full-time director. Ufford-Chase was the son of a Presbyterian Church (USA) minister and had experience connecting theology and activism. During its first decade, liberal Christian theologians and religious activists helped construct BorderLinks' mission and identity, including Robert McAfee Brown, Mary Anne Lundy, and Ched Myers. These figures and others, all tied in some way to the Central American peace and Sanctuary movements, used religious narratives to frame social, political, and economic problems, displaying religious symbols in their public work. The movements linked progressive groups and individuals across denominational boundaries, resulting in a syncretic religious identity distinctly opposed to the growing Christian Right religious activism of the era. Their style of liberal, Christian engagement with social issues blended the direct activism of 1960s and 1970s social movements with messages of biblical prophets in the Old Testament. Both movements also drew on extensive international networks to relay information from Central America as well as to host delegations of American travelers investigating the foreign effects of US policy.[4]

BorderLinks' immersion travel was set up to resemble trips organized by other immersion travel producers, like The Center for Global Education, the Cuernavaca Center for Intercultural Dialogue on Development (CCIDD), and Witness for Peace. These organizations, and others like them, introduced North Americans to a wide range of communities throughout Latin and South America by creating transnational contact and educating travelers about the political and social aspects of global poverty, violence, and militarization. Witness for Peace, for example, took US religious groups to Central American conflict zones.[5] The visiting religious groups would stay with families, visit destroyed villages, and return home to "witness" the suffering to their churches. Upon return, travelers were mobilized to publicize the effects of US foreign policy in the

[3] John Lofland, "Charting Degrees of Movement Culture: Tasks of the Cultural Cartographer," in *Social Movements and Culture*, ed. Hank Johnston and Bert Klandermans (Minneapolis: University of Minnesota Press, 1995).

[4] Nepstad, *Convictions of the Soul*; Smith, *Resisting Reagan*; Héctor Perla Jr, "Si Nicaragua Venció, El Salvador Vencerá: Central American Agency in the Creation of the US–Central American Peace and Solidarity Movement," *Latin American Research Review* 43, 2 (2008).

[5] Edward Patrick Griffin-Nolan, *Witness for Peace: A Story of Resistance* (Louisville, KY: Westminster/John Knox Press, 1991).

press, to lobby politicians, to provide aid to refugees, and to prepare for strategic acts of nonviolence.[6]

Compared with immersion trips in the conflict zones of Central America, BorderLinks' immersion trips to the US-Mexico border required less financial investment, less time, and less risk for travelers, as they did not move beyond the border region of Mexico. With these trips, BorderLinks' goal was to link the prophetic vision of religious progressives to tangible evidence of suffering by Central American refugees at the US-Mexico border. BorderLinks' mimicking of other organizations' practices was not surprising given the interlocking connections between activists in the movements, as well as the wisdom among practitioners about what immersion travel could produce.[7] Even in 2009, there were still personal connections to this founding historical milieu. Hope, a staff member, went on trips with Witness for Peace and The Center for Global Education in the 1980s. BorderLinks' Executive Director, Delle McCormick, had arrived in 2005, after serving as the director of CCIDD. Patricia, a Mexican national staff member, first encountered BorderLinks in the 1980s as she worked with Central American refugees.

Rick's Story: A Founding Myth about Immersion Travel

Two decades after its founding, when BorderLinks staff members recounted the organization's history for a just-arrived group of trip participants, they usually began with "Rick's story." Rick's story was repeated because it was, literally, the founding myth of the organization. As Ufford-Chase himself recounts:

[In] 1986, I had the good fortune to make my first trip to Central America with a group called Witness for Peace. I stayed with a family in Esteli, Nicaragua for five nights during the trip. On the last night, deeply moved by my direct experience of the effect of war in Nicaragua, I had a long conversation with my host father (with the help of a translator). I told him I believed that God was calling me to learn

---

[6] Sharon Erickson Nepstad and Christian Smith, "Rethinking Recruitment to High-Risk/Cost Activism: The Case of Nicaragua Exchange," *Mobilization: An International Quarterly* 41, 1 (1999).

[7] Sharon Erickson Nepstad, "The Process of Cognitive Liberation: Cultural Synapses, Links, and Frame Contradictions in the U.S.-Central America Peace Movement," *Sociological Inquiry* 67, 4 (1997); Sharon Erickson Nepstad, "Oppositional Consciousness among the Privileged: Remaking Religion in the Central America Solidarity Movement," *Critical Sociology* 33, 4 (2007).

Spanish and to move to Nicaragua to be a part of their struggle for justice. Gently, but firmly, this Nicaraguan peasant told me that I had misunderstood God's will. "We Nicaraguans are quite capable of building a new society," he said, "but we can't do it while trying to fight a war against the most powerful nation on earth." My job, he believed, was to go home and work with people in my own country to help them understand the impact of our actions on the rest of the world. I vowed on that trip home that I would start by learning Spanish, and that I would do my best to honor his words. That conversation has been the north star of my faith journey ever since.[8]

Various versions of Rick's story existed in practice, taking on the fluctuations familiar to oral traditions in which the specific details vary but the main themes remain. While traveling with a group from St. Michael's Church, I heard the BorderLinks staff leader Janice recount the story this way: "Rick was told by someone in Honduras to go back and tell their stories." With the traveling group from Eastern College, the staff leader Alicia related the organization's connection to the Sanctuary movement. Then, she described that, "Rick was inspired by a feeling of conversion when he was in Nicaragua. He figured out in talking with people there that the best thing to do was to return and educate the U.S." She continued, "He started BorderLinks as a faith-based response about education for transformation and social change."

In the quasi-official version, longtime BorderLinks supporter Jerry Gill writes the following:

In Nicaragua, Rick was so moved by the faith of the peasant people in the midst of their oppressed situation that he decided to return home, learn Spanish, and come back to help the Nicaraguans in their struggle. When he told the elderly 'campesino' (peasant farmer) with whom he was staying about his fresh commitment and his plan, the latter looked him straight in the eye and said: 'You have misunderstood the call of God. We Nicaraguans are more than capable of taking care of ourselves. What we can't do is what you must do—return home and work to change U.S. policy toward Nicaragua.'[9]

Some of the details in the versions differ; for example, the country Rick visited (Honduras vs. Nicaragua) and the description of what he did upon return (tell stories vs. work to change policy). Yet the narrative arc of

---

[8] "Rick Ufford-Chase: Elder, Mission Co-Worker, Peacemaker," www.rickuffordchase .com/index.html.
[9] Jerry Gill, *Borderlinks: The Road Is Made by Walking* (Tucson, AZ: BorderLinks, 1999), p. 4.

these different versions is similar, involving personal relationships, a feeling of transformation, and a reversal of insight. The generic form of the story, what Arlie Hochschild refers to as the deep story, goes something like this: a naive American traveler goes to a foreign location and is made aware of reality by the acuity of locals' understanding and faith.[10] He is shocked by conditions of suffering but misunderstands what he has to offer by way of a solution. His path to right action is revealed by the cross-cultural relationships made during travel. In the end, he works on himself and his native country.

Rick's story is a conversion story. This transformational narrative draws on a template that exists throughout Western culture; it is found in conversion narratives among the religious and nonreligious alike.[11] The template embeds psychological and emotional experience in a timeline that symbolizes the shift from ignorance to knowledge.[12] In conversion stories, the discovery of realities beyond the self leads to discoveries of one's self, resulting in surprising identity and behavioral shifts.

BorderLinks used Rick's story to summarize and promote its vision of individual change and social transformation. Stories like Rick's have practical pedagogical functions, suggesting to immersion travelers what could happen to them and what they could do after their travel experience.[13] Rick's version identifies international travel and cross-cultural engagement as the precipitators of discovery and change. The story has religious elements, but ones based less on dogmatic belief than in the personal discernment of spiritual meaning. In her analysis of the transformation of well-educated, middle-class churchgoers in the United States during the Central American peace movement, Nepstad showed how similar conversion stories, like that of Oscar Romero, provided a template for conversion from privilege to social engagement, with spiritual truths found along the way.[14] These sorts of stories suggested to hearers a

---

[10] Hochschild, *Strangers in Their Own Land: Anger and Mourning on the American Right.*

[11] DeGloma, *Seeing the Light.*

[12] Ibid.; John Lofland and Norman Skonovd, "Conversion Motifs," *Journal for the Scientific Study of Religion* 20, 4 (1981).

[13] Francesca Polletta, *It Was Like a Fever: Storytelling in Protest and Politics* (Chicago: The University of Chicago Press, 2006); Rhys H. Williams and Susan M. Alexander, "Religious Rhetoric in American Populism: Civil Religion as Movement Ideology," *Journal for the Scientific Study of Religion* 33, 1 (1994).

[14] Nepstad, "Creating Transnational Solidarity: The Use of Narrative in the U.S.-Central America Peace Movement," *Mobilization* 6, 1 (2001); *Convictions of the Soul*; "Oppositional Consciousness among the Privileged."

template of what was possible without being didactic, inviting individuals to imagine how their commitments could unfold.[15]

In the background of the story is an ongoing, unjust relationship between the United States and a Central American country. The impoverished conditions in the story, and above all the stories of those living in those conditions, have a motivational effect on the traveler. Having seen and heard, the traveler should respond: "What can I do?" Rick's tale, though, adds a twist: the initial response of traveler is *wrong*. The traveler's first response is simple and presumes that the problem is in the foreign country, as if there is something deficient about that place. However, an unnamed foreigner corrects his interpretation and redirects his newfound commitment. As the Nicaraguan antagonist points out to Rick (and to future BorderLinks travelers), the problem is with the United States.

The outsider in Rick's story remains nameless, playing the role of a stranger whose gift is challenging as well as priceless.[16] Indeed, it is exactly this type of stranger, and this type of interaction, that immersion travel through BorderLinks purports to offer to travelers. If personal interactions with suffering foreigners are vital in gaining right knowledge and making personal decisions about future action, then BorderLinks is the way to make this happen.

The story's dramatic reversal is especially inviting to BorderLinks travelers because it intensifies the expectation of what might occur during travel. It also attempts to resolve the criticism by Ivan Illich and others, as recounted in Chapter 1.[17] Rick's story upholds the usefulness of travel abroad, contra Illich's critique, but uses the travel experience to redirect the focus of travelers' actions to the US domestic sphere. This piece of the story is a symbolic statement about the organization's attempt to avoid reproducing historical relations of paternalism, dependency, and inequality between the United States and Central America. The Nicaraguan tells the American traveler *not* to come to the country, but to focus his energies in the United States. BorderLinks is meant as an organizational tool to skip the stage of misunderstanding in the story, so travelers could return home and get to work.

---

[15] Brian M. Lowe, *Emerging Moral Vocabularies: The Creation and Establishment of New Forms of Moral and Ethical Meanings* (Lanham, MD: Lexington Books, 2006).

[16] Georg Simmel, "The Stranger," in *The Sociology of Georg Simmel*, ed. Kurt H. Wolff (New York: The Free Press, 1950).

[17] Ivan Illich, "To Hell with Good Intentions," in *American Midwest Regional Meeting of the Conference on Interamerican Student Projects* (Chicago: 1968).

Pedagogical Roots

Rick's story encapsulates a pedagogical vision that was part of a progressive, religious culture connected to Central and South American social and religious movements. This pedagogical vision was most often associated by the organization with Paulo Freire, a Brazilian intellectual who led national-level social welfare and educational offices before writing numerous works of educational philosophy.[18] In the 1960s, Freire implemented a radically new educational program in Brazil that created small learning groups among the poor to acquire literacy skills through concrete analysis of social and political life. His efforts quickly came to be seen by repressive governments as subversive, leading to his eventual exile. On half of the trips I participated in, Paulo Freire was explicitly mentioned by trip leaders at the very beginning of the trip as the pedagogical inspiration for the organization's work.

At the same time that Freire was experimenting with new educational techniques, pastoral workers and priests in South and Central America were laying the early roots of the liberation theology movement.[19] Because of connections between Freire, his ideas, and religious intellectuals, his "popular education" model shared clear philosophical and pragmatic overlap with the ideas of liberation theology. Both gave special attention to understanding the social structural and economic roots of oppressive poverty. Freire proposed the idea of education through "conscientization," emphasizing the power of poor people in local communities to understand themselves, develop skills, and produce political change.[20] By the 1980s, both Freire's popular education model and liberation theology had disseminated widely within progressive, religious communities in the United States.

After mentioning Freire, BorderLinks trip leaders would give a short explanation of his work in Brazil, claiming that BorderLinks was opposed to the "banking model" of education. According to Freire, the banking model of education saw people as empty vessels to be filled by the words

[18] Paulo Freire, *Pedagogy of the Oppressed* (New York: Sebury Press, 1970); Mary Breunig, "Critical Praxis and Experiential Education," in *Sourcebook of Experiential Education: Key Thinkers and Their Contributions*, ed. Thomas E. Smith and Clifford E. Knapp (New York: Routledge, 2011).

[19] Smith, *The Emergence of Liberation Theology.*

[20] Manuel A. Vásquez, "Structural Obstacles to Grassroots Pastoral Practice: The Case of a Base Community in Urban Brazil*," *Sociology of Religion* 58, 1 (1997); Paulo Freire, "Cultural Action and Conscientization," *Harvard Educational Review* 40, 3 (1970).

and opinions of those with expertise. A central theoretical concern in Freire's work was the ideological role of expertise in systems of education. In banking systems of education, students were malleable objects, not respected for their emerging autonomous capability of acquiring skill and knowledge. Quoting from Freire's *Pedagogy of the Oppressed* in one its fundraising mailers, BorderLinks wrote:

Education either functions as an instrument which is used to facilitate integration of the younger generation into the logic of the present system and bring about conformity or it becomes the practice of freedom, the means by which men and women deal critically and creatively with reality and discover how to participate in the transformation of their world.

BorderLinks' goal was to help travelers realize their ability, as church-goers, college students, or nonexperts, to discover reality without the filters of political propaganda or political frames that legitimated unjust economic and social policies. From the liberation theology tradition, the perspectives of powerless or suffering people – like undocumented immigrants – were especially useful ("privileged") to travelers for their truth-bearing power. While the conscientization approach designed by Freire and liberation theologians had poor people doing education through a questioning praxis about the truths of their lives, BorderLinks had travelers questioning the truths of their lives through an encounter with truths from the lives of suffering others.

To illustrate what this pedagogical process should look like, Border-Links staff members often mentioned the "cycle of praxis." This phrase referred to a conceptual model, borne of mid-twentieth-century Catholic Action groups, that was developed to explain stages of both motivation and action.[21] Known as the See-Think-Act or the See-Judge-Act cycle, it encoded a process of careful observation, critical thought through shared values, and action-oriented decision-making. The cycle imagery became a powerful metaphor as it moved through a network of Catholic organizations, turning up over ensuing decades in a papal encyclical, Vatican II documents, liberation theology, and progressive religious movements.[22] Noting its presence among Brazilian Catholic activists as late as the

[21] Anthony J. Pogorelc, "Movement to Movement Transmission and the Role of Place: The Relationship between Catholic Action and Call to Action," *Sociology of Religion* 72, 1 (2011).

[22] Edward L. Cleary, "The Brazilian Catholic Church and Church-State Relations: Nation-Building," *Journal of Church and State* 39, 2 (1997); Luiza Beth Fernandes, "Basic Ecclesiastic Communities in Brazil," *Harvard Educational Review* 55, 1 (1985).

1990s, Mische referred to it as a vision of "transformative learning from reflection on everyday life."[23]

The cycle imagery displays the ideals of experiential education that BorderLinks supports. The three stages of the cycle – seeing, thinking, and acting – are mentioned in BorderLinks' publicity materials as well as in the narrative the organization shares with travelers about its immersion travel. This framework was crucial to BorderLinks' self-understanding, with the trip leader, Molly, who had served the organization across two executive directors, noting, "The framework that's been the most continual [since the beginning of the organization] is the See-Think-Act pedagogy." With a sense of these roots, we can now examine what BorderLinks' emergence and existence made possible.

A HYBRID ORGANIZATION: BRIDGING EDUCATION, RELIGION, AND HISTORY

At first blush, the founding of BorderLinks appears to be a straightforward story about a new organization created to solve a problem. The organization had an animating story, a distinct pedagogy, and a seemingly clear purpose: to raise awareness through immersion travel so that other social movement organizations could focus on the work of activism.

While this portrayal reflects the strategic choices that the organization's founders began with, it does not explain why this particular style of immersion travel appeared legitimate to the feeder organizations that have sent travelers over the decades. BorderLinks appears to bridge to meanings of education and religion in a way that resonates with a specific set of feeder organizations and travelers. For organizations and travelers across 30 years, this resonance comes from BorderLinks' provision of a space to nurture new identity. Organizations and travelers that came were seeking out a way to connect social awareness, experience, and personal transformation beyond institutional constraints. By analyzing why this bridging to a new constellation of meaning has been attractive, the BorderLinks case provides insight into three topics in the study of civil society and social movement organizations.

First, BorderLinks provides intriguing evidence about how specialized organizations support a social movement sector.[24] Most studies of social

[23] Mische, *Partisan Publics*, p. 191.
[24] Sarah A. Soule and Brayden G. King, "Competition and Resource Partitioning in Three Social Movement Industries," *American Journal of Sociology* 113, 6 (2008).

movements focus on core organizations that mobilize activists to take part in activities that express collective identities and target political goals. Those organizations are "where the action is at." Behind the action, though, a broad collection of organizations support social movements without themselves producing activism.[25] These other organizations specialize in forming and motivating individuals, raising awareness, and creating consciousness.

The best theoretical understanding of this organizational work comes from Aldon Morris' description of "movement halfway houses" in the civil rights movement.[26] Organizations like the Highlander Folk School and the American Friends Service Committee did not represent a group of people, and did not organize direct activism. But, as Morris explains, they could help to develop "skilled activists, tactical knowledge, media contacts, workshops, knowledge of past movements, and a vision of a future society."[27] For example, the Highlander Folk School held trainings in nonviolence and oppositional consciousness that were attended by a range of eventual activists, including Rosa Parks. Such organizations helped to straddle the distance between sentiment pools of possible supporters and mobilized activists, attempting to turn the former into the latter.[28]

Given the special role of halfway houses as the point of motivational contact for potential movement participants, it is surprising that studies have rarely analyzed how these organizations work to generate a shared focus among a diverse population of people. The boundary straddling they do – being "halfway" to activism – is an attractive service not just to activists but to feeder organizations. Feeder organizations, like colleges and churches, can remain symbolically distant from activism while fostering awareness among their members that *might* lead to activism. Social movement organizations can spend less time on the inefficiencies of participant recruitment while at the same time hoping for an expanded supply of adherents.[29]

---

[25] Andrews and Edwards, "Advocacy Organizations."; Bob Edwards and John D. McCarthy, "Social Movement Schools," *Sociological Forum* 7, 3 (1992); Mayer N. Zald, "Theological Crucibles: Social Movements in and of Religion," *Review of Religious Research* 23, 4 (1982); Verta Taylor, "Social Movement Continuity: The Women's Movement in Abeyance," *American Sociological Review* 54, 5 (1989).

[26] Morris, *Origins of the Civil Rights Movement.*   [27] Ibid., pp. 140.

[28] Klandermans and Oegema, "Potentials, Networks, Motivations, and Barriers."

[29] McCarthy and Zald, "Resource Mobilization and Social Movements: A Partial Theory."

A second insight from BorderLinks is how different organizational styles emerge in a field of practice. BorderLinks has continually distinguished itself against other styles of immersion travel, such as service trips and short-term mission trips, both of which have been widely popular among American religious organizations. By doing so, the organization has created and legitimated a space for a progressive, religious identity within the population of US religious organizations that promote international engagement. How this happened sheds light on the way that distinctions of a similar civic practice emerge through positioning against other organizations that deploy a similar practice.[30]

Third, BorderLinks provides a case study of the long-term benefits and challenges of organizational hybridity. Hybrid organizations combine resources, logics, and activities that originate from distinct institutional fields.[31] As a religiously inspired organization founded on the border between education and activism, BorderLinks combined the logics and practices of multiple institutional fields. BorderLinks' broad resource environment and its identity as educational, instead of activist, enabled its survival after Sanctuary movement organizations declined in the 1990s, allowing it to outlive the conditions of its birth. Yet its identity and pragmatic message were challenged by changes in the political and economic context. The results of this indicate that hybridity can help to keep an organization alive while slowly constraining an organization's identity over time.

The rest of the chapter visits these three topics under the rubric of bridging, showing how BorderLinks bridged meanings and practices of education and religion over historical eras to survive for three decades.

BRIDGING TO EXPERIENTIAL EDUCATION

The religious and educational feeder organizations that connect to BorderLinks are seeking to move their members in a new direction. These organizations may be oriented toward changing the world, but they do so

---

[30] Martin, "What Is Field Theory?"; Emirbayer and Johnson, "Bourdieu and Organizational Analysis."

[31] Minkoff, "The Emergence of Hybrid Organizational Forms: Combining Identity-Based Service Provision and Political Action."; Dekker, "Civicness"; Steven Rathgeb Smith, "Hybridity and Nonprofit Organizations: The Research Agenda," *American Behavioral Scientist* 58, 11 (2014).

through activities that are not primarily activist, such as teaching classes, directing worship, and serving the community.[32] They share four broad characteristics that make BorderLinks' experiential education especially appealing.[33]

First, for each of these organizations, politics is a sensitive boundary, such that partisan political speech in the name of the organization is generally considered an inappropriate activity. Organizations like these might be wary of connecting with an "activist" organization but much more willing to connect with one that promotes an educational approach. Second, for each of these organizations, the curriculum, daily activities, and practical wisdom are, at a deep level, aimed at shaping individuals into different future selves. As David Baker has recently argued, the roots of modern educational institutions in religion reveal an emphasis on the primacy of developing individuals' capacities.[34] Educational and religious organizations alike support opportunities for individual transformation. Third, feeder organizations usually do not have extensive programs for investigating specific social issues, especially from afar. The ability to outsource to an external organization like BorderLinks makes it easier to please organizational members who are interested in complex, distant social issues. Fourth, feeder organizations contain a diverse membership, with only a small portion looking for ways to expand moral commitments or explore specific social issues. BorderLinks provides a venue where feeder organizations can bring self-selected members for an awareness-raising experience.

Trip leaders from feeder organizations sought out BorderLinks as an alternative educational space to motivate persons in ways more potent than within their home contexts. Before coming, one group leader noted that, "[BorderLinks] has tried to set itself off from a classic service-learning piece. It's much more experiential than service-based." This group leader continued, "There's really only so much that you can get

---

[32] Patricia H Thornton, William Ocasio, and Michael Lounsbury, *The Institutional Logics Perspective: A New Approach to Culture, Structure, and Process* (New York: Oxford University Press, 2012); Nancy Tatom Ammerman, "Golden Rule Christianity: Lived Religion in the American Mainstream," in *Lived Religion in America*, ed. David D. Hall (Princeton, NJ: Princeton University Press, 1997).

[33] Bradley J. Koch, Joseph Galaskiewicz, and Alisha Pierson, "The Effect of Networks on Organizational Missions," *Nonprofit and Voluntary Sector Quarterly* 44, 3 (2015).

[34] *The Schooled Society: The Educational Transformation of Global Culture* (Redwood City, CA: Stanford University Press, 2014).

across to them [students] in the classroom. I mean even with films and things like that. . . . I just find that [the trip] is the kind of thing that they, you know, really don't forget." This theme about taking students beyond the classroom, physically and pedagogically, recurred.

During an interview, one group leader commented on the importance of breaking away from expert-driven education, describing that, for her, a BorderLinks trip,

is not just an intellectual experience, it's something much, much deeper. . . . I'm very co. . .mmitted to the notion of education outside of the classroom . . . we need to be demonstrating and modeling life learning, something that's much deeper. So often our education encourages a kind of split in our students where they compartmentalize their lives. . . . If you can find a way to take the classroom out to the enfleshed, real material of people's lives, something happens.

For leaders like this, BorderLinks was a place to do education differently. In the midst of an activity with the group of college students that she brought from Eastern College, Dana exclaimed to a student and me, "*This* is the work I want to do . . . not all the administrative stuff" that is part of a professor's life. Later, she explained that this is "transformative education." She noted that her institution was "behind the curve" in this trend of "going beyond the books," so BorderLinks could help to bend that curve.

Group leaders like this were not only introducing their students to a different mode of education; they were also using BorderLinks to pass along the concerns and commitments of their own identities. In my survey, 2 percent of BorderLinks travelers reported having participated in the Central American peace movement or Sanctuary movement. This percentage may seem low, but it is much higher than the American population at large. The people who were old enough to have participated in those movements in the 1980s were, by 2009, bringing travelers to BorderLinks from the feeder organizations in which they had made careers. They were pastors, seminary professors, and college professors, like the ones quoted above. They were using BorderLinks to introduce a new generation to the issues and styles of participation that had been part of their histories. And they were excited about what this could mean. One trip leader recalled with pride that some students who had gone with her to BorderLinks "went on to do incredible social justice work. One worked with [a farmworker labor group], then she worked at an [immigrant resource center], now she's going to law school. Three of them are going to law school now, with a focus on immigration." While I could not verify these claims, they nonetheless articulated the hopes leaders had of bridging to a powerful version of education.

BRIDGING MEANINGS OF TRAVEL

Just as BorderLinks provided a form of engaged education distinct from mainstream pedagogy, so too it produced a form of transnationally engaged religion.

BorderLinks' style of immersion travel emerged in the late 1980s as religious organizations in the United States were increasingly embracing short-term travel after being nearly nonexistent a few decades before. International travel had become significantly easier, which, when connected to global changes in religious demography, made it possible for US religious groups to partner with religious peers across the globe. Just as importantly, neoliberal economic policies decreased foreign nations' resources for internal development, providing a locale for American religious organizations to deploy small-scale aid projects that expressed ideals of community development.[35] As a result of these changes, immersion travelers had a vast arena where they could engage and aid international communities and persons.

American religious groups were especially drawn to immersion travel because it allowed for a personalist approach to international aid in an American cultural moment that lionized participation in civic engagement. Personalism – the prioritization of face-to-face relationships as an essential feature of human life and the belief in the power of individual relationships over institutional ones – has long been a defining feature of American civil society and a critical feature of practicing religion and solving social problems.[36] This valuation of personalism cut across lines of religious theology and orthodoxy.[37] The personal interactions that

[35] Mostafanezhad, *Volunteer Tourism*; Immerwahr, *Thinking Small*.
[36] Paul Lichterman, *The Search for Political Community: American Activists Reinventing Community* (New York: Cambridge University Press, 1996); Baggett, *Building Private Homes*; Robert N. Bellah et al., *Habits of the Heart* (Berkeley: University of California Press).
[37] Penny Edgell Becker, "Making Inclusive Communities: Congregations and the "Problem" of Race," *Social Problems* 45, 4 (1998).

religious immersion travelers sought in foreign locales were not an after-thought or a by-product of travel; they were constitutive of what made immersion travel attractive.

Immersion travel had also become attractive to religious organizations for its ability to reconstruct identity through the "de-routinization of religious life" in the religious careers of members.[38] Viewing religious identity among the American middle class, Madsen has argued that both progressive and orthodox persons in American religion navigate between personal religious seeking and community commitment.[39] Some individuals engage in an ongoing pursuit of religious novelty, with this seeking behavior made possible by the structure and activities of religious organizations and communities. Such activities become part of the active way that people build up their faith identity by connecting them to institutions but also providing material for individual identity creation.[40] By the 1980s, immersion trips had become a prime example of a community-based, other-focused religious practice that also aided individual identity projects.

Distinctions in Religious Immersion Travel

The problem for BorderLinks was that most religious immersion travel was "short-term mission" travel, a style that BorderLinks' religious identity rejected.[41] In the eyes of most progressive religious groups, the phrase "mission trip" had negative connotations with classic missionary work. In the eyes of progressive religious groups, short-term mission trips were seen as naive engagements with vulnerable foreign communities that reproduced paternalism, inequality, and faulty understanding of global social reality. BorderLinks' style of immersion was constructed

---

[38] Iddo Tavory and Daniel Winchester, "Experiential Careers: The Routinization and De-Routinization of Religious Life," *Theory & Society* 41, 4 (2012).

[39] Madsen, "The Archipelago of Faith: Religious Individualism and Faith Community in America Today."

[40] Nancy T. Ammerman, "Religious Identities and Religious Institutions," in *The Handbook of the Sociology of Religion*, ed. Michele Dillon (New York: Cambridge University Press, 2003).

[41] There was a historical basis to the "mission trip" language used by practitioners and scholars alike, since some short-term religious travel arose as a recruitment tool for long-term missionary work, before ultimately failing. Brian Howell, "Roots of the Short-Term Missionary, 1960–1985," Building Church Leaders, www.buildingchurchleaders.com/articles/2006/rootsmissionary.html.

TABLE I *Forms of international immersion travel*

Sphere of Action	Organizational Public Identity	
	Secular	Religious
Political	Zapatismo solidarity trips The Minuteman Project	Witness for Peace delegations Birthright Israel
Charitable	Disaster relief trips Alternative spring breaks	Habitat for Humanity Short-term mission rips

in contradistinction to this image. BorderLinks' position in the field of immersion travel was a historical accomplishment that marked out a distinct way of being religious.

Table 1 shows a simple categorization scheme of the two dimensions that structure different styles of immersion travel. The rows denote a continuum between political and charitable orientations. The political row denotes travel that attempts to understand, critique, and/or change political conditions of foreign places, focusing on political policies and solutions. The charitable row denotes travel that focuses on charitable activity for the benefit of foreign others. The columns denote whether the public identity of the immersion travel producer is nonreligious or religious. As discussed in Chapter 1, and as the table makes clear, immersion travel could be used for political and charitable purposes, by nonreligious and religious organizations alike. Since its founding, BorderLinks has been positioned in the right-side column, more toward the political orientation given its topical focus, historical connection to social movements, and avoidance of charitable activity.

The founders of BorderLinks rhetorically positioned the organization's style of immersion travel in opposition to *both* tourism and mission trips. In the semi-official organizational history of BorderLinks, Gill writes, "the entire BorderLinks enterprise is a far cry from the usual approaches to crossing the border, which generally involve short-term mission trips aimed at lending a helping hand to needy people or leading tourist visits to beachside resorts."[42] During an interview for a national religious news

---

[42] Jerry H. Gill, *Borderlinks II: Still on the Road* (Tucson, AZ: BorderLinks, 2004), p. 152.

source in 1994, the founding director Rick Ufford-Chase succinctly stated, "We [BorderLinks] are not a tourism office."[43]

These concerns, and the organization's distinction work, remained throughout the organization's history, combining into the executive director's continued warning to travelers against thinking they were "going on a vacation with Jesus." In an interview, she explained to me that the organization's model was meant to be a step beyond the "reverse mission" idea where people think, "'We go in [to a country], we're transformed … and we come home changed.'" She continued, "That's not enough. In fact, that is sinful. That is oppressive. That is consumerism of the worst. And we need to make sure that we are also about transformation on the other side. And how we [are] building lasting relationships with those people."

To drive home the symbolic distinction of what the organization did, the trip leader Janice explained in an interview, "We don't call them mission trips, we call them educational delegations or educational seminars, things like that." Aware, though, that so many religious groups, including the congregation of her upbringing in the Midwest, used the terminology of mission trips when they came to BorderLinks, Janice would play with the language to help groups along. She said, "I think that for helping congregations understand what it is and see the need for it, that it's helpful to talk about it that way. That this *is* mission. And as far as short-term mission goes, I think that it is short-term mission at its best." Whatever the word, BorderLinks' trips were different than the dominant form of short-term mission travel.

Equally important as language for distinguishing against short-term mission travel, BorderLinks eschewed religious conversion work, embraced a religious social justice history, and invited nonreligious partners and travelers into a space open to diverse spiritualties. By the late 2000s, the religious nature of the organization was present in ways familiar to scholars that study progressive, religious groups.[44] Religion could be found in its public autobiography, in the types of feeder organizations that came, in the words of activists and migrants that the organization connected to, and in the spiritual meanings those involved gave to their work individually, but *not* in the constant presence of distinct religious language or religious ritual within the organization itself.

---

[43] Demetria Martinez, "Pressing for Justice along the Border; Borderlinks Activists Work with the Poor at the U.S.-Mexico Line," *National Catholic Reporter*, March 4 1994.
[44] Bender, *Heaven's Kitchen*.

Indeed, despite the director being an ordained minister and half the delegation leaders sharing a religious identity with me during their interviews, Janice commented, "My sense is that as an organization [religion] is something we don't talk about very much. It's not very central to the actual workings of the organization." In saying this, Janice appeared to make the mistake of looking for coherent religious vocabularies and religious actions to find religion. She seemed to catch her mistake, though, commenting a moment later, "That said, we are supported by a lot of churches, a lot of our funding comes from churches, a lot of our delegations are from faith-based organizations."

In reality, the organization could turn the "volume" of religion up when it was appropriate for a group coming from a religious feeder organization. In these situations, self-identified religious staff members, like Janice, Hope, Graham, and Pam, were assigned to guide the religious groups. On these trips, Janice explained, trip leaders would plan a visit to a religious service organization, schedule a talk from a local pastor, schedule attendance at a local worship service, or use biblically based materials for evening reflections.

There were downsides to the default organizational approach of keeping the volume of religion turned down. As some scholars have argued about the styles of progressive, religious organizations, the tendency to "quiet" religious language and identity in public work can move the educational, emotional, and moral resources of religion into the background.[45] Delle, the organization's director, explained, "We're so self-conscious about religion here. . . . [Some of] the [staff] leaders don't consider themselves religious or don't want to put a bet over on anybody." This religious quieting helped to achieve inclusivity, but did so at the cost of tabling differences and removing some elements of the organization's deep story.[46]

As an example, one staff member, Sarah, had been very active with the movement to close the School of the Americas. She was part of a national religious group that attended an annual protest and supported religious people that served jail time. Yet the only time I heard her bring it up was in a one-on-one conversation she was having with a college student who

---

[45] Robert Wuthnow, "Beyond Quiet Influence?: Possibilities for the Protestant Mainline," in *The Quiet Hand of God: Faith-Based Activism and the Public Role of Mainline Protestantism*, ed. Robert Wuthnow and John H. Evans (Berkeley: University of California Press, 2002); Lichterman and Williams, "Cultural Challenges for Mainline Protestant Political Progressives."

[46] Edles, "Contemporary Progressive Christianity and Its Symbolic Ramifications."

asked about the movement. Sarah lowered her voice as they had this conversation at the front of the van, trying to keep others from hearing too much about this aspect of herself. Another staff leader, Pam, explained to me that she self-censored some of her religious language with nonreligious groups. The impact of this for her was that she found it difficult to communicate her understanding of the issues because, as she said, "I don't know any other stories than biblical ones." During an interview, Janice related, and Hope later confirmed, that a nonreligious group from the local university had complained about Hope's references to Bible stories and religious themes during their trip. Both Janice and Hope saw this as a reminder to do a better job of gauging their audience(s), of being inclusive.

But there appear to have been upsides to keeping the volume of religion turned down as well. John, who brought a group of college students from Sojourner University, the majority of whom weren't religious, commented,

BorderLinks, for me, is the answer to a prayer. I say that partly tongue in cheek, and partly not, because it embodies, epitomizes exactly the kind of religiosity that I'm trying to, first of all, persuade students exists because their stereotypes of religion are so first grade ... You know, I want to say to them, 'Look you guys, this [BorderLinks and its work] is what organized religion looks like.' ... It's not all about getting inside your head and filling it with sexual repression. It's about getting out on the border and giving a crap when people are suffering. . . . It's subtle, and it's humble, and it's not a big media story. ... That makes me that much gladder that BorderLinks is there doing what it does.

Overall, BorderLinks developed a style of immersion travel that was both simultaneously progressive and religious in its engagement beyond the United States, attractive to feeder organizations making similar distinctions and expressive of a religious identity decreasingly familiar in American public life.

BRIDGING ACROSS ERAS

The last dimension of bridging at BorderLinks was the difficult work of bridging history. As it began producing immersion trips, BorderLinks was in close alignment with the Sanctuary movement's framing of undocumented immigration. BorderLinks diagnosed undocumented immigration to be the result of US-supported military regimes in Central America, constructing this interpretation with frequent visits to the Immigration and Naturalization Service (INS) and with testimonials from undocumented immigrants who were smuggled into the United States by activists. An anthropologist studying the Sanctuary movement in the early 1990s wrote that BorderLinks, "didn't provide just any kind of immersion but one that resonated with Sanctuary's political critique of the US state."[47] Reflecting on the purpose of having travelers visit with state agencies, Hilary Cunningham related that, "BorderLinks participants were to see the inscription of this state in the encounters with the INS and Border Patrol."[48]

Within a decade of BorderLinks' founding, however, the Central American peace movement and Sanctuary movement had declined in response to changes in Central American wars and US policy. Border-Links remained. The organization's history notes a shift in focus during this period. As the Central American refugee plight ended in the early 1990s, BorderLinks' focus moved from themes about US political and military policy to the economic forces structuring the border.[49] The ratification of the North American Free Trade Agreement (NAFTA) in 1993 soon increased the visibility of one form of global capitalism in BorderLinks' backyard: *maquilas* owned by international companies that hired cheap labor, assembled finished products in nonunionized conditions, and exported the finished products to the United States for consumption. In the early years of NAFTA's implementation, the *maquilas* and their impact became a key part of BorderLinks' focus. *Maquilas* introduced a host of issues that drew groups to BorderLinks to learn about labor rights, ecological destruction, labor mobility, and Fair Trade consumption.

BorderLinks continued its immersion travel work, but, by the early 2000s, its trip-leading was characterized by uncertainty. The same anthropologist that studied BorderLinks at the end of the Sanctuary movement returned a decade later to find that the shift in political and economic terrain had changed the organization.[50] In those 10 years, BorderLinks transitioned from a focus on Central America politics, with clear marking of the US government as the controller of the border, to a broader focus on free trade and neoliberal economics. In this new global focus, the machinations of nation-states were less the problem than "stateless" policies related to free trade. The breadth of policies had

[47] Cunningham, "Transnational Politics at the Edges of Sovereignty," p. 373.
[48] Ibid., p. 380.   [49] Gill, *Borderlinks*.
[50] Cunningham, "Transnational Politics at the Edges of Sovereignty"; Cunningham, "Transnational Social Movements."

implications for BorderLinks' pedagogy, making its interpretive frame more difficult to connect to processes at the physical border. Federal agencies had also become savvier.[51] BorderLinks staff reported that the Border Patrol had decided to deploy one point person for public relations who presented a coherent, agreeable message and face that BorderLinks travelers had difficulty rebutting. As an example, Cunningham observed sympathetic reactions from trip participants to a Border Patrol officer, something that seemed impossible a decade earlier. To make matters even more complicated, the close connections that BorderLinks once had with social activists and movements in southern Arizona had evaporated.

It took another historical change, one that entailed tangible, evocative evidence of the broader political and economic forces in the border region, to produce a refocused era at BorderLinks.

Dead Bodies in the Desert

In the first few years of the new millennium, the structure of border politics changed again as increasing numbers of persons crossed the US-Mexico border through the "Tucson sector," a stretch of Sonoran Desert from Yuma to the New Mexico border. Dead bodies began appearing more frequently in the desert. In 1999, nineteen bodies of undocumented border crossers were found, rising to 169 in 2004, and peaking at 224 in 2010.[52]

Until NAFTA, and for some years after, when Mexican migrants came to the United States, it was often for seasonal purposes to work the harvests. Mexican nationals would come to the United States for stretches of time to earn money before returning home.[53] However, under NAFTA's restructuring of land rights, formerly shared pieces of land were divided and became even less productive for sustaining families.[54] NAFTA also allowed US agricultural grain dumping on Mexican agricultural markets, which suppressed the profits that Mexicans could derive

[51] David S. Meyer and Suzanne Staggenborg, "Movements, Countermovements, and the Structure of Political Opportunity," *The American Journal of Sociology* 101, 6 (1996).

[52] Martinez et al., "Structural Violence and Migrant Deaths in Southern Arizona: Data from the Pima County Office of the Medical Examiner, 1990–2013."

[53] Douglas S. Massey, Jorge Durand, and Nolan J. Malone, *Beyond Smoke and Mirrors: Mexican Immigration in an Era of Economic Integration* (New York: Russell Sage Publications, 2003).

[54] Elizabeth Fitting, *The Struggle for Maize: Campesinos, Workers, and Transgenic Corn in the Mexican Countryside* (Durham, NC: Duke University Press, 2010).

from their agricultural production.[55] This international economic policy shift correlated with Mexican governance problems, including the peso devaluation of 1994, which increased the differential wages between Mexico and the United States. A cumulative effect of these many forces was an increase in labor migration to the United States.[56]

The critical change that made immigration deadlier was in border enforcement policy at numerous points along the US-Mexico border, spurred by the example of Operation Gatekeeper in El Paso in the mid-1990s.[57] The new enforcement policies funneled immigrants away from traditional urban crossings into the deserts. More lights, walls, and federal agents in urban areas made the unknown challenges of the Mexican desert more appealing for migrants. Eventually, this move to remote, dangerous routes increased the economic incentives for organizations, both opportunistic and criminal, to organize a black market crossing trade in the forbidding desert.

As dead bodies in the desert increased, so too did social movement activity along the border. In the mid-2000s, a new cycle of social movement activity began in southern Arizona, with groups like Humane Borders and No More Deaths providing water and humanitarian aid in the desert, and others like Border Action Network and Derechos Humanos advocating for civil rights of immigrants and Hispanic citizens against the backdrop of intense border militarization.

By 2008, when I first made contact with BorderLinks, the vast majority of its trip activity was about undocumented border crossing: the economic conditions that "push" migrants, the dangers of desert crossings, the care of migrants by local humanitarian organizations, and the deadly policies of border enforcement. This immigration focus was quite clear in BorderLinks' building. Outside the door that travelers entered in their first moments at BorderLinks was a bright-blue barrel, recently retired from serving duty as a desert water station with the humanitarian aid group Humane Borders. The central meeting area at BorderLinks had an immigration history timeline on pieces of paper taped to the walls around the

---

[55] Timothy Wise, "Agricultural Dumping under NAFTA: Estimating the Costs of U.S. Agricultural Policies to Mexican Producers," in *Mexican Rural Development Report* (Washington, DC: Woodrow Wilson International Center for Scholars, 2010).

[56] Raúl Delgado-Wise and Humberto Márquez Covarrubias, "The Reshaping of Mexican Labor Exports under NAFTA: Paradoxes and Challenges," *International Migration Review* 41, 3 (2007).

[57] Joseph Nevins, *Operation Gatekeeper and Beyond: The War on "Illegals" and the Remaking of the U.S.-Mexico Boundary* (New York: Routledge, 2010).

room, reminiscent of an information-filled grade school classroom. Each piece of paper highlighted a moment of immigration history in the United States, pointing out moments of especially dark history such as Chinese exclusion or indentured servitude. In the winter of 2010, the entry hallway to BorderLinks was repainted to show the US-Mexico border region known as the Sonoran Desert, with markings to indicate the major immigrant border crossings that BorderLinks groups visited. The previously broad vision of BorderLinks' had contracted to the border while the political and economic forces driving undocumented immigration had grown more complex.

When travelers came to BorderLinks in these years, they were walking into an organization with a long history of activity at the border, a distinct style of using travel, and a renewed focus on a social problem with connections throughout North America that was especially visible in BorderLinks' backyard.

CONCLUSION

For 30 years the work of BorderLinks reflected its name, but in ways beyond the apparent linkages across the geographic border. Beginning at its founding, the organization was bridging in its vision of education, its meaning of travel, and in its role in the history of border-focused social movement activism. The founders of BorderLinks came from a movement culture that linked progressive religion, political consciousness, and personal transformation, and they embraced immersion travel as a way to encourage the same in travelers. The deep story of the organization symbolized by Rick's story displayed the power of immersion travel, inviting travelers to see the organization as a way to build equitable cross-cultural relations and receive unexpected enlightenment.

For the organizations that brought travelers in 2009, BorderLinks offered an opportunity to bridge the ambiguous distance between education and activism. The organization provided travelers with an experience that was potentially more formative and informative than the traditional learning routines of feeder organizations from which they came. For group leaders, the time they spent with their members in immersion travel was an opportunity to introduce them to a way of living that valued personal growth and social justice simultaneously.

The deep meanings of BorderLinks' immersion travel formed in clear distinction to the way most American religious groups did immersion travel. BorderLinks rejected the dominant model of short-term mission trips as too paternalistic and temporary, incapable of grasping the complex realities of injustice and imagining just responses.

Though BorderLinks survived across the decades, it had to keep shifting its focus in response to changes in the political and economic realities at the US-Mexico border. By the late 2000s, BorderLinks' focus was on undocumented immigration, but the social forces prompting undocumented immigration were more complex, and the possible actions that travelers might take were less clear than they were 30 years before.

This background of BorderLinks takes us to the threshold of a trip. As travelers arrived, they entered a time and space in which the organization attempted to make its deep story of bridging real. How the organization did this day by day is the topic of the next chapter.

3

The Problems of Finding Truth through Travel

We have no set idea of action. . . . we just hope something happens.

BorderLinks trip leader

In the spring of 2009, I met up with the group from Central College for its trip with BorderLinks. Three professors and five students had flown across the country from their small, faith-affiliated, liberal arts college. They landed late in the evening at the airport in Tucson, where I introduced myself as they picked up their baggage. A theology professor had organized the trip as the unique midsemester activity for her class on postcolonial theology. The students and professors chatted excitedly in the van ride to the BorderLinks building. George, a BorderLinks staff member, would lead the group, joined by Lizbeth, a seasoned leader from Mexico.

By the time I met the travelers from Central College, I had been on three immersion trips with BorderLinks. In the midst of focusing on travelers, I had begun to notice that BorderLinks staff members spoke and acted in ways that surprised me given the organization's progressive identity and mission. The growing observations in my notebooks indicated that they hid their own opinions about immigration, avoided talking politics, and offered little guidance about what travelers could do after they left BorderLinks.[1] During the trip with Central College,

---

[1] Other researchers concur that BorderLinks staff members avoided leading discussions, suggesting political action, or providing a unified, overarching view of immigration. Perin,

74

these patterns became even more evident to me. One of the group members, Mike, asked George on the second day of the trip: "Will we get *your* ideas on the solution [to undocumented immigration]?" George avoided answering the question and kept doing so until the end of the trip despite Mike's continued persistence. George described BorderLinks in a way that hints at the organization's self-understanding of how to do immersion travel. George said, "We are not activists here, so we're not doing lobbying or things like that. We do education." Later in the trip, while discussing what they should do when they returned to Central College's campus, group members kept asking George for his ideas. Looking exasperated, George finally replied, "I have no idea, but I hope you do something."

Why wouldn't George or other BorderLinks staff members, almost all of whom were active in progressive advocacy and activist groups, provide answers or advice for immersion travelers? George's behavior was similar to other staff members, indicating that BorderLinks had a unique local culture.[2] As the previous chapter showed, BorderLinks' history, identity, and context placed it within a tradition of progressive, religious commitment to social justice at the US-Mexico border. However, the ambiguities implicit in its "deep story," its institutional hybridity, and its experiential learning pedagogy limited how the staff, in practice, were able to "do education" through immersion travel. These unexpected challenges, like George's vague avoidance, are the themes of this chapter.

FAITH AND FRACTURES IN THE ORGANIZATION OF IMMERSION TRAVEL

One of the most challenging aspects of studying immersion travel is understanding how those who produce immersion travel think that it "works." An obvious place to begin is with an organization's deep story and articulated purpose, which we encountered in the previous chapter. Those provide a public articulation of identity, of what staff and supporters believe they are doing through an organization. But, as my recurring field observations and the brief vignettes of George and Central College

"Educational Travel for Societal Change"; Piekielek, "Visiting Views of the U.S.-Mexico Border."

[2] Rhys H. Williams, "The Cultural Contexts of Collective Action: Constraints, Opportunities, and the Symbolic Life of Social Movements," in *The Blackwell Companion to Social Movements*, ed. David A. Snow, Sarah A. Soule, and Hanspeter Kriesi (Malden, MA: Blackwell Publishing Ltd., 2004).

suggested, the translation from ideals to actual practice was garbled. In fact, as we will see, some of what BorderLinks did during immersion travel was at odds with its assumptions about how immersion travel works.

BorderLinks' sense of the appropriate way to do immersion travel reflected a *faith* in the power of experience to reveal and to transform. This faith came from the tradition of experiential education articulated by Paulo Freire and familiar to the founders and staff of the organization.[3] Following the logic of experiential education, BorderLinks introduced travelers to information and human voices that travelers would otherwise never encounter. Travelers were supposed to leave the world of books, news, and mainstream expertise behind to discover new truths about immigration, from new sources. BorderLinks did not want to spoil travelers' authentic sense of moral discovery through experience. Yet this faith in experiential education was *fractured* in numerous ways.

The way this happened at BorderLinks provides an opportunity to understand how a nonprofit organization converts its founding ideals into practice. Despite the beneficent assumption that nonprofit organizations and altruistic individuals are translating clear ideals into behavior, many studies of volunteerism and activism show that basic social processes interrupt this translation.[4] BorderLinks was no different.

The problems BorderLinks encountered in turning its idealized meanings into civic action are the problems of civil society more generally. As Nina Eliasoph comments in light of her research on the tacit inequality at the heart of the volunteer role, "It is the matches and mismatches between the moral narratives [of actors] and the situations [of actual behavior] that should attract our attention" as scholars.[5] Some of the most illuminating research on civic organizations and social movements has been directed at these mismatches. For example, Francesca Polletta demonstrated how the Student Nonviolent Coordinating Committee (SNCC) used deliberative decision-making at one point in its civil rights activism, but also how those practices reproduced racial identity and inequality,

[3] Freire, *Pedagogy*.
[4] Baggett, *Building Private Homes*; Lichterman, *Elusive Togetherness*; Lee, *Do-It-Yourself Democracy*; Eliasoph, *The Politics of Volunteering*; Dekker, "Civicness."
[5] Nina Eliasoph, "Beyond the Politics of Denunciation: Cultural Sociology as the 'Sociology for the Meantime'," in *Culture, Society, and Democracy: The Interpretive Approach*, ed. Isaac Reed and Jeffrey Alexander (Boulder, CO: Paradigm Publishers, 2007), p. 92.

TABLE 2 *BorderLinks' formal neutrality and resulting cultural fractures*

Stage	Organizational Ideal	Unintentional Practice	Results of Fractured Ideals
See	"We're not the experts"	Whack a mole	Inequality of staff roles; inadvertent staff expertise; interventions against ignorance
Think	Dialogue with "real people"	Testimonial economy	A partial field of discursive positions; power of eloquent experts; suppression of dissent; complexity, not clarity
Act	"Do something"	Heart-knowledge processor	Individualization of moral stances; emotionality over analysis; exclusion of politics; "Share the story"

leading to the organization's demise.[6] A more recent example comes from Krause's analysis of humanitarian relief INGOs.[7] Far from being rational attempts at coordinating aid for those most in need, Krause showed that those organizations fell prey to expectations of efficiency and immediate success, resulting in the pursuit of "good projects" to fulfill abstract ideas of relief.

In the case of BorderLinks, observing the "matches" means paying attention to the practices the organization deployed that appeared to align with the organization's vision. Understanding the "mismatches" means tracing how these practices produced unintended outcomes and new meanings in tension with founding ideals. I follow the matches and mismatches at BorderLinks by using its own "cycle of praxis" imagery, which we encountered in the previous chapter (see Table 2, column 1).

The matches of organizational meaning to practice resulted in an internal organizational culture that I call formal neutrality.[8] Formal neutrality is an organizational stance of nonpartisan openness to discovery that protects individual conscience, while encouraging experience and

---

[6] Francesca Polletta, *Freedom Is an Endless Meeting: Democracy in American Social Movements* (Chicago: University of Chicago Press, 2002); Polletta, "How Participatory Democracy Became White: Culture and Organizational Choice."

[7] Krause, *The Good Project.*

[8] Gary J. Adler, Jr. "'Neutral' Talk, Conscience, and Political Legitimacy," in *Religion and Progressive Activism: New Stories about Faith and Politics*, ed. Todd N. Fuist, Ruth Braunstein, and Rhys H. Williams (New York: New York University Press, 2017).

promoting knowledge that are expected to lead people in a particular value direction. A formally neutral stance, like the one at BorderLinks, promoted the noncoerced discovery of truth by travelers, while at the same time constructing a set of authoritative voices, experiences, and relationships that were assumed to provide a direction to that discovery. This stance allowed personal transformation to occur in an organizational context that implicitly and indirectly guided the social meaning of that transformation. In place of the expertise, coherent frames, and explicit action scripts characteristic of many advocacy organizations, the formal neutrality at BorderLinks was accomplished by downplaying organizational expertise, emphasizing authentic voices, and being nondirective about action possibilities. The organization's identity, history, and staff all suggested a progressive orientation about undocumented immigration and social change, but the organization's practices constructed a neutral, noncoercive context. BorderLinks held faith in the power of experiential education to fill out this formally neutral approach.

This formally neutral approach comports with the nonpartisan, conscience-oriented methods of personal formation characteristic of many churches, seminaries, and universities. It is reminiscent of the way that political socialization occurs through homeland tourism, in which discovery through experience is promoted over ideologically coherent, political messaging. According to Kelner's analysis of Birthright Israel, the organization prioritized the message and experience of Jewish Israelis over non-Jewish Israelis and Palestinians, but the way this was accomplished produced many nonexclusive meanings and made possible a range of interpretations.[9] The result was not socialization into a coherent, politicized frame but an awareness that *might* be mobilized by some other organization, down the road.

The organization's formal neutrality leads to mismatches between its vision and practice. These mismatches help us account for the ways that organizational work does not seamlessly lead to action. I characterize these mismatches as cultural "fractures," using the concept introduced by Paul Willis in his study of working-class British schoolboys.[10] A cultural fracture, as I use it, are the unexpected and unintentional practices and meanings that develop as an organization attempts to correct or channel

---

[9] Kelner, *Tours That Bind.*
[10] Paul Willis, *Learning to Labor: How Working Class Kids Get Working Class Jobs* (New York: Columbia University Press, 1977).

problems that arise when ideals encounter day-to-day difficulties (see Table 2, columns 3 and 4).

Making experiential education work through immersion travel was often more difficult than expected at BorderLinks. By the end of an immersion trip for a BorderLinks traveler, the See-Think-Act cycle had gone round, but not in the way the organization hoped or expected. In the following sections, I walk through each stage in BorderLinks' cycle to show the problematic distance between ideals and unintended practice in immersion travel.

SEEING, WITHOUT EXPERTS

The initial moments of an immersion trip, when travelers were wide-eyed and expectant, were also the beginnings of BorderLinks' attempts to encourage discovery through experience, not expertise. At the beginning of a trip with Midwestern Theological Seminary, the trip leader Pam exemplified this spirit when talking about what she called "education for change." She explained that, at BorderLinks, "instead of sitting on your duff, you get to move around" to explore issues and confront "touchy barriers" in your life and the life of your community. She told the travelers that this experience was "not just for your education, but the local community and the world as well."

Once travelers arrived at the BorderLinks building, the staff members assigned bunks and reviewed a schedule of events for the coming week. In English, a US staff member explained that she/he and her/his Mexican counterpart would be facilitating the events of the week. They would introduce travelers to people on both sides of the border, who in turn would discuss their views of undocumented immigration. But, they emphasized, they would *not* be doing everything for the group. As a practical way of reinforcing this, the staff members asked the group to divide up responsibilities: someone to introduce the group throughout the week, someone to keep time and corral the group to the next activity, someone to fill up the communal jug of purified water, and someone to check the emotional well-being of the group.

BorderLinks staff wanted to guide travelers through an experience but not be experts about that experience. They wanted to be seen as facilitators, organizers, or educators. The staff members were ushering travelers into the "popular education" model of Paulo Freire. The key element in this process was a noncoercive, open approach to learning. As one staff member, Alicia, said to travelers during an orientation session, "We're all teachers, we're all learners."

The Reappearance of Expertise

The achievement of this approach was not easy, though, as demonstrated by BorderLinks' navigation around objects that symbolized expertise. One such category of symbolic objects included books. On one trip, the St. Michael's group was having a conversation with Burt, a BorderLinks staff member. The group was in a room with large bookshelves on two different walls. Burt was describing how important experiential learning was in his own life: "I did contextual education [in school] – a real experience like this, not just book knowledge." No one in the room balked at the apparent conflict between the space and Burt's comment.

Despite BorderLinks' claim that real learning occurred outside of the classroom ("off your duff"), books were actually an important part of BorderLinks. There were hundreds of books on bookshelves scattered throughout the space; on liberation theology, spirituality, or economics. BorderLinks sold books written by local authors in the entry hallway. As Burt's situation suggests, it was "book knowledge," not books per se, that was symbolically problematic. Book knowledge symbolized static information and connoted an antiseptic environment, not discovery through experience. In the realm of book knowledge, critical issues such as immigration occurred at a remove and were owned by "experts," leaving ordinary people powerless to discover truth through the voices of the powerless. Books might be helpful during travel with BorderLinks; book knowledge was the problem to be avoided.

To keep the book knowledge atmosphere from developing, the most difficult symbols of expertise that BorderLinks staff leaders had to navigate were themselves. Their presence provided a real challenge to experiential education since it was quite difficult for an expert-driven division of labor *not* to emerge.

One reason was the entrance of travelers into new space. Travelers entered a new structure of time, guided by BorderLinks staff members. An imprinting process familiar to tour guides occurred: to know where to go, when to eat, or what was planned, travelers looked to staff members.[11] I became aware of this difficulty when I realized that just-landed BorderLinks travelers would ask *me* – a researcher whom they had never met before – questions about the social world that they had entered. During the first few moments of a BorderLinks trip, they asked

---

[11] Erik Cohen, "The Tourist Guide: The Origins, Structure, and Dynamics of a Role," *Annals of Tourism Research* 12 (1985).

me questions like, "What does the name Nogales mean?" or "Where does this area gets its water from?"

Avoiding answering these questions was the tip of the iceberg for the antiexpertise struggle of BorderLinks staff. After all, staff members were experts in comparison with travelers. The American delegation staff members had collegiate backgrounds based in the social sciences, international studies, or Hispanic studies. The Mexican staff members had lived along the border for most of their lives, and some had themselves been immigrants at one time.

As travelers turned to staff members for expertise, they tended to reproduce an inequality between trips leaders, thereby accentuating the expert division of labor even more. For most of each trip's first few hours, the staff leader talking to the group was the US staff member, using English. The organization was aware that this could introduce role inequality to the ideal of doing experiential learning as a community. To rebut this tendency, BorderLinks tried "simultaneous translation" so that the Mexican staff member could immediately understand what travelers were saying and travelers could understand what was said in Spanish. The listeners' focus was always supposed to remain on the speaker, not the translator. The method of simultaneous translation was explained to travelers as a means of maintaining fair relationships among all members of the group. Ideally, language would not exclude, creating the goal, if not the reality, of equality.

Using simultaneous translation was difficult to do, though, as I found out when I failed miserably in a trial run to do so. Pam had our group practice our body postures. We practiced this in a sly way, having the "translator" and the "speaker" both speak English. However, we were only supposed to look at the speaker. I had a difficult time doing so, often looking to the translator instead of the speaker. I was so bad at this that the group laughed as I failed. In the end, it was easier for me to look at the person who happened to be talking, to follow the trail to easy expertise.

When travelers like me messed up simultaneous translation, US staff members would encourage them to ask the Mexican leader their questions directly. But these attempts and correctives usually petered out within the first few days of the trip. It was easier for English-speaking travelers to ask English-speaking US staff members their questions. And it was easier for a US staff member to respond directly to a traveler instead of eliciting and translating comments from Mexican staff members.

The difficulty of translation exposed a deeper inequality between the binational staff leaders, which reinforced the emergence of US leaders as experts. Despite publicly cordial relations, my notes contained instances of clashes between the trip leaders: US leaders who stopped simultaneous translation; Mexican leaders who refused the translation when they were the only non-English speakers present; and US leaders talking over Mexican leaders or reinterpreting what they said. By the time that a Mexican leader was "in charge" on the Mexican side during a trip, usually a few days into the week, a pattern of the US leader as the primary leader – and source of expertise – had been set.

As an example, the group from St. Michael's seemed particularly attuned to this inequality, but they perceived it negatively affecting the US leader. One afternoon in Mexico, I sat in the back of the van near three of the travelers as they speculated on the division of labor between the trip leaders. One traveler guessed, "Janice is the leader, so maybe Marco organizes everything?" One of the other travelers, in a hushed, secretive tone, said she had background information on Marco that she could share with us later. I never heard that information, but another traveler's reply to this suggested she thought Marco was not pulling his weight: "He should do all the driving [in Mexico] since she does the translating, the organizing, and checking to make sure everyone is here!" This experience in the field prepared me for an interview with the Mexican trip leader, Patricia, months later, during which she described that, "I've often felt that I'm often viewed as just the chauffeur in delegations."

"Whack a Mole" against Requests for Expertise

The continuous presence of experts who were trying *not* to be treated as such generated unusual patterns during a trip. One of these patterns is best described by reference to the familiar carnival game, whack a mole. In the actual game, stuffed moles pop up at random from the dozen or so holes in the game table. Players, armed with a weighted mallet, do their best to whack the moles back into the table. The game is challenging because the moles appear quickly and in different locations. On a BorderLinks trip, travelers' attempts to engage a staff member's expertise resembled ever-present moles, a behavior that popped up and threatened the experiential learning ideal. An extended example from the Central College group helps to illustrate this.

Near the beginning of their trip, the group sat in the back of the BorderLinks building. By happenstance, there was a local humanitarian aid activist there; he was cleaning up from a meeting he had had with other activists in the building. He was dressed in desert tones and walking boots, carrying a backpack with supplies. The Central College group, still new to Tucson, began peppering him with questions. None of us (including myself) knew who this person was or his name, but we all treated him as an authority. We asked lots of questions and, unlike staff members, he obliged with answers to all of them: "How should we solve the immigration problem?"; "Is Janet Napolitano pushing for something, or open to it?"; "Are there outdoor markets in Mexico, or are they all inside?"

After a few minutes, George, the BorderLinks staff member, entered the room and the activist left. The stream of questions continued but now focused on George. Unlike the activist, he actively avoided access to his expertise. Mike looked at George and asked: "Are prices higher or lower in the US or Nogales?" In reply, George said, "We'll do that [topic] with the Market Basket Survey," referring to an experiential activity that BorderLinks used to show the challenge of buying food on a budget in Nogales. One mole whacked.

Becoming excited about our upcoming trip to Nogales, Jim asked "How much of the industrial park [of *maquilas*] will we get to see? Can we explore the buildings?" George replied rather curtly: "We'll drive through and get out to look at one point. Ophelia [a Mexican staff member] can talk about changes in Nogales over time." Another mole whacked.

Susan then asked: "With all the news about drug cartels that we've been hearing about, how does it affect immigrants?" By this point, George was seated but did not look comfortable. He blew the air out of his mouth with a sense of deflation, ran his hand through his hair, and squirmed in this chair. George gave a vague answer: "The war on drugs and the war on immigrants have parallels. In my mind, they are the same dynamic." The moles kept coming. Sensing that George was willing to reveal some expertise, Mike asked an especially challenging question of George: "Will we get *your* ideas on the solution?" George squirmed some more and looked frustrated.

Like staff members, I picked up the habits of whack a mole and self-censoring to encourage an environment of open learning and nonexpertise. Despite having visited places many times during my fieldwork, I tried to redirect travelers' questions to me by either saying "I don't know" or suggesting they ask someone else. Ignoring requests was challenging to do because I wanted the travelers to learn as much as they could and to have their curiosity rewarded with useful information. But, according to BorderLinks, indulging this too much would contradict the vision of the experiential learning model.

Exceptions to Showing Expertise

There were, however, a few times when staff members would assert their expertise. In a book on democratic social movements, Polletta gives an example of how the Highlander Folk School was sometimes forced against the staff's desire to provide expertise and guidance.[12] In instances when a group failed to sharpen its analysis, the Highlander staff challenged the group to think in new ways. When an assertion of expertise occurred at BorderLinks, it showed that the organization, despite its public commitment to an open process, was on guard against undesired ends. The only times I observed this happen involved the assertion of expertise in a corrective way, when travelers' interpretations or words appeared insensitive, ignorant, or wholly inaccurate.

During Midwestern Theological Seminary's trip, there had been news about a rash of kidnappings in Mexico. At lunch one day, Benjamin joked that, "I'm getting a pot of money together for ransom." Mitt replied, with a sense of playfulness, "I don't want to be kidnapped here, please." A few other travelers and I chuckled at this exchange, with its distant possibility. The BorderLinks staff member Pam, though, had been listening and seemed uncomfortable with the conversation. Describing her experience with groups who do nonviolent civil disobedience, she said in a voice without humor, "It's a position of privilege to be ransomed and rescued." The room was silent while she talked. We stopped making eye contact with each other, staring at our plates. In an attempt to keep the conversation light-hearted, the group's leader replied, "I hope that isn't Border-Links' policy!" All of us, except for Pam, laughed, followed by comments from two travelers about the many liability forms they had to sign before the trip.

Later that evening, Pam came back to the issue in the most potent example of rebuke I saw during my time with BorderLinks. The group had rolled out sleeping bags on the chilly floor of a school in Mexico. A traveler offered a prayer, then invited us to share our thoughts from the day. During the evening reflection, Pam said, "I'm uncomfortable with the ransom joke that has been going on. People are really kidnapped and can't pay." The air in the room became tense as everyone stopped moving and became quiet. After a few moments, both Benjamin and Lucie

---

[12] Polletta, *Freedom Is an Endless Meeting*.

apologized for having joked about this. The ransom jokes never reappeared during the trip.

Another, more mundane, example provides a sense of how the assertion of expertise could discourage the process of experiential learning. Janice had planned to take the group from St. Michael's Church to a display of art on the University of Arizona campus.[13] This piece of art was made from the same material as the border wall in Nogales, with two 15-foot-tall stylized figures on each side interacting with the wall. Because parking was tight on the university campus, Janice dropped us off while she went to park the van.

The ensuing moments felt like a prime example of experiential education. The group walked around the art piece, touching it, peering through various holes, and trying out different interpretations with each other. Derek shared a range of reasons with me about why the figures on one side appeared to be working feverishly to build the wall. About ten minutes later, Janice caught back up to the group. She immediately said, "I don't know how much Marco [the Mexican staff member] told you, but you can probably tell which side's which." Marco had not offered any expertise. A silence hung in the air for a few seconds, in stark contrast to the free-flowing conversation we had been having. Janice explained that the Mexican side was the side with figures that are "striving," while the figures on the US side looked lazy, leaning against the wall to hold it up while benefitting from the economic benefits it created. As this was the opposite of Derek's interpretation, he sheepishly commented to me on the side, "I think I had it wrong." As we walked away, another traveler, Dan, cracked a joke that unexpectedly pointed up the breach that had occurred: "An artist would ask [us], 'What do *you* think it is?'" And so would a BorderLinks staff member if, in fact, it was easy to avoid being an expert in practice.

THINKING, WITH REAL PEOPLE

If staff members avoided expertise on a BorderLinks trip, what stood in its place?

At the beginning orientation of a BorderLinks trip, the staff member Alicia hinted at BorderLinks' answer, explaining to a group that,

---

[13] "Border Dynamics" is a piece of public art, created by Guadalupe Serrano and Alberto Morackis, which resides on the campus of the University of Arizona (artmuseum.arizona .edu/public_art/border-dynamics).

"at BorderLinks we start with lived experience. Rather than experts that tell us *about* real people, we talk with real people." This focus on talking to "real people" about their experience of social reality was a long-standing feature of the organization. In his official history of BorderLinks, Gill explained:

True learning and helping can only take place as the result of experiential inter-action between those who learn and help and those who are taught and helped, and in this process both parties are the teachers and helpers, both are taught and helped.[14]

Alicia's mention of "real people" showed that priority on a BorderLinks trip was given to certain voices; that certain accounts of lived experience were more important, more "real," than others. This orientation toward the truth of certain voices was central in BorderLinks' history. As Gill writes:

There is a way in which the work of BorderLinks can be understood as an attempt to educate those of us living in the First World, the 'oppressors', concerning the nature and basis of the world created by the Global Economy—as well as what might be done about it. The goal here is neither defensiveness nor guilt, but honest encounter with the people and realities of the border.[15]

Gill further explains that at BorderLinks this "encounter must be structured with a minimum of direct teaching or of pressure to come to any specific conclusions."[16] The factuality of an encounter should speak for itself. If authentically achieved, the encounter would require no overlay to be authoritative and motivating. This orientation resonated with Rick's story, part of the collective memory of a movement culture institutionalized in experiential education pedagogy and a "preferential option for the poor."

On a BorderLinks immersion trip, "real people" were those whose life experiences (as Mexicans, as immigrants) were otherwise inaccessible to participants. Participants were not likely to meet these people in their daily lives, and they were not likely to hear them represented in the media. At BorderLinks, these encounters usually included time for a testimonial of a "real person" sharing their story. In theory, testimonials allowed an organization like BorderLinks to have a frame of suffering built by

---

[14] Gill, *Borderlinks*, p. 36.   [15] Gill, *Borderlinks II*, pp. 100–1.
[16] Gill, *Borderlinks*, p. 37.

sufferers themselves.[17] In later chapters, I will address how travelers reacted to such testimonials. Here, I focus on the role of testimonials during an immersion trip and the organizational work required to put this ideal into practice.

BorderLinks had to create many ways of presenting the stories of "real people." For a week-long immersion trip, it was not possible to have one testimonial; instead, the organization had to get numerous testimonials so that travelers could discover the realities of the US-Mexico border and undocumented immigration. And the organization had to create conditions for the repeated replication of testimonials, so that it could meet the demand of the dozens of immersion trips each year. BorderLinks had to devise a way to bring the ideal to life, again and again. It did this by creating a "testimonial economy."

The Rules of the Testimonial Economy

The testimonial economy refers to the enduring set of relationships between BorderLinks and individuals or organizations, through which BorderLinks provided testimonials for its travelers. This economy included a range of possible voices for the organization to draw from to fill out any given week-long immersion trip. Testimonial-tellers received various goods in return for participating in the economy: access to travelers, a sense of helping to educate others, and occasionally payment for their efforts. The testimonial economy for an organization that hosts thousands of travelers a year was a complex structure to sustain over time. As a consequence, BorderLinks articulated rules and expectations that would leave the economy intact for future groups of travelers. These rules helped sustain the visible testimonial activity seen by a group of travelers, but also made invisible BorderLinks' organizing work to keep the economy going.

The privileged voices in this economy were the "real people" who experienced the suffering of border city poverty or undocumented immigration, speaking for themselves from their own experience. One of the central elements of this economy were homestays. In a homestay, small groups of travelers (two–four people) within a larger traveling group would stay in the house of a Mexican family in a border town. Travelers would eat dinner and breakfast with the family, then have time in the

[17] Grace Yukich, "Constructing the Model Immigrant: Movement Strategy and Immigrant Deservingness in the New Sanctuary Movement," *Social Problems* 60, 3 (2013).

evening or morning to talk (sometimes with the help of a translator). The homestays were also part of BorderLinks' attempt to support local neighborhoods and women's incomes in border communities. For any host family, a homestay provided a vital source of income, since the family was reimbursed for expenditures besides being paid a small amount of money.

BorderLinks, though, tried to prevent travelers from knowing this. The discovery of this income might raise doubts in the minds of travelers since it added an economic motive to the personal connections that were supposed to occur during the visit. I was not aware of how many BorderLinks travelers knew about the payments to homestay families. On only one trip did I hear the group discuss this openly, and their awareness of payment in the testimonial economy appeared to tarnish this aspect of the trip. On the final night of their trip, I sat with Bob, Alice, and Susan, talking about the highlights and lowlights of the week. They were all disappointed by the homestays, feeling like the hosting families did not offer much by way of conversation or knowledge to the travelers. Susan summed up the implicit critique of the group: "A lot can go wrong with homestays, especially if you feel like they're doing it for business." The travelers gave no public thought to the production of hospitality required of families that may have been hosting week after week for months or years on end, and what a cost such an altruistic relationship would entail.

Besides homestays, the main venues for meeting "real people" were immigrant shelters. There, travelers could talk with undocumented migrants one on one or sit as a group to listen to their stories. In this setting, a slightly different set of rules applied because BorderLinks did not have one-to-one, predetermined relationships with immigrants. BorderLinks provided a small amount of supplies for the shelter's work. This donation was meant to be off-stage so that travelers would be unaware that this was occurring.

Travelers were instructed by BorderLinks staff members not to give money to migrants. This rule was couched in the language of avoiding dependency. During the orientation with Eastern College, the trip leader Alicia told the group that "there's no need to give any gift [to anyone they encountered]. Donations just created conflicts or precedents, which other [BorderLinks] groups down the road [would] have to follow." As the van from Midwestern Theological crossed into Mexico, Pam shared some last-minute guidelines: "Two things. Don't take pictures [at checkpoints] because you could get in trouble. Don't give money to anyone, even if they are desperate and look like a person who could use a quarter. It causes dependency and can get us involved in things." Giving money was seen as a species of trouble to be avoided, a recurring theme in the sphere of transnational civic action.[18] Moreover, the organization had some internal stories about times when money led to problems. During an interview with Patricia, she recalled two such stories, one at a migrant shelter and one related to homestays. She explained that, at the migrant shelter, "we had about four immigrants that approached the delegation and they were requesting funds to purchase a bus ticket back home." After the group gave money to one immigrant, with the understanding it would be shared with the others, "at the last moment, he decided not to give the money to anybody. . . . [Then], we had a big fight break out." Of the homestays, she explained the travelers are encouraged to give a simple, personal gift, like a postcard. Otherwise, "if one family received a nice gift from one of the [groups], and the other family doesn't, unfortunately those families start debating with each other."

These rules attempted to remove the overt appearance of money in exchanges with economically vulnerable Mexicans. The truths of a testimonial were vulnerable to suspicion if listeners suspected false motives or a hidden agenda, which the logic of payment signaled.[19] In theory, the suppression of public giving maintained value for the "freely given" stories from "real people" that travelers wanted to hear. Moving monetary exchanges into the background, away from individual interactions, helped to decrease visible status inequality and heighten feelings of connection.[20]

Despite these rules, I witnessed travelers on at least three occasions attempt to give money secretly to migrants, demonstrating the impulsive philanthropy that often characterizes interactions across severe economic divides.[21] The rules of the testimonial economy did not fail because of travelers' willful nonadherence. The real problem was that the rules were not known to the individual immigrants that were *outside* the stabilizing structure of the testimonial economy. Since the tacit agreement about offstage remuneration was unavailable to these "real people," requests for assistance were often forthcoming. The troubles of this misalignment between the regime of rules and the expectations of "real" people were

---

[18] LiErin Probasco, "Prayer, Patronage, and Personal Agency in Nicaraguan Accounts of Receiving International Aid," *Journal for the Scientific Study of Religion* 55, 2 (2016).

[19] Viviana A. Zelizer, "The Social Meaning of Money: "Special Monies," *American Journal of Sociology* 95, 2 (1989).

[20] Adler Jr. and Offutt, "The Gift Economy of Direct Transnational Civic Action."

[21] Erica Bornstein, "The Impulse of Philanthropy," *Cultural Anthropology* 24, 4 (2009).

made clear in a situation that happened with the St. Michael's group during their trip.

Early one morning, while staying in Agua Prieta, just south of the American border town of Douglas, the St. Michael's Church group headed to an immigrant service center. The service center was not open yet, so Janice told us about the various services that deported migrants needed. The group was standing in a parking lot, in the shadow of a building. As we stood there, a woman walked up to our group. The woman had disheveled hair and wore garments that one day may have been dress clothes but were now dirty and ill-fitting. She inserted herself very close to three group members. In the ensuing lull in our group conversation, she gave an account of her recent troubles in accented English. She talked rapidly. We stood, some of our group looking at her; others were staring at the ground or looking at the buildings. I found myself thankful that I could pay attention to the others instead of her since her presence was both disruptive and demanding.

When the woman paused for a moment in a rambling story about her problems, a group member, Lisa, looked at her and only said, "Thank you for your story." While delivered with sincerity, and resonant of BorderLinks' focus on hearing stories from those who suffer, it also felt like an attempt to close the interaction. To our shared surprise, the woman replied angrily, saying that what she said was the truth, not a story. Lisa was visibly shaken at this retort, realizing that her words did not have the intended effect of ending the interaction. At this point, Janice said to the woman: "We don't have any money to give." Not satisfied with this answer, and not allowing Janice to speak for the whole group of Americans, the woman then looked at each of us as she asked for money. Most of us quietly said, "No." After flashing a look of disgust, and waiting for a response that did not come, she walked off.

Somewhat to my surprise, the moment turned into a session of sharing stories about beggars and their demands. After a few quiet moments, Lisa said, "She went for me." She said it with a tone of impatience but indicated that she had navigated us through the interruption. Another traveler told a story about watching a beggar work a restaurant with the same sad story table after table. After another traveler mentioned that people can make "good money" with these strategies, another added a quick joke: "And they don't even have to pay tax on it!" Lisa had the last word about the interaction with the woman, and one that was strangely in line with BorderLinks' vision behind the encounter with "real" people: "But that was a good experience to learn." The problem was that the experience provided by the testimonial economy was meant to be smooth, fair, and meaningful, but travelers' knowledge about the invisible structure and their encounters with people outside the structure made that difficult.

The Other Part of the Testimonial Economy: Somewhat Real People

While BorderLinks prioritized the testimonies of "real people," the majority of a BorderLinks trip was taken up with talking with what I came to call "somewhat real people": experts who spoke on some facet of immigration. Each BorderLinks trip had a collection of experts who provided talks that lasted thirty to ninety minutes. These could be humanitarian aid activists, local pastors, shelter workers, attorneys, ranchers, or even Immigration and Customs Enforcement (ICE) agents. The experts used various repertoires to articulate their ideas about immigration, framing themselves as part of an organization or profession tasked with confronting undocumented immigration. While I analyze their effect in later chapters, here I note the existence of these "somewhat real people" and point out the conflict they present to BorderLinks' ideals.

For the fundamental educational goals of BorderLinks, experts were crucial since they could provide concise overviews of large amounts of history and information in a short amount of time. But explaining this authoritative role of experts to travelers was rhetorically tricky, as it was a pivot toward expertise, away from the preference for direct engagement with the suffering of "real people." On one trip the staff member Alicia struggled to explain to travelers how these speakers fit into the organizational priority of talking with the "real people." Alicia seemed unsure, but determined, as she wove together an explanation that might work for travelers even if it did not seem to work for her. Her explanation ended up going something like this: border enforcement authorities, humanitarian aid activists, immigration lawyers, and local pastors were indeed "real" people in an ontological way, and we should listen to them, but they were "real" in a different way than the other "real" people (e.g., immigrants). The difference was that experts would represent positions on "sides" of the immigration issue, as opposed to presenting the unvarnished reality of suffering.

The admission about sides being represented by "somewhat real people" was a noticeable departure from the ideal of discovering truths only from those who suffer in lived experience. In allowing for the representation of diverse voices, BorderLinks attempted to balance such viewpoints. In practice, this meant:

A concerted effort was made to provide an opportunity for participants to hear and respect a wide spectrum of voices and points of view. Indeed, a positive balance is sought between the perspective of a manager of a maquiladora and that of its workers, as well as between that of a Border Patrol agent and a migrant person. There is no attempt to stack the deck in favor of the Mexican experience since the realities of the border will always manage to reveal themselves.[22]

By including diverse voices, BorderLinks displayed its commitment to a discursive model of civil society, in which opinions were best formed when all sides of an issue were represented.[23] In this part of its testimonial economy, BorderLinks was unintentionally moving toward discursive representation in its work, allowing a range of "opinions" about immigration and immigrants to reveal a complex discursive field.[24] This approach was evidence that the organization was partially built on a Habermasian vision of the public sphere, in which diverse ideas about social life and reality could be presented and interrogated through interaction and discussion.[25] Theoretically, travelers could sift through the discourses, deciding which had the best rationales and which should be accepted.[26]

The Problems of Representing "Both Sides"

Unfortunately for BorderLinks, a diverse discursive field was difficult to achieve in practice. BorderLinks struggled to recruit enough voices for the number of trips it organized. For example, the availability of border enforcement authorities fluctuated. In 2008, BorderLinks was told they could have one visit with Border Patrol officials each month. The organization had similar trouble scheduling speakers from other governmental organizations, such as Customs and Border Protection (CBP) or ICE. In the six trips that I participated in, I only heard two presentations by US

---

[22] Gill, *Borderlinks II*, p. 21.   [23] Lee, *Do-It-Yourself Democracy.*

[24] John S. Dryzek and Simon Niemeyer, "Discursive Representation," *American Political Science Review* 102, 4 (2008).

[25] Jurgen Habermas, *The Theory of Communicative Action*, trans. Thomas McCarthy, vol. 1 (Boston, MA: Beacon Press, 1984 [1981]); Mische, *Partisan Publics.*

[26] Diana C. Mutz, *Hearing the Other Side: Deliberative versus Participatory Democracy* (New York: Cambridge University Press, 2006).

Customs agents and one presentation from an ICE official. At times, BorderLinks had relationships with ranchers who would speak to the economic costs of migration and their feelings of political impotence. In six trips, however, I only heard one rancher address a group. Despite BorderLinks', and travelers', commitment to hearing all sides, not all sides wanted to be heard. By assuming the existence of an identifiable field of positions that needed to be heard, BorderLinks was respectful of discursive openness, but this commitment was derailed by being unable to represent this field for travelers to engage with easily.

Sometimes when it tried to represent both sides, its faith was betrayed. After hearing one group's disappointment about not meeting the controversial Minuteman Civil Defense Corps, I asked the BorderLinks staff member Sarah why Minuteman were not on the list of possible speakers. Sarah said that they were at one point – until they violated BorderLinks' trust. According to her, Minuteman secretly took pictures of a Border-Links group during their meeting with travelers, then posted these pictures to a website as evidence of support for the Minuteman cause. A similar explanation came up on the trip with St. Michael's, which allowed an opportunity for BorderLinks to reiterate its commitment to showing all sides. When asked why the group could not meet with the Minuteman, Janice replied, "We try to be neutral, but this is where that flies out the window. We don't deal with them anymore because they took pictures" of a group one time and posted them without permission. Being neutral for BorderLinks meant trusting both sides would do likewise.

Respectful Bodies

As part of engaging diverse voices, BorderLinks instructed travelers to use distinct listening practices that embodied a commitment to openness. Just inside the door to BorderLinks' dorm area, travelers could read a list of values written in large font. One of the values was "open communication." During orientation, the trip leader Janice explained to the group the need to use a "listening posture" with experts, which she said would be modeled by her throughout the week. This posture meant looking at the speaker, showing interest in the conversation and, if the need arose, doing whatever it took to avoid falling asleep.

BorderLinks' goal of respecting speakers was taken quite seriously. Travelers did not challenge what speakers said; they discussed their negative comments once the actual interaction was done and the speaker was no longer with the group. Not surprisingly, some speakers, such as border enforcement authorities, elicited more reaction. But a line of respect was policed by BorderLinks staff, who did not publicly push against what these speakers said to groups. I only came across one firm example of a staff member who had challenged a speaker, and she shared the story as a morality tale about why staff members could not do so. During my interview with Patricia, I asked her why staff members didn't challenge speakers if they were saying things a staff leader, like her, thought were untrue or unjust. She replied,

I can't do it, because I've already been called to attention. One example is we [e.g., she and a group of travelers] were meeting with a manager from Chamberlain [a *maquila*] and at the time he was talking with all the students and telling them that forty pesos a day was a good salary at the time. Which is equivalent to four dollars. But, I told him, there with all the students, "How is it that you can lead this business and still sleep with a full conscience?" And, from there they haven't ever received us again.

To avoid this outcome, she changed her approach. She explained that, now, "at the conclusion [of the visit] we bring everybody together, and then we tell them from our perspective what we've lived and how the policy really works." Patricia reported that, as new staff members came on board, they're told that "we have an internal policy that we can't ever confront contradictions because it closes doors on us."

The importance of showing respect despite harboring disagreement was made evident to me one day with my reaction to something Pam said. It was the end of a long day, and Pam said that the next day we would have a visit from "ice, ice baby," using a sing-song tone which referred to the 1990s popular music hit by Vanilla Ice. She was, of course, mocking the actual visit we would have the following day from ICE. As our group chuckled at the cheesy tune, Pam noticed how much she was overstepping a line of respect by commenting, with a devilish grin: "We should sing this tomorrow, it'd be very disrespectful." The group, of course, did no such thing and Pam herself would not have let that happen.

Notably, these postures of respect and nonconfrontation were quite a step away from the free-flowing questioning and problematizing advocated by BorderLinks' sources, like Paulo Freire. BorderLinks' inclusion of a range of voices and positions introduced the possibility that travelers might be swayed by the rhetorical strategies of the "somewhat real people" they heard. After all, the experts that spoke to BorderLinks groups had positions to represent and a vested interest to draw travelers toward their interpretation of the border.

I was able to interview an ICE agent about his willingness to make agents available for the many hours required to make presentations to BorderLinks. He saw BorderLinks as an important part of the agency's mission to communicate its work to the public. As he recounted in an interview with me, which I was not allowed to audio record, BorderLinks' groups were an opportunity for the agency to point out the real danger from terrorists and drug dealers, while also letting them know that the public image of raiding immigrant residences was inaccurate. To him, BorderLinks was doing his agency a service by constituting small publics that his public relations efforts could influence. ICE was able to take part in the testimonial economy on terms for its own benefit.

In procuring this expanded array of voices, BorderLinks went to great lengths to maintain an ideal of open, noncoerced, diverse exploration of the border. Visibly stacking the deck of speakers would mean violating both the reality of a preexisting discursive field with opposing positions, as well as impinging on the ability of travelers to sort through those positions. Of course, the deck *was* stacked in a BorderLinks trip, in the sense that the organization and its travelers already prioritized immigrant voices. Still, the organizational willingness to represent a discursive field suggests a profound organizational belief in the truth power of testimonials from "real people" to win out over the truth of represented positions.

This work of including diverse voices was also expected by travelers, as they were attuned to whether the deck was stacked during a BorderLinks trip. Other examples of awareness-raising through travel note that travelers were aware of whether activities and discussion provided little interpretive space.[27] During follow-up interviews, I asked travelers whether they thought BorderLinks had an agenda. A number said, yes, that BorderLinks' message was that border policy was broken, migrants were mistreated, and that travelers could be involved to help improve these problems. Mary with the St. Michael's group explained to me that BorderLinks was "leading us [her fellow church members] to a feeling of sympathy for the plight of immigrants."

When pointing this agenda out, though, no traveler mentioned feeling pressured to accept a certain conclusion or ostracized for differences of opinion. More frequently, travelers stated that BorderLinks' agenda was "to be aware" of what was happening at the border. One termed the

[27] Kelner, *Tours That Bind.*

BorderLinks message "incredibly complicated," which "showed complexity" of the border and "opens more questions than it closes." One of the few overtly conservative travelers I traveled with, who told me he was watching for liberal bias, stated that BorderLinks' message, in the end, was "to reevaluate and come to your own conclusions." On the last day of a trip with Southern Seminary, another conservative traveler, Paul, commented that "there would be some people [back home in the South] who would worry about the message [from the week] and [question] 'where's the other side?', but now I can say it's not just a bunch of leftist propaganda."

BorderLinks' respectful inclusion of many different positions always left open the possibility that wrong conclusions were taken away from a BorderLinks trip. Travelers were left with the difficulty of sorting through a complex discursive field without organizational criteria about what was accurate and what was just. This organizational outcome was in tension with the orientation of the pedagogues that inspired BorderLinks' work to begin with. As Freire said in a recorded dialogue with Myles Horton: "While having on the one hand to respect the expectations and choices of the students, the educator also has the duty of not being neutral. . . . The educator as an intellectual has to intervene. He [*sic*] cannot be a mere facilitator."[28] Swapping BorderLinks for educator in this quotation, and travelers for students, the duty to intervene was a duty that the organization tended to avoid. It placed its faith in travelers and groups to sort through a complex discursive field, hoping that the truths portrayed by "real people" would make the difference.

The resulting organizational confusion was noticed by its staff, who struggled with it. While speaking with Janice, I asked her why she had said to a group I traveled with that she needed to be neutral. She replied by saying that "you kind of get conflicting messages about this at BorderLinks." She explained that, on the one hand, the organization urged her not to take sides during travel, but also that it was "impossible to be viewed as neutral" by travelers. When I asked the trip leader Molly why trip leaders acted this way, she said, "I feel like they think if they inserted their own opinion, it would be given this extra power and people would grab onto that instead of hearing the different voices."

---

[28] Brenda Bell, John Gaventa, and John Peters, *Myles Horton and Paulo Freire: We Make the Road by Walking: Conversations on Education and Social Change* (Philadelphia: Temple University Press, 1990), p. 180.

To the organization's director in 2010, who was preparing to leave, this was evidence that the Freirian model was breaking down. Her tenure as the first director to follow Rick had been rocky, involving extensive staff turnover, budget tightening to deal with financial instability from the purchase of the group's building, and personality conflicts. She felt the organization had stagnated, that it hadn't been able "to really create progressive minds, really critically thinking minds." I asked why. She replied, similar to Molly, that,

> I think that it is a self-consciousness that comes with white privilege, of knowing enough that you don't want to misuse your power. But not knowing enough that you have a responsibility to your voice in certain instances, particularly as facilitators here. Somehow they've misunderstood what popular education is about, to think that it is about tolerance, anything goes.

The director was possibly right about some individual staff members, but what I've argued is that this tension derived from the organization's work, as it navigated diverse voices and kept a testimonial economy going for the next group of travelers.

ACTION, WITHOUT EXPECTATION

The BorderLinks building was an aesthetically rich, spirit-filled environment. The décor and structure of BorderLinks' space suggested to travelers that the issues they encountered about immigration were one piece in a web of issues. A prominent poster in the "living room" that hung on the wall above an upholstered, dilapidated rocking chair reinforced this image. The six-foot by four-foot black-and-white poster showed a massive spider hovering over an intricate web, with various unfortunate objects caught in the web. Stepping close to the poster, you might be surprised to see this was an evocative visual aid describing the modern economy: the spider of neo-liberal capitalism pulled the strings (literally) of multinational corporations, resulting in mismanaged national governments and a subdued mass of humanity mired in poverty and injustice. With the addition of immigration, the picture would provide a rather accurate depiction of BorderLinks' view of the global economy.[29]

But what could a person do against such an all-encompassing, complex web? This takes us into the domain of the third theme in BorderLinks'

---

[29] The poster was the "Free Trade Area of the Americas" design from the Beehive Design Collective (www.beehivccollective.org). It was never publicly discussed on any trip.

organizational vision: action. BorderLinks' self-stated purpose for existence was "to inspire action." Both travelers and staff, before trips, during
trips, and after trips, expressed a faith that immersion travel did inspire
action. The primary organizational way for talking about action was by
reference to transformation. Describing a BorderLinks trip he attended,
Gill commented that, "Like nearly all BorderLinks excursions, this trip
was truly a transformative experience for everyone."[30]

   At the beginning of trips, as BorderLinks staff members oriented
travelers, they often noted how transforming the week would be for
people. I came to refer to this in my notes as staff efforts to "prep the
change." Prepping the change happened in numerous ways. The repeti-
tion of Rick's founding myth was the most obvious example, but the
reference to transformation was omnipresent. On the first night with
Southern Seminary, the US BorderLinks leader, who had been on immersion trips herself, told the group the "truth" of the transformative experience that was about to happen to them. The Mexican BorderLinks leader
at dinner that night shared how, on her very first day with BorderLinks,
her life changed. Now, she said, she could see the change happen in other
people during the week by looking at their faces. The BorderLinks Executive Director would share her own transformative story with groups as a
way of inviting travelers to embrace the idea of transformation. Speaking
with the group from Sojourner University, she said that the BorderLinks
trip could be a "life-changing experience" and that people in the area had
a saying about the desert that could apply to the BorderLinks experience:
"You either get burnt up, or you catch fire." Two weeks after a Border-
Links trip, travelers usually received a follow-up letter with thanks from
their trip's BorderLinks staff leaders and gentle encouragement for continued transformation. The second paragraph of one letter I received
began: "We hope that your time here was transformational." In another
newsletter, the message from the Executive Director was even more
assured: "We know that most travelers in our programs come away
transformed by the experience."

   This language of transformation was generally agnostic about the
details of travelers' lives before their participation in BorderLinks. For
example, many BorderLinks travelers were *already* attitudinally committed to pro-immigrant positions and/or had been involved with immigration causes. What the language of transformation added was emotional

---

[30] Gill, *Borderlinks*, p. 28.

motivation to do *something more* upon returning home. The frequent use of the word was universalizing in its implications: how could a traveler *not* be transformed? This, after all, was why feeder organizations sent their members on such trips.

Behind the word transformation was an intricate organizational anthropology about how travelers cared for suffering and the emotional processes that had to occur for a traveler to eventually act. The organization's attempt to inspire action was understood as a complicated move of commitment from "head" to "heart." BorderLinks' staff members described how BorderLinks trips were meant to produce "heart knowledge" in addition to "head knowledge." Head knowledge, like book knowledge, referred to the problematic learning of facts and knowledge separated from the context in which humans experienced the brute reality of the facts. Head knowledge was the gathering of information with little or no regard for the ethical implication of such knowledge. Heart knowledge meant becoming aware of how facts and information affected moral sensibility and encouraged future action.

One of BorderLinks' stances was that, in most discussions of immigration or the border, head and heart knowledge were separated, even opposed to one another. BorderLinks seemed to ask of travelers: "If head and heart knowledge were joined, would we build an expensive wall in the desert that people scale? Would we allow hundreds of deaths in the desert each year?" BorderLinks' methodology was meant to bring these two together. Doing so, however, was not easily accomplished. If Border-Links' goal was to connect heart knowledge and head knowledge, the preexisting pathway between head knowledge and future action had to be disrupted. Freeing travelers' hearts meant stopping the patterns by which head knowledge dominated the move to action.

The Heart-Knowledge Processor

To do this, staff members added a spiritual-psychological element to experiential education pedagogy, which I came to call the "heart-knowledge processor." On the majority of trips I traveled with, Border-Links staff members would discuss the heart-knowledge concept as they introduced a period of group discussion or reflection. BorderLinks staff members explained to me that they would hold off on processing heart knowledge since travelers were not ready or "in a place" to experience its benefits until after a few days. The staff member Janice explained to me that most groups began to tire, became frustrated, disengaged from speakers, and stopped asking questions about midway through the week. When this happened, she said, groups "need the hold-it-in-your-heart talk." She explained that the purpose of this talk was to convey to travelers that they "don't need to fix it [e.g., the suffering and injustice], they don't need to be American." In the middle of the week with Southern Seminary, Janice sensed that the group was confused, having had a difficult experience on a desert walk. During a reflection, she encouraged the group: "Don't worry about action yet, we'll get to that. [Instead], put the stories in your heart, *then* move them to your head." For travelers to be changed by the experience and to move into good action, they had to spend processing heart knowledge.

One way was through reflections. One evening with Midwestern Theological, the trip leader, Pam, began a reflection by asking, "How is your heart?" She explained that this was a "Mayan way of saying, 'How are you doing?'" This particular group was feeling disturbed. Benjamin said that he felt "conflicted. . . . I'm going to be different [after this trip], but I don't know what that means." Mitt followed this, commenting, "I need a different way to live but to be the same person. I see it in practical terms. I feel a call to change. It's radical to change and to have a call to radical change." He explained that doing a BorderLinks trip was "like doing a tough diet because you fail because you are so used to doing what you were doing before." Lucile followed on these, saying:

My heart is heavy. I see the faces of people from the room last night [when we spoke with Mexican church members in a border town]. I see faces that depend on me, on us, to help make a difference, to help with their situation. . . . The heaviness is to go home and figure out what my role is.

This group was picking its ways through the complicated minefield of heavy emotions. Heart-knowledge processing required this work, lest the heaviness remain and prevent future action.

The focus on processing emotions, and on the process of dealing with heart knowledge before moving to action, could disrupt the trip. During a trip with Southern Seminary, while looking at the border wall in Nogales, which was fifteen feet high, topped with razor wire, monitored by security cameras, and adorned with resistance art, the group had become engaged in a political and economic conversation about the wall. Janice stopped the conversation and asked us to consider migration through reflecting on our identity and personal history. She seemed worried that the group was getting ahead of itself on its first day in Mexico. She suggested that we

FIGURE 2 Artwork on Mexican side of border wall

should take in our own stories, and the stories we hear, to our hearts: "See where they [the stories] pull us or rub us raw."

Another way to engage the heart processor was an activity that involved outlining a human body on a sheet of paper. At the head, travelers could write down all the things they had learned during the week: their head knowledge. At the heart, travelers could write down the emotions they were experiencing and/or the aspects of the trip that most triggered the reaction of their heart. When she introduced this activity, Janice explained that the heart was the container that would hold the valuable experiences that travelers would take away from the week. The group divided into three small groups, scattering on the cool floor of open space in a church.

Table 3 provides a list from this activity. On the right-hand side of the table, the heart contains both heavy and inspiring emotions. BorderLinks hoped to turn these emotions into motivation, which then generated action informed by the head knowledge listed on the left-hand side of the table.

Another way that the heart processing worked was to call on the expertise of someone who could talk about emotions. This could involve

TABLE 3 *Head knowledge and heart knowledge on a BorderLinks trip*

Head Knowledge	Heart Knowledge
Facts	Dreams of people
Importance of water	Faces
Statistics (about migrant deaths)	Desperation
Justice system (and deportation)	Fear
Cost of living in Mexico	Hopelessness
Living environment in Mexico	Passion
International law	Determination
	Sense of care
	Guilt
	Embarrassment
	No more deaths!
	Inspiration
	Commitment

Mexican staff members sharing their "story" about low wages in *maquilas*, poor housing quality, and the difficulties of migrant work, followed by encouraging comments about how travelers should feel. The testimonial was usually given its own time slot in a day, a moment dedicated to hearing a narrative about a struggle that, through the work of the storyteller, could be emotional, informative, and inspiring. The emotional impact of these particular stories was multiplied by the personal familiarity that trip members had with the storyteller. This evoked Rick's founding myth, in which the traveler's confusion was given clarification by a foreign person he met. After sharing her story with the Central College travelers, the Mexican BorderLinks staff member Lizbeth commented, "Take stories you heard here back, along with the faces of people [you met]. Tell people about the border, especially those with the least knowledge."

These multiple ways of processing heart knowledge fit seamlessly with the embodied metaphor of heart common in linguistic usage, which makes the domain of its meaning rather large. There is a clear linkage in Border-Links' language between heart, emotion, and suffering. During a trip with Sojourner University, I noted many times travelers talking about their hearts: breaking when hearing about the mistreatment of immigrants, or as the mode of connection when hearing an immigrant's painful story.

The effects of the heart-knowledge processor were numerous. It made emotional management public, with travelers following an organizational rule that not only elicited emotionality but that found motivation in emotion.[31] During these moments, travelers reflected on what they had seen but also began to manage anxieties of what this meant in the course of their lives. As Janice reminded the St. Michael's group at the beginning of the activity, "This is the point of turning to action. The first steps are the hardest, but with more reflection you can move on to other action."

The logic of the heart processor provided travelers a language to understand what might happen to them, as well as what might not. Heart-knowledge processing regulated the emotional, even moral, pressure that built up for individuals during a trip. It allowed control over something that could feel out of control: the overwhelming system of injustice that travelers learned about. Through this process, action became a *personal* issue, based on travelers' discernment of their own hearts and their lives.

However, this process simultaneously minimized the pressure for action by suggesting that the movement to action must be slow and must be discerned by the individuals themselves. The heart-knowledge processor was specific in its demands for something, but vague about what direction this demand should go. Deep feelings could become a reason for releasing travelers from obligation. On the last day of the Central College trip, the BorderLinks Executive Director explained to the group, "It's common to expect the eventual outcome [of this trip] is outrage. . . . But don't be ashamed as your feelings change, because they will." As Alicia suggested to the group from Eastern College:

Be gentle with yourself when you return to school because there is so much going on. Don't worry about fitting in social justice goals into your college life. There are other opportunities for graduates. Let it shape your life, but you do have responsibilities now to deal with [in college]. Shifting priorities and making space is important. Be gentle on yourself. You got a lot of changes this week from all of this.

---

[31] Arlie Russell Hochschild, *The Managed Heart: Commercialization of Human Feeling* (Berkeley: Univeristy of California Press, 1983); Erika Summers-Effler, *Laughing Saints and Righteous Heroes: Emotional Rhythms in Social Movement Groups* (Chicago: University of Chicago Press, 2010).

Action, Maybe?

After heart-knowledge processing, BorderLinks' encouragement of action was anything but straightforward. Gill indirectly provides evidence of the problem from the organization's history, writing, "While BorderLinks is not essentially an activist organization, it is committed to the belief that all real learning leads naturally and inevitably to action."[32] There is certainly the *expectation* of action, to which Gill writes:

> Ultimately it is the hope of those of us who work with BorderLinks that those who participate in its programs will find ways to improve the conditions along the US/Mexico border by helping to alter the political policies that initiate and maintain the destructive and dehumanizing realities there. Some former travelers go home and organize economic boycotts of products assembled in maquiladoras, while others may protest at the School of the Americas or work to elect responsible legislators. Many more help to disseminate information about unjust political and economic policies, and hopefully everyone gets out and votes![33]

In practice, BorderLinks' staff members went to great lengths to avoid suggesting what travelers could do – including not suggesting the list that Gill wrote. While "action" as a general category was encouraged, political action was usually missing. Thus, the most surprising fracture in BorderLinks' attempts to inspire action was the disappearance of politics: the disappearance of a systematic, critical discussion about the action that could use political behaviors and structures to rearrange what they saw at the border.[34] This absence was curious given the identities of the staff at BorderLinks. The second time I pulled into BorderLinks' parking lot with an immersion group, I saw cars with "Obama 08," "No Border Wall," and "ACLU" bumper stickers. The staff leaders' office was decorated with posters supporting immigration reform and other local, progressive causes. During our interview, Molly confirmed to me that, "Pretty much everyone [on the staff] is disgusted by the [border] deterrence strategy, the buildup of the wall, that kind of thing," with nearly all involved in progressive advocacy groups.

Yet on six trips I heard no discussion from BorderLinks staff members about high-profile pieces of legislation, such as the DREAM Act, that

---

[32] Gill, *Borderlinks*, p. 37.   [33] Gill, *Borderlinks II*, pp. 151–2.

[34] Stephen Hart, *Cultural Dilemmas of Progressive Politics: Styles of Engagement among Grassroots Activists* (Chicago: Chicago University Press, 2001); Nina Eliasoph, *Avoiding Politics: How Americans Produce Apathy in Everyday Life*, (New York: Cambridge University Press, 1998).

travelers could advocate for in their home districts. Even the phrase "comprehensive immigration reform" was not much used by BorderLinks staff despite its ubiquity in political and journalistic conversation at the time. One of the few times I heard it mentioned was by the Executive Director in a short conversation at the end of St. Michael's trip. She said it in passing, first mentioning "little things" people could do, such as conserving water and recycling, then quickly saying, "We also want you to get involved with immigration reform, humanitarian aid, that type of thing." "That type of thing" – of political action – was hoped for but was not an end to which BorderLinks pointed.

Here, some of BorderLinks' formal neutrality was due to confusion. On three different occasions, I heard staff members refer to a limit on political advocacy by nonprofit groups as one reason to avoid politics. But this understanding was factually incorrect, failing to distinguish off-limits electioneering from the critique of political figures, policy analysis, and discussion of particular policies.[35] These activities were all legal territory for BorderLinks; it just did not do them. During an interview with Molly, who was in charge of the overall educational offerings and training for the organization, I pressed her on this point. She replied,

Because of our nonprofit status we've always been a little confused about how much we can do about educating people about legislation. Like encouraging direct actions. I think there's more we could do about that, but I think we've sort of shied away from it, mostly because we're not quite sure where the line is.

As of 2010, the organization hadn't figured a way out of this confusion even though the contrast this created with its founding era, and with other immersion producers, was something that staff members talked about. A few minutes later in the interview, Molly continued,

As new staff have come on they've been, like, 'Why do I see these other organizations, like Witness for Peace or other organizations doing this type of work, do this direct policy and advocacy stuff? And we're told we can't do that because of our status or maintaining our contacts.' I think we've talked about it, but we haven't [changed as an organization]. I think there's something in our bylaws that says like fifteen percent of our time can be devoted to legislative activity. No one has ever really known how to do that. One of the trip leaders last year made this immigration policy packet that we've sometimes used with groups. I think we need to resurrect it with the current people. We've made efforts for immigration policy

[35] Jeffrey M. Berry and David F. Arons, *A Voice for Nonprofits* (Washington, DC: Brookings Institute Press, 2003).

to be more tangible for people to know the specifics of by the time they leave, know what's up for debate in Congress and that sort of thing.

I never saw such a packet. As a result, travelers could leave BorderLinks with a deeper understanding of the spider web of systemic injustice that caused the suffering of immigrants, but travelers might become "stuck" on one thread in that web, thinking of some avenues of action that appeared legitimate, but not others.

On the trip with Central College, the resistance of BorderLinks' to providing clear directions came through as a group repeatedly kept asking George what he thought they should do. George's final reply to the group, given with a look of impatient exasperation, was, "I have no idea, but I hope you do something." When the BorderLinks staff member Nancy spoke with groups, she often gave a similar message: "We don't tell you what to do. It's about falling in love. Go back and get connected and do something. And, hopefully, something with the poorest and the marginalized. We didn't bring you here to be worker-bees in immigration reform. We want that [immigration reform], and people do need it, but just become involved!"

Story Telling as Action

The primary way that BorderLinks tried to encourage future action was by helping travelers' turn their stories into a tool. On the last night of my trip with the groups from both Sojourner University and St. Michael's College, the BorderLinks staff members had us make lists of actions we could do when we got home. Table 4, composed of notes I took from the groups' lists made on butcher paper, displays the action ideas of these two groups, one of college students and another of church members.

The majority of the suggestions focused on individual development, such as reading the newspaper, keeping alive the spirit of resistance learned at BorderLinks, and learning about immigration reform. A few suggestions included connecting to institutionalized politics, such as elected officials or civic groups focused on immigration. A significant portion focused on some aspect of "sharing the story." Storytelling was the default action that BorderLinks encouraged most often.

When asked by a group halfway through the week what to do, Alicia responded evasively, "I will give you a 'Toolkit for Action' at the end of the week, when you can learn more." She was suggesting that the practical demand for action was something they could deal with after their

TABLE 4 *Possible actions brainstormed by two BorderLinks delegations*

Sojourner University		
Group One Suggestions	Group Two Suggestions	Group Three Suggestions
Keeping alive the spirt of resistance	A BorderLinks delegation next year	Spread the word on a personal level
Restless struggling to understand	Take Gary's survey	Encourage community volunteering
Communication of border realities	Host humanitarian aid speaker	Establish volunteer system on campus
Planting date trees	Tell our families about what we saw	Expand our "borders"
Finding your place along the spectrum	Blog about our experience	
Imperative to act ethically	Thesis about immigration	
	Summer volunteer along the border	
	Share the story with the campus	
	Read the paper	
	Economic development	
	Talk with others	
	Be politically involved	
	Research	
	Learn about immigration in other countries	
	Watch Obama! [Hold him accountable]	

St. Michael's Church	
Group One Suggestions	Group Two Suggestions
Connect locally to immigrant organizations	Understand "immigration reform"
Talk to friends, Congress about experience	Investigate *maquilas*

(*continued*)

TABLE 4 (*continued*)

St. Michael's Church	
Group One Suggestions	Group Two Suggestions
Letter to editor about immigration	Talk to people about the experience
Talk to people in Hispanic neighborhood	Read books about issue
Show pictures from the trip at church	Contact elected officials
Pray for immigrants	Collect shoelaces to send to Mexico
Worship	Change to Fair Trade coffee at church
Adult education at church on immigration	Worship Adult education at church on immigration

hearts had been moved. While this "Toolkit for Action" sounded promising, it echoed the patterns in the brainstorming session, if it was used at all. I participated in three BorderLinks trips before hearing any Border-Links staff member discuss or provide this resource. Finally, after seeing a staff member copy it hurriedly at the end of a trip that she was leading, I asked for a copy. When I read the fourteen-page document, I saw it had four pages dedicated to books, news sources, or documentaries, and two pages dedicated to contact information for immigration-related organizations. Three pages of the Toolkit for Action were devoted to helping travelers tell their stories. This focus on story was reflected on the organization's website as well: the *one* webpage in mid-2011 devoted to travelers' actions after their delegation was about sharing the story of their travel. The Toolkit for Action suggested the following:

As you re-enter your community, it is the perfect time for storytelling. By articulating what you learned during your time on the border through specific and intentional stories, you build a bridge from your experience to your community, causing others to think about perspectives and people that are often overlooked. Indeed, your words and pictures describing those people whose lives are affected by injustice in trade and border policy are a vivid and powerful expression of why this trip is important.

BorderLinks wanted travelers to be strategic in their storytelling, balancing information and emotions to represent distant suffering.[36] In this vein, the document suggested the following:

- Put a *human* face on the impact of trade/border policies ... tell names and describe places.
- Be intentional in your *language*, so as to not cause your listeners to be defensive.
- Refrain from stating harsh generalizations about a certain political leader or policy that could immediately lead to an argument.

There was no specific story to tell; there was no specific policy to discuss; there were no ready-made facts provided for travelers to use. The tone of the story was to personalize without politicizing. This fit with Border-Links noncoercive orientation, which allowed individual conscience to decide which direction transformation might go. But did travelers feel that stories were a powerful response?

When I spoke with one of Sojourner University's members, Wilbur, months after the trip, the problem of what to do with "story" came up. I asked Wilbur what he had told his family and friends about the trip when he returned. He explained that "I didn't know where to start talking [because] it was just a big experience." After a few attempts, he only shared his story with "someone in the right mindset," which he explained meant someone with a preexisting progressive tilt toward immigration. In the end, while the BorderLinks experience had been powerful for him, he was resigned about the power of sharing this story with others, saying, "I can't convert someone with my experience of BorderLinks, but Border-Links itself can."

CONCLUSION

BorderLinks tried to "do education" in a way that placed faith in the ability of travelers to discover the truths of unjust social reality and be moved to action. To make this possible the organization created a context that was formally neutral, allowing the noncoercive encounter with voices of "real people" to lead to the individualized discernment of action.

However, as we have seen, the translation of ideals into practice was fractured along the way. The organization squelched the expertise of its

---

[36] Boltanksi, *Distant Suffering*.

staff, created a testimonial economy that could be hard for travelers to navigate, downplayed overt political talk, and provided vague guidance about future action. Travelers felt noncoerced and inspired by Border-Links, but they also felt confused about what to do next. In an interview after his trip with Midwestern Theological Seminary, David explained that he was deeply affected, but was not sure what BorderLinks wanted him to do beyond "Don't forget the stories."

As other scholars have noted, the use of Freirian pedagogy with privileged persons confronts some inherent challenges.[37] Freire's original method of liberatory learning was localized and connected to practical activities for people without power.[38] For travelers with advanced educational backgrounds, far from home, the sinews between experiential education and social change appear complex and winding. For an organization enacting the Freirean vision with nonpartisan groups while balancing its own survival, these challenges were difficult to resolve. The ideals of experiential learning through immersion travel did not easily translate to practice. As a result, BorderLinks formed a felt awareness through the encounter with the US-Mexico border while respecting the boundaries of individual conscience and diverse feeder organization logics. By the end of a BorderLinks trip, travelers had done experiential education, but it is unclear what experiential education had done to them.

BorderLinks provides a twist to what Eliasoph has shown about Americans' avoidance of talking politics as an outcome of apathy.[39] The people in Eliasoph's research were socially engaged and aware of current events but excluded political talk from the course of normal group conversation because of perceptions about politicians' weak power and hypocrisy. By contrast, BorderLinks flipped the process. It purposefully avoided talking politics as a way to avoid producing apathy in the first place. It wanted empathy to arise, leading to engagement. The organization relied on the epistemic power of others' suffering and an individual process of discernment to orient new opinions and actions. If apathy was avoided, then travelers might do something after their trip. BorderLinks provided cultural elements that *could* motivate action, but what to do was left unresolved.

[37] Ann Curry-Stevens, "New Forms of Transformative Education Pedagogy for the Privileged," *Journal of Transformative Education* 5, 1 (2007).
[38] Breunig, "Critical Praxis and Experiential Education."
[39] Eliasoph, "Making a Fragile Public: A Talk-Centered Study of Citizenship and Power," *Sociological Theory* 14, 3 (1996); Eliasoph, *Avoiding Politics*.

Reflecting on his work at the Highlander Folk School, Myles Horton discussed a similar organizational problem: how to do education without being didactic, ideological, or exclusive of personal discovery.[40] Because Highlander encouraged participants to confront social injustice, the work was not viewed as educational. But, since the organization did not push a slate of candidates with packaged solutions for social change, it was not viewed as political. Instead, like BorderLinks, it hoped that the experience it introduced would influence participants in new ways. The BorderLinks of today shows the difficulty in translating this sort of vision into practice.

Yet, even with these fractures, the organization felt like something happened to travelers. How did the immersion travel experience actually affect travelers? In the next chapter, we go inside the content of immersion travel, observing how the activities of immersion travel matter.

---

[40] Bell et al., *Myles Horton and Paulo Freire.*

PART II

ACTIVITIES, EMOTIONS, AND EMPATHY

4

What Immersion Travelers Feel All Day

They're not coming for a Disneyland experience, they're coming here to see the underbelly of the beast.
                Hilary, Federal Public Defender

When travelers settled into the BorderLinks building, they were provided an itinerary for the week ahead. Each itinerary was packed with activities that staff members had painstakingly arranged to show travelers the border, to produce the testimonial economy, and to provide space for reflection. By the end of a weeklong trip, a BorderLinks traveler crossed hundreds of miles and stopped at two dozen or so different places to talk, look, and listen. How did the activities of this itinerary affect travelers?

This question gets us close to a puzzle that lurks in the background of research about transformative experiences and experiential education: whether the generic experience of immersion travel matters more for civic outcomes than the specific activities of any given immersion trip. In the pages ahead I argue that the generic form for travel sets a context, but that the specific activities matter for what transformation feels like and becomes. At BorderLinks, anger and sorrow are the emotional products of immersion travel, but they arise from very different types of activities.

THE TRIP OR WHAT'S INSIDE THE TRIP?

Travel away from home is often understood as a liminal experience: time and space away from the familiar places and routines of ordinary life. Liminal experiences, like an immersion trip, are temporally structured by a pattern of anticipation, separation, return, and reintegration. Travelers are reliant on guides, they inhabit foreign spaces, they enact new daily routines, they make new relationships, and they forego personal privacy. One well-trodden avenue for analyzing liminal experiences focuses on the generic structure of the liminal experience. In his description of such experiences, Victor Turner noted that "liminality may be partly described as a stage of reflection," during which individuals could reorient their futures in relation to the past, based on new experience.[1] For Turner, liminal experiences provided an opportunity for personal reorientation in conjunction with social reintegration.

In this interpretation, a liminal experience influences travelers as a function of a generic social pattern. The stages of leaving, becoming a stranger, and temporarily living in a new way are supposed to create a changed person upon returning home.[2] Neil Smelser's analysis of "odyssey experiences," a reference to the journey of Homer's well-known Greek hero, illustrates the theorized tie between generic trip structure and transformation.[3] Smelser writes that, "a finite period of disengagement from the routines of life and immersion into a simpler, transitory, often collective, and often intense period of involvement ... often culminates in some kind of regeneration."[4] The logic in this line of argument is that the generic structure of a form of culture is itself effective in causing a change in people's lives. DeGloma has shown how powerful a cultural form can be in his analysis of awakening narratives.[5] Awakening narratives are story templates that are semiotically structured to point toward enlightenment as people use them "to account for discovering truth in one's life."[6] Those who use these awakening narratives, similar to those who participate in odysseys and other liminal experiences, create something new merely by using a cultural form that provides structure for articulating the occurrence of newness. In this line of interpretation, liminal experiences will shape individuals no matter what happens in the experience. Not surprisingly, those who study immersion travel report that nearly every traveler reports a sense of being changed.[7] The underlying cultural form generates this response.

---

[1] Victor Turner, *The Forest of Symbols: Aspects of Ndembu Ritual* (Ithaca, NY: Cornell University Press, 1967), p. 105.
[2] Turner and Turner, *Image and Pilgrimage.*   [3] Smelser, *The Odyssey Experience.*
[4] Ibid., p. xi.   [5] DeGloma, *Seeing the Light.*   [6] Ibid., p. 19.
[7] Kelner, *Tours That Bind*; Vrasti, *Volunteer Tourism in the Global South.*

A significant weakness in this line of interpretation is that the particularities of a given experience – its content – are downplayed. For example, DeGloma shows how awakening narratives structure individuals' accounts of transformation, no matter whether the transformation is to or from religion, to or from a sexual orientation.[8] The problem with this approach is that causal efficacy is attributed to the cultural form alone. As a result, cultural forms are implicitly portrayed as homogenous, demoting the importance of particularities and difference within a cultural form.

Yet instantiations of cultural forms do vary in their effects. For example, after-school involvement, volunteering, and small groups are generic forms with generic effects, but also with significant difference by content.[9] After-school sports, band, and chess club may all have a similar pattern of voluntary participation and group bonding, but the *content* of these activities generates distinctly different civic outcomes. For example, band and chess make adult political participation more likely, while sports activities have little or even adverse effect.

My purpose here is not to deny the raw power of liminal experience in immersion travel. The liminal pattern in immersion travel makes it possible for individuals to anticipate the value of the experience and to activate its possibilities.[10] As William Sewell writes, "To engage in a cultural practice is to make use of a semiotic code to do something in the world."[11] BorderLinks travelers partook of liminal experience as a cultural form when they expected interesting things to occur and when they inhabited liminal roles that helped to produce these interesting things.[12] But we also need to know more about these interesting things: immersion travel's internal activities. By looking at the activities within a trip, we observe what immersion travel producers can do to foster intensity and direct a traveler's sense of transformation.

The approach I follow for categorizing and analyzing trip activities draws from two decades of research on collective action. This tradition

---

[8] DeGloma, *Seeing the Light.*

[9] McFarland and Thomas, "Bowling Young"; Lichterman, *Elusive Togetherness*; Eliasoph, *Avoiding Politics.*

[10] Jeffrey Alexander, Bernhard Giesen, and Jason L. Mast, *Social Performance: Symbolic Action, Cultural Pragmatics, and Ritual* (New York: Cambridge University Press, 2006).

[11] William Sewell, "The Concept(s) of Culture," in *Beyond the Cultural Turn*, ed. Victoria E.; Hunt Bonnell, Lynn (Berkeley: University of California Press, 1999), p. 51.

[12] Bornstein, "Volunteer Experience."

has grappled with understanding how information and emotion are produced and transmitted in a way that changes individuals' propensity to care and to act.[13] In the pages that follow, I highlight three processes within immersion travel. First, I construct a typology of trip activities by categorizing them as attempts to frame undocumented immigration.[14] Second, I show how BorderLinks' activities engendered two types of emotion that have often been identified as crucial to generating moral concern, particularly for distant sufferers.[15] Finally, I show how the complex emotional and informational picture that emerges through a BorderLinks trip created motivational potential.

I begin with a brief description of how the organization arranged the activities of an immersion trip. Then, I use the evaluation forms that BorderLinks travelers completed on their last day of travel to analyze activities and travelers' emotional responses. The chapter concludes by considering what this analysis reveals about immersion travel as both a form of liminal experience and a specific type of awareness-raising process. Overall, this chapter gives a sense of what immersion travelers felt, what they valued doing, and what moved them.

THE PRODUCTION OF IMMERSION TRAVEL ITINERARIES

The pressure on BorderLinks staff members to produce a "good" trip was intense. Staff members were aware that some travelers had never been to the US-Mexico border. They were also aware, from the comments of

---

[13] The source literature for this approach is quite voluminous. I generally draw from the "cultural" stream of research on social movements, though that itself is wide, including framing, identity, and emotional approaches. The most relevant aspects of collective action for understanding the topic of immersion travel have to do with motivation and mobilization.

[14] Benford and Snow, "Framing Processes."; Yukich, "Constructing the Model Immigrant."

[15] Kraig Beyerlein and David Sikkink, "Sorrow and Solidarity: Why Americans Volunteered for 9/11 Relief Efforts," *Social Problems*, 55, 2 (2008); James M. Jasper and Lynn Owens, "Social Movements and Emotions," in *Handbook of the Sociology of Emotions*, ed. Jan E. Stets and Jonathan H. Turner (New York: Springer, 2014); Jo Reger, "Organizational 'Emotion Work' through Consciousness-Raising: An Analysis of a Feminist Organization," *Qualitative Sociology* 27, 2 (2004); Thomas et al., "Transforming 'Apathy into Movement'."; Erika Summers-Effler, "The Micro Potential for Social Change: Emotion, Consciousness, and Social Movement Formation," *Sociological Theory* 20, 1 (2002).

group leaders, that past travelers had had transformative experiences that future travelers were excited about. Sarah, a staff member, explained to me that group leaders who had come before to BorderLinks would sometimes expect the same schedule of activities that they had the previous year in hopes that their group members would have the same reactions.

Fulfilling these expectations had contradictory effects on staff members, as they were also aware of the resource pressures that ensued from not booking trips or losing bookings. The resource flow into BorderLinks was punctuated by high travel times in midwinter, late winter, and late spring. These periods coincided with space in academic calendars when students could leave home for a week. Reservations for these peak periods were accepted more than a year in advance. However, BorderLinks' capacity during these peak periods was limited by its sleeping space, the number of its vans, and the number of its staff.

When a reservation was made, BorderLinks took a $500 deposit, which would not be returned if the trip was canceled. Even with this deposit retained, the cancellation of a trip was a major financial problem for the organization. A canceled five-day trip of ten travelers traveling at the cost of $125/day meant $6,250 of lost income. There was almost no way for BorderLinks to fill a trip booking that was vacated within three months of the actual trip, which meant that cancellations could be devastating. In response, BorderLinks' staff members worked to arrange delegation schedules that, through the testimonial economy and heart-knowledge processing, would work best to inform and emotionally move travelers.

In the weeks before a group's arrival, a BorderLinks staff member made arrangements for all the activities of an upcoming delegation, sometimes tailoring trip activities to a group's interests. Patricia, a Mexican trip leader, explained, "We base it off of the group's interest. Many groups that come have often been here before. They might call and let us know, 'This is what we need. We want homestays; we want interactions with community people.'"

Staff leaders considered the process frustrating, mostly obscured to the groups themselves, who did not understand the flexibility needed when arranging schedules with dozens of speakers and organizations. Beyond confirming the availability of speakers, staff members had to rotate speakers so that they did not become overtaxed with too many requests. One of the trip leaders, Molly, explained that they did a regular check-in with speakers and organizations to confirm that "they didn't feel like we were using them for free talks whenever we wanted." This was especially important because speakers were not usually reimbursed for their participation. Molly explained that, "In Mexico, we give [honorariums] sometimes to speakers. And material aid to migrant aid stations. We'll try to bring socks, stuff like that. In the US, rarely. Sometimes we'll pay someone's gas if they're taking us on a desert walk."

Across a trip itinerary, specific activities were sacrosanct. BorderLinks staff worried if travelers had not met key speakers, had not done a homestay, or had not had a chance to talk with immigrants. After we dropped the Sojourner University group at the airport, I spoke with Sarah, the BorderLinks staff leader, about how she felt about the trip she'd just led. She replied, "I was worried about this group. At first, they were really heady, trying to figure out and fix everything. By the end, though, they were talking more about their feelings of the situation." I asked her what she thought caused this shift. Sarah replied "Well, definitely [hearing] the immigrants' stories at AFA. And the desert walk . . . Also, I think having that interaction with John Fife." From Sarah's comments, the ideal structure of an immersion trip was to introduce different types of activities that, as we will shortly see, represented immigration and created an emotional response in distinct ways.

Sarah also alluded to an emotional-temporal rhythm in the trip. Trip leaders attempted to build this rhythm into each trip if they could, having certain activities that prompted emotions and knowledge in a certain order. When I asked Janice how she organized a trip to highlight the immigrant stories that she and others prioritized, she explained:

There are some things that ideally I would like to happen before we have those interactions . . . like having some border history and just having some time together as a group to start to get any context at all for what is going here. . . . Then, I really prefer to have some visits, at least a couple of visits, with people who are helping migrants. . . . It's providing context, and it's providing context from a point of view that is much closer to the participant's point of view. And I think that that's helpful, I think that's it's easier to hear.

Planning a good trip and getting a group to the border were difficult prospects, but, once there, the immersion itinerary filled the experience.

WHAT DO TRAVELERS DO ALL DAY?

Once travelers arrived, the day-to-day activities of a BorderLinks trip were scheduled around the economy of testimonial-telling at the

US-Mexico border.[16] More than 90 percent of groups visited with an immigrant service organization in Mexico. For example, one oft-visited organization was the local office of Grupos Beta, a Mexican immigrant-protection agency that alerted would-be migrants to the dangers of immigration through the desert and provided short-term help and travel vouchers for recently deported migrants. Another typical immigrant service organization was La Corazon, a daily feeding program for deported immigrants. On a weeklong BorderLinks trip, the median number of visits to immigrant service organizations was four.

Every group visited with organizations or activists in the United States that were focused on the injustices of immigration. This might include No More Deaths, an organization that set up humanitarian aid camps in the desert; Humane Borders, an organization that placed water barrels in the remote desert; Derechos Humanos, an organization that educated immigrants about their legal rights, assisted with identifying human remains found in the desert, and publicized unjust policies; or the local office of the Sierra Club, which worked to change border wall policy that imperiled sensitive nature areas. On a weeklong trip, the median number of visits with such proimmigrant voices was four.

About half of all groups met with an agent from either ICE, CBP, or the Border Patrol. During these talks, the agents discussed the specific duties related to their job and the missions of the agencies. Nearly all groups observed proceedings of Operation Streamline, a judicial deterrence initiative that placed detained immigrants in criminal proceedings with the threat of future jail time in exchange for quick repatriation.[17] Conducted at the DeConcini US Courthouse in Tucson, the sessions included the mass processing of non-English-speaking immigrants, who appeared in court in hand and leg irons.

Nearly 85 percent of trips took time to visit the border wall, usually at a point in Nogales, Mexico, where artists had decorated the wall with graffiti in plain sight of US surveillance cameras. About three-quarters of groups spent up to half a day on a walk in the Sonoran Desert along

---

[16] Information on trip activities comes from evaluation forms given to travelers in the last few hours of their time at BorderLinks. The descriptive statistics in this section are at the group level since all travelers on a trip are a part of the same group activities.

[17] Joanna Jacobbi Lydgate, "Assembly-Line Justice: A Review of Operation Streamline," *California Law Review* 98, 2 (2010).

FIGURE 3 Border wall through urban Nogales

immigrant trails. Other activities were interspersed during a BorderLinks delegation and included a homestay with Mexican families in Nogales or Agua Prieta, informational activities run by BorderLinks staff members, or viewing of art exhibits.

Beyond these activities, each day was filled with many other aspects of group life. Groups ate all their meals together; traveled together for hours in a van; and slept in shared, or sex-divided, communal settings.

What Activities Do Travelers Value?

Table 5 is a listing of the activities in which more than fifty travelers participated during 2009. The activities are ranked according to their mean scores on a Likert scale, ranging from one (highest) to five (lowest), based on the following prompt: "Please rate the following activities in terms of their importance for helping you to understand border issues."

In the second column, activities are categorized into ideal types of presentation mode within the testimonial economy. *Talks* were usually given by activists or individual state agents, though some talks were also

TABLE 5 *Trip activities, types, and mean scores*

Activity	Type	Mean Value Score	n
Operation Streamline	Visit (immigrant viewing; State)	1.11	207
Border Enforcement Agent	Talk (state)	1.11	96
AFA	Visit (immigrant interaction)	1.17	99
John Fife	Talk (activist)	1.17	116
Desert walk	Simulation	1.18	158
Rancher	Talk (activist)	1.19	80
Grupos Beta	Visit (immigrant interaction)	1.2	123
Ayuda Place	Visit (immigrant interaction)	1.23	83
Homestay	Visit (Mexican interaction)	1.23	147
Hospitality house	Visit (immigrant viewing)	1.26	54
Plaza in Ciudad de la Luz	Visit (immigrant viewing)	1.26	58
Border wall	Visit (state)	1.27	156
BLX final reflection	Talk (BLX)	1.28	164
La Corazon	Visit (immigrant interaction)	1.3	64
Delle McCormick	Talk (BLX leader)	1.31	83
US attorney	Talk (activist)	1.31	179
Sierra Club	Talk (activist)	1.32	91
House of hope	Visit (immigrant interaction)	1.35	52
Lighthouse Service	Visit (immigrant interaction)	1.36	61
"Crossing Arizona" film	Video	1.37	71
Just Coffee Cooperative	Visit (economic)	1.39	84
BLX Immigration Game	Simulation	1.41	111
Migrant Respect group	Talk (activist)	1.42	59
Reverend D	Talk (activist)	1.42	76
BLX Dinner Game	Simulation	1.53	59
Lighthouse Worship	Visit (religious)	1.54	59
Artist	Talk	1.55	98
Microloan	Visit (economic)	1.69	58
BLX Shopping Game	Simulation	1.69	185
BLX orientation	Talk (BLX)	1.69	161
Nogales industry viewing	Visit (economic)	1.81	110
BLX Food Talk	Talk (BLX)	1.81	134
Comida Place	Visit (service)	1.91	54

n=210
Means adjusted for clustering at group level. BLX is an abbreviation for BorderLinks.

given by artists, pastors, ranchers, or BorderLinks staff. Talks provided information and distinct discursive frames about immigrants and immigration, from the point of view of nonimmigrants who spoke as representatives of organizations or groups. *Visits* were brief tours organized at a specific location, usually an organizational setting, but occasionally a geographic place. Most of the visits were to places at which immigrants could be seen or interacted with. Some of the visits were to locations marked by state control (e.g., the border wall or Operation Streamline deportation proceedings). A few visits were to locations that illustrated economic processes, such as a *maquila* industrial park, a Fair Trade coffee co-op, or an NGO microloan agency. Visits involved less formal presentation in comparison with talks. Instead, travelers were meant to see and engage in conversation with those present, especially immigrants. *Simulations* were activities or games, organized by Border-Links, that simulated processes, conditions, or experiences endured by undocumented immigrants (see Chapter 5).

The two highest-rated activities both involved the state: the top-rated activity was the viewing of Operation Streamline, while the second was a talk by a border enforcement agent. Of the top eleven activities, about half (six) involved the presence of immigrants.[18] Three of these six were viewings of immigrants (the courtroom in Operation Streamline, a town plaza near the US-Mexico border, and a for-profit "hospitality house" in a town near the US-Mexico border). Another three of the top eleven activities were visits that intentionally provided personal interactions with immigrants. Other top activities included a talk with a rancher, a homestay, and a desert walk simulation. While seven of the top eleven activities involved visits, particularly visits with the presence of immigrants, visits were less prominent among the very highest-ranked activities. Only two of the top five highest-ranked activities were visits involving the presence of immigrants. Only one of the top five was an occasion for direct interaction with immigrants.

From this evidence, travelers appeared to value the sorts of activities that they could not do from a distance, such as viewing sites of immigrant suffering or talking with individual immigrants at the border. These were the precise opportunities that immersion travel affords travelers in

---

[18] The activities rated tenth and eleventh had identical ratings of 1.26.

contrast to staying at home. BorderLinks' attempt at balancing discursive positions was also valued. The two most-valued activities, talks by state agents and viewing a judicial process, were often recounted as disagreeable or distasteful by travelers but were nonetheless something that travelers could not observe back at home. Despite the strong organizational orientation toward prioritizing personal contact with "real people," travelers did not rate *interactions* with immigrants as the most valuable of trip activities. In fact, a simulated desert walk was rated nearly as highly as the highest-rated immigrant interaction and higher than all other immigrant interactions.

What Activities Don't Travelers Value?

Activities overtly involving economics, including visits to alternative economic institutions, were in the bottom half of the valued activities. This, and the minimal presence of economic activities among the full list of activities to begin with, reflects the difficulty that BorderLinks had portraying economic topics related to undocumented immigration.

Most of the simulation activities used by BorderLinks, which were generally economics focused, were in the bottom third of the ratings. One reason for this may be that some simulation activities could, theoretically, be done without travel to the US-Mexico border. For example, the BorderLinks Dinner Game consisted of travelers cooking and eating a typical meal that would be consumed by a Mexican living on a *maquila* worker's wages. Other organizations use a version of this eating game because it allows the living conditions of distant persons to be simulated without having to travel to or even know much about foreign locations.[19]

Another reason for the low rating of simulations may have been their confusing design. The BorderLinks Shopping Game asked travelers to gather the prices of the items at a supermarket that a family living on a *maquila* worker's wages would buy in their weekly "market basket." The travelers were to record these prices then, during a discussion session, compare these prices with US prices and the equivalent cost in a US worker's budget. My observation notes showed numerous ways that the game broke down.

[19] Oxfam America, "Our Signature Event: The Oxfam America Hunger Banquet," actfast .oxfamamerica.org/.

It could break down through lack of knowledge about typical US commodity prices or even simple math, like the conversion of pesos to dollars. In one example I observed, the BorderLinks staff leader, George, asked the Central College group, "Any observations about the comparisons of prices?" Beth immediately replied, "My brain is not good at working with math." George suggested a shortcut that might help: use "ten to one" to convert pesos to dollars. Tricia, a college student, immediately replied with shock at the US price, "That's expensive for milk!" Beth, the college professor, replied that *that* conversion landed on the right price for milk, pointing out to Tricia, who didn't regularly purchase milk in the United States, that, "Yeah, milk in the United States *is* expensive." George seemed to want to rein in the discussion to drive home a point that the group wasn't getting to: "They say things cost less here – but not really if you look." The next step in the activity was to convert *maquila* wages into dollars per hour, then write on the board how many hours one would need to work to afford basic commodities. The discussion bogged down in an attempt to get the math right, with Bob taking out his iPhone to use as a calculator and the rest of the group watching him tell George what to write on the board. Eventually, the conversation turned toward whether *maquilas* provided good jobs or not. The group got the general point of the activity, but it was a bumpy ride.

After simulations, the two lowest-rated activities likely received those ratings because they violated the organization's boundaries in two ways: by not focusing on undocumented immigration and by overtly advocating specific actions. The lowest rated activity was service work done at a local emergency food aid organization in Tucson. According to BorderLinks staff members, this activity was avoided unless a group requested some "service" aspect to their trip. The connection to undocumented immigration was tangential, and the focus on volunteer service work was at odds with the organization's "education not charity" approach.

The second-to-lowest-rated activity starkly highlights what themes and practices were considered illegitimate by travelers as part of BorderLinks' immigration-focused work. BorderLinks had a vision of food justice that it articulated as part of a talk on sustainability, what I termed the "Food Talk." This was a presentation by a BorderLinks staff member about food; about the purpose for BorderLinks' vegetarian diet; about the benefits of buying local, organic food; about the injustice of the food industry; and about the power of consumer behavior to influence basic dynamics of undocumented immigration. The general point was that an unjust and unhealthy food system existed as a result of bad government policy, overreaching corporations, and alienation from the food production process. According to BorderLinks, this system affected immigration in many ways: by undermining Mexican food exports, by increasing the demand for farm labor in the United States, and by endangering farmland in other countries for meat raising.

The Food Talk was one of the rare occasions during the week that a BorderLinks staff member would speak authoritatively, exercising expertise and directly suggesting specific actions that travelers could do. Notably, this presentation was *not* done by the BorderLinks staff member that was leading a group, but instead by a staff member charged with food shopping, cooking for groups, and developing the organization's permaculture garden.

The travelers from one group used space on the evaluation form to write that they felt they had been preached to during this talk, a rather severe charge given BorderLinks' practice of formal neutrality. Not incidentally, this group was from an area of a state with large meat-processing facilities, making this message challenging to swallow. Other travelers expressed frustration with the imposition of vegetarianism during the trip. For them, vegetarianism was onerous, not a voluntarily chosen action related to immigration. This displeasure appeared to be especially the case with groups who, because of geographical region, age, or political leaning, were not oriented toward a change in diet that removed meat. The travelers with Southern Seminary, mostly from rural backgrounds, expressed relief when we had our first meal in Mexico – because they would get meat in their food.

The BorderLinks staff presenters who gave the food talk did seem wary that they were crossing a boundary in displaying their authority. When giving the Food Talk to the St. Michael's Church group, the staff member Beatrice made sure to say "I'm not an expert" to the group three different times, referring to the fact that she had read about these topics in specific books. She was trying to locate the authority outside of herself, but this was difficult to do since the presentation was at odds with staff leaders' normal roles.

The occurrence of skeptical attitudes toward the Food Talk and economics-focused activities indicated the limits of the organization's expansive experiential education vision.

Which Activities Move Travelers?

Table 6 is a listing of trip activities by their value ranking, along with the means of anger and sorrow reported by travelers for each activity.[20] The last two columns include the mean for the cooccurrence of emotions within a traveler for each activity, as well as the mean for the nonoccurrence of either emotion within a traveler for each activity. The table is ordered according to the mean activity value ranking derived from Table 5. Within each of the columns, the top five values are shaded light gray, and the bottom five values are shaded dark gray. So, for example, in the mean anger column, Operation Streamline, the border enforcement agent talk, the hospitality house visit, the Sierra Club talk, and the Migrant Respect group talk had the highest mean values for reported anger. Alternatively, the Lighthouse visit, the Just Coffee Cooperative visit, the Lighthouse Worship visit, the artist talk, and the BorderLinks orientation talk had the lowest mean values for reported anger.

One takeaway is that activities' value to travelers were related to the amount of emotion they produced. The last column in the table makes clear that no activity produced an emotion for every traveler. About half of the activities produced one or both emotions for 50 percent of travelers. The five activities that produced one or both emotions for the greatest portion of travelers included immigrant viewings, an immigrant interaction, a simulation, and a documentary video. The activities with the highest means of emotional nonoccurrence (e.g., those that did not produce much emotion at all, shown in dark gray in the final column) were the artist talk, the BorderLinks orientation, the Comida Place service visit, the Lighthouse Worship visit, and the Just Coffee Cooperative visit. From field notes, these activities tended to involve little public emotion work, instead consisting of viewing or listening to information being relayed in a didactic fashion, similar to the "book knowledge" approach BorderLinks was trying to avoid.

---

[20] Only two emotions were solicited for ranking due to space limitations on the evaluation form. The emotions were selected because they have been well researched and appear to articulate different emotional pathways toward concern and engagement. On two forms, travelers wrote marginalia to suggest the inclusion of a third emotion to rank: hope. This was written in connection with John Fife's talk. Intriguingly, his talk did not produce much anger or sorrow among the vast majority of travelers. But, as the marginalia suggests, it may have produced hope.

TABLE 6 *Trip activities and emotional production*

Activity	Type	Mean Value Rank	Mean Anger	Mean Sorrow	Anger-Sorrow (A-S)	Emotional Cooccurrence	Emotional Nonoccurrence
Operation Streamline	Visit (immigrant viewing; state)	1	0.74	0.68	0.06	0.54	0.11
Border enforcement agent	Talk (state)	2	0.53	0.17	0.36	0.16	0.46
AFA	Visit (immigrant interaction)	3	0.29	0.66	-0.37	0.26	0.31
John Fife	Talk (activist)	4	0.19	0.16	0.03	0.07	0.72
Desert walk	Simulation	5	0.25	0.68	-0.42	0.20	0.27
Rancher	Talk (activist)	6	0.33	0.19	0.14	0.14	0.61
Grupos Beta	Visit (immigrant interaction)	7	0.26	0.44	-0.18	0.17	0.48
Ayuda Place	Visit (immigrant interaction)	8	0.18	0.50	-0.32	0.16	0.49
Homestay	Visit (Mexican interaction)	9	0.04	0.19	-0.15	0.03	0.80
Hospitality house	Visit (immigrant viewing)	10	0.44	0.52	-0.08	0.30	0.35
Plaza in Ciudad de la Luz	Visit (immigrant viewing)	11	0.32	0.22	0.10	0.19	0.68
Border wall	Visit (state)	12	0.39	0.37	0.02	0.23	0.47

(continued)

TABLE 6 (*continued*)

Activity	Type	Mean Value Rank	Mean Anger	Mean Sorrow	Anger-Sorrow (A-S)	Emotional Cooccurrence	Emotional Nonoccurrence
BLX final reflection	Talk (BLX)	13	0.06	0.21	-0.14	0.05	0.79
La Corazon	Visit (immigrant interaction)	14	0.11	0.43	-0.32	0.07	0.54
US attorney	Talk (activist)	15	0.40	0.30	0.10	0.20	0.52
Delle McCormick	Talk (BLX leader)	16	0.06	0.34	-0.28	0.04	0.65
Sierra Club	Talk (activist)	17	0.43	0.25	0.18	0.16	0.48
House of hope	Visit (immigrant interaction)	18	0.05	0.19	-0.14	0.05	0.81
Lighthouse service	Visit (immigrant interaction)	19	0.02	0.21	-0.19	0.02	0.79
Crossing Arizona film	Video	20	0.40	0.56	-0.16	0.25	0.29
Just Coffee Cooperative	Visit (economic)	21	0.00	0.01	-0.01	0.00	0.99
BLX immigration game	Simulation	22	0.34	0.28	0.07	0.13	0.52
Migrant Respect group	Talk (activist)	23	0.45	0.30	0.15	0.19	0.45
Reverend D	Talk (activist)	24	0.10	0.11	-0.02	0.05	0.84
BLX Dinner Game	Simulation	25	0.23	0.26	-0.02	0.06	0.57

Lighthouse Worship	Visit (religious)	26	0.00	0.04	-0.04	0.00	0.96
Artist	Talk	27	0.04	0.09	-0.05	0.03	0.90
BLX shopping game	Simulation	28	0.22	0.24	-0.03	0.11	0.65
Microloan	Visit (economic)	29	0.06	0.04	0.02	0.00	0.90
BLX orientation	Talk (BLX)	30	0.02	0.08	-0.06	0.00	0.92
Nogales industry viewing	Visit (economic)	31	0.17	0.18	-0.01	0.08	0.75
BLX food talk	Talk (BLX)	32	0.09	0.06	0.03	0.03	0.89
Comida Place	Visit (service)	33	0.07	0.02	0.05	0.02	0.93

Light shading indicates activity is within the top five in a column; dark shading indicates activity is within the bottom five in a column. Means adjusted for clustering at group level. BLX is an abbreviation for BorderLinks.

In Table 6, the top anger-producing activities are talks or visits to view immigrants. One type of talk was given by border enforcement agents, whose comments connecting immigration to drug trafficking or the prevention of terrorism usually generated antipathy from travelers, with anger resulting as a reflex emotion based in moral opposition to the speakers' positions.[21] At the outset of one talk, a CBP agent said they usually used public presentations as a recruitment talk. Jason, a traveler, quickly said, "Wrong crowd!" The ensuing talk focused on terrorism and smuggling prevention, with statistics about trade flows ("65 to 70 percent of salad comes through here"; "Thirty-two million [people] pass through"), the possibility of an agricultural terrorist attack, and the number of drugs ("You name it, we've seen it, or are going to see it."). When it was over, the agent left behind squishy red chiles with contact information. As he went, only two of the nine people in the room shook his hand. Within a minute after the door closed, Derek said, "That guy is an asshole, he must have been picked on in high school." The group didn't object to this characterization. Dan said they just joined the CBP to ride ATVs, pointing at a left-behind brochure with an ATV-riding agent.

The other top talks were by the Sierra Club and the Migrant Respect group. These speakers were adept at prompting an emotional response from travelers, with anger again a reflexive, moral emotion, but tutored by the speaker to be in alignment with his or her own emotion.[22] The Sierra Club speaker used a visual presentation that included high-quality documentary footage of environmental destruction done by border policies. The video showed a mother mountain lion panicking at being separated from her cub, which had crossed the border wall and could not return. He commented about the origins of the video: "The Border Patrol was having a good time, running around, taking pictures of this cat." A few minutes later he showed a picture of a recent, massive flood in Nogales. He attributed blame to the stark image: "It was caused by Homeland Security building a wall in [an underground] tunnel that *already* had cameras and remote pepper spray [to deter immigrants]." Then, drily, he added, "It was later determined that the wall was built illegally in Mexico." In response, one traveler immediately gasped. Another traveler interjected with visible anger, "Who comes up with this stuff?!" These speakers, both professional activists, were adept at relaying

---

[21] James M. Jasper, "The Emotions of Protest: Affective and Reactive Emotions in and around Social Movements," *Sociological Forum* 13, 3 (1998).

[22] Jasper and Owens, "Social Movements."

information and coordinating emotional indignation, which travelers appear to have responded to.[23]

No immigrant *interaction* produced anger in more than 30 percent of travelers. Talks by nonactivists and homestays also failed to produce much anger. These were interactions centered on new information or finding commonality. As Janice explained about homestays to one group of travelers, "The people are [performing] an act of radical hospitality." The Mexican delegation leader, Patricia, described homestays as "one of the most human experiences for any delegation." When I asked why, she replied, "Even if it's just one day, it closes the circle of knowledge, from the point of, here's how you work in the *maquila* and here's how you work with the family. Or, how another family who doesn't depend off of the wages of the *maquila* lives as well."

In Table 6, the top sorrow-producing activities were immigrant viewings, a simulation, a documentary video, and immigrant interactions. In comparison with the anger-producing activities, sorrow-producing activities were not likely to be talks. An immigrant interaction was more likely to produce sorrow than anger. Overall, more activities produced higher levels of sorrow than anger. Six activities produced sorrow for 50 percent or more of travelers. And more activities produced at least moderate levels of sorrow. If the table were ordered by the mean levels of sorrow, only the final third of activities would show sorrow levels below 20 percent of travelers.

Emotions, Together?

So far we have considered how anger and sorrow are produced separately by activities. This separate consideration is for a good empirical reason: the "cooccurrence" column in Table 6 shows that anger and sorrow did not tend to cooccur within travelers as they experienced activities.

It is important to note that the activities that seemed to specialize in producing a particular emotion – immigrant interactions for sorrow and talks by activists for anger – also tended toward the high end of emotional cooccurrence rankings. Thus, neither of those activities is dominated by one emotion alone. The middle column of Table 6 shows the difference between the mean level of anger and the mean level of sorrow of an activity (Anger-Sorrow). It shows that, while both types of activity could

[23] Reger, "Organizational 'Emotion Work' through Consciousness-Raising: An Analysis of a Feminist Organization."

include both emotions, each leaned more toward one than the other. Activist talks overwhelmingly had positive A-S values (e.g., more anger than sorrow), while immigrant interactions had negative A-S values (e.g., more sorrow than anger).

Only one activity – Operation Streamline – produced both emotions in more than 50 percent of travelers. This activity was distinctive in its visual impression: dozens of shackled immigrants quickly processed in a large courtroom through proceedings that occurred in their nonnative language. It was also an activity that provided numerous potential targets for anger, which travelers talked about afterward and mentioned in interviews months later. These included private lawyers hired by the federal government who did crossword puzzles in the courtroom; Border Patrol officers who sternly escorted detainees; armed guards who looked bored as they stood by courtroom doors; and a presiding judge that worked in dispassionate legal language.[24]

When I attended Operation Streamline with Sojourner University, I sat alongside students as seventy-seven names of detained immigrants were called. The judge explained that they were being charged with illegal entry: "Without a plea, the court can give six months sentence," while with a plea the "court can impose a sentence of the misdemeanor." As the procedure unfolded, one of the lawyers sitting nearby shared the charge sheet for his client with our group, on which he had written, "This guy is a victim of receiving the maximum of this stupid policy that is ineffective." As the proceedings continued, some immigrants provided details of their cases during sentencing: a sick wife who needed money for surgery, an elderly parent with medical bills, a child dying without medical care. When each immigrant left the courtroom, their chains clinked as they came within five feet of the travelers' seats. As soon as the session ended, the students gathered in the hallway. Julia said, "that makes me want to be a lawyer even more." Jennifer followed, "I was so mad at those two marshals [that escorted immigrants out]. They were rude and laughing the whole time – and they were Latino!" Jessica jumped in, "This is the most racial tension I've seen [on the trip]. . . . It's like they grabbed all the people who were indigenous, chained them up, and brought them in."

---

[24] This is not to say that travelers accurately understood what was occurring as a precondition to anger. My field notes and other research suggest confusion among travelers about the rules of the spectacle they were watching. This was confirmed in my interview with Hilary below.

The courtroom viewings were usually followed by a conversation with one of the half-dozen US federal public defenders that would talk with BorderLinks groups about what they had just seen. Hilary shared frustrating stories of meeting with numerous clients for a only few minutes in the morning before representing them *en masse* in the courtroom. Hilary's goal in meeting with BorderLinks travelers was to "give my opinion and give my experience" in order to clarify for the "95 percent of groups, of people within groups, [who] don't understand" what went on in the courtroom.

Beyond Operation Streamline, only four activities produced both sorrow and anger in more than 20 percent of travelers. The difference between which activities produced anger, which produced sorrow, and which produced both suggests there is a division of emotional production labor at BorderLinks. The organization deploys many activities, but these activities themselves produce emotions in distinctly different ways.

Talks by activists have a clear role to play in producing anger more than sorrow. No activist talk produced both emotions in more than 20 percent of travelers. This reaffirms a conclusion in research on motivation: that moral anger may feel spontaneous, but its production rarely is. Activists speaking to travelers constructed anger through articulating causes of injustice, blaming the suffering on clear social forces, and modeling the emotions themselves.[25] While immediate or "hot" anger was possible as the result of a spontaneous event, like viewing the courtroom deportation proceeding of Operation Streamline, mediating figures like activists were likely to be especially crucial in turning a complex topic such as the suffering of undocumented immigrants into a focus of indignation.[26] When a speaker from the Migrant Respect group came to talk to Eastern College, she reviewed how the border policy was leading to

---

[25] Marshall Ganz, *Why David Sometimes Wins: Leadership, Organization, and Strategy in the California Farmworkers Movement* (New York: Oxford University Press, 2010); Jasper, *The Art of Moral Protest*; Jasper and Owens, "Social Movements."

[26] James M. Jasper and Jane D. Poulsen, "Recruiting Strangers and Friends: Moral Shocks and Social Networks in Animal Rights and Anti-Nuclear Protests," *Social Problems* 42, 4 (1995); Paul Dimaggio, "Culture and Cognition," *Annual Review of Sociology* 23, 1 (1997); Jasper and Owens, "Social Movements."; Nepstad, "The Process of Cognitive Liberation."; Nepstad, "Oppositional Consciousness among the Privileged."; Verta Taylor and Lisa Leitz, "From Infanticide to Activism: Emotions and Identity in Self-Help Movements," in *Social Movements and the Transformation of American Health Care*, ed. Jane C. Banaszak-Holl, Sandra R. Levitsky, and Mayer N. Zald (New York: Oxford University Press, 2010).

deaths in the desert. Thirty minutes in, she stopped and said, "You should be horrified to hear this!" Activists who gave talks to BorderLinks groups were representing undocumented immigration, communicating its meaning through their words and bodies in their displays of anger.

Immigrant interactions, on the other hand, appeared to mostly generate sorrow. Only one immigrant interaction activity, the AFA visit, produced both emotions in more than 20 percent of travelers, but it still tended to produce sorrow more readily. This evidence that face-to-face interactions mostly produced sorrow is at odds with earlier research that reported the power of interpersonal interactions to generate anger.[27] The difference in my research findings about the emotional results of interpersonal interaction is likely due to a methodological difference. The earlier research did not measure emotions soon after the activities of immersion travel, instead using retrospective accounts of travelers. Those accounts came from activists who had been successfully mobilized into activism, looking back at activities in their past. The angry emotions they reported as connected to interpersonal actions were likely due to ensuing processes of interpretation, possibly through the work of other activists. In other words, in previous research the interpersonal interactions of the past could be recalled with anger, even if anger was not a dominant part of the original emotional response. Another problem with earlier research is that, by focusing on people that became activists, it did not represent how face-to-face interactions were experienced by *all* travelers at the time, whether they became activists or not. When we examine interactions in time among all travelers, the evidence suggests that the modal emotional experience of face-to-face interaction is sorrow.

This association of sorrow with personal interaction is well documented in psychological research. One worry from that research is whether sorrow can incapacitate those who feel it.[28] At the very least,

[27] Nepstad, "Oppositional Consciousness among the Privileged."; Sharon Erickson Nepstad and Christian Smith, "The Social Structure of Moral Outrage in Recruitment to the U.S. Central America Peace Movement," in *Passionate Politics: Emotions and Social Movements*, ed. Jeff Goodwin, James M. Jasper, and Francesca Polletta (Chicago: The University of Chicago Press, 2001).

[28] Thomas et al., "Transforming 'Apathy into Movement'."; C. Daryl Cameron and B. Keith Payne, "Escaping Affect: How Motivated Emotion Regulation Creates Insensitivity to Mass Suffering," *Journal of Personality and Social Psychology* 100, 1 (2011); Arthur Kleinman and Joan Kleinman, "The Appeal of Experience; the Dismay of Images: Cultural Appropriations of Suffering in Our Times," *Daedalus* 125, 1 (1996); Iain Wilkinson, *Suffering: A Sociological Introduction* (Maldin, MA: Polity Press, 2005).

the sorrow experienced in such interactions needs to be managed so that the emotional costs of further engagement do not overwhelm any urge to action.[29] From the evidence presented here, if immersion travelers only did what BorderLinks most prioritized – meet suffering face to face with "real" people – they might only be left with sorrow from an immersion trip.

CONCLUSION

This account of what immersion travelers do all day suggests the rich array of activities that occur during immersion travel with BorderLinks. Despite a growing set of descriptions about what occurs during immersion trips, the activities of immersion travel have been something of a "black box." Very little research has categorized the different types of activities that occur and how those differences matter for the way that immersion travel works.[30] Instead, analyses of immersion travel that attempt to understand its influence on travelers have mostly stayed at the level of cultural form, emphasizing generic characteristics of liminal experience. This chapter helps clarify the range of activities that may occur in immersion travel and how variation in their relative presence can distinguish different styles of immersion travel. For example, the evidence of this chapter suggests why some types of immersion travel sponsored by religious groups, which contain lots of face-to-face interaction but little if any engagement with political and social realities, may produce more sorrow, less anger, and less potential for critical awareness.[31]

What do the activities of BorderLinks' immersion travel do for travelers? *Talks* are meant to construct the positions of the discursive field about undocumented immigration, what I have termed as the work of constructing the testimonial-telling economy. *Visits* provide an opportunity to see organizational and state process that either aid, coerce, or punish immigrants. Given how highly travelers valued these types of activities, it seems clear that BorderLinks' immersion travel succeeds at a fundamental level in providing experiences that travelers could not have had at home. In this sense, the immersion travel of BorderLinks is

---

[29] Cameron and Payne, "Escaping Affect."

[30] Beyerlein et al., "The Effect of Religious Mission Trips."

[31] Adler Jr. and Offutt, "The Gift Economy of Direct Transnational Civic Action."

accomplishing what we might expect it to. It does this in a multipronged way, providing many different modes of encountering information about undocumented immigration.

Yet we can also conclude that the model of immersion travel held up by BorderLinks, with its emphasis on hearing from "real people" that suffer, has mixed outcomes in practice. Travelers tended *not* to highly value interactions with immigrants. Instead, the visual power of viewing conditions of suffering, the rhetorical strategies and information provided by expert talks, and a desert walk simulation were rated as highly, if not more highly, than face-to-face interactions with immigrants. Despite the way that face-to-face interaction is lionized by supporters of cosmopolitanism and transnational civil society, it is not the highest-valued activity among immersion travelers for achieving understanding about undocumented immigration. The ensuing chapter will have more to say about why this is so, but the evidence here makes clear that other activities (talks by emotionally adroit activists and the viewing of immigration conditions) are crucial to the awareness that is raised by immersion travel.[32]

A key insight from this chapter is that immersion travel is emotionally complex due to its diverse activities, within the emotionally elastic time of travel. The activities that make up immersion travel produce different emotional configurations, some intentionally and some not. The presentations of activists appear to be central in representing immigration and producing a sense of anger. On the other hand, the personal interactions with "real people" who suffered appear to generate sorrow more readily. The activity of viewing suffering in the courtroom landed somewhere in between, generating both emotions. Immersion travel not only produces a complex emotional palette but it does so through activities that represent immigrant suffering in distinctly different ways.

Many studies of social movements discuss the centrality of cultivating anger in motivation, but studies of distance-focused concern have recently shown that sorrow can motivate prosocial action as well.[33] The results here show how both anger and sorrow are part of immersion travel, and thus may be part of how any motivation ensues. The immersion travel of BorderLinks appears to bring together distinct modes of emotional

---

[32] Vetlesen, *Perception, Empathy, and Judgement*; Reger, "Organizational 'Emotion Work' through Consciousness-Raising."

[33] Beyerlein and Sikkink, "Sorrow and Solidarity."; Justin Farrell, "Moral Outpouring: Shock and Generosity in the Aftermath of the BP Oil Spill," *Social Problems* 61, 3 (2014).

production that are usually seen as belonging to *either* social movements (anger) or international humanitarian organizations (sorrow). The blending of distinct emotions and modes of analysis recalls the bridging identity of BorderLinks. Here, on the terrain of emotions, we see that BorderLinks' immersion travel is a space for bridging different emotional avenues toward motivation. Given what we have already learned about the organization straddling institutional boundaries and constructing a complex economy of testimonies, this is not surprising. At the same time, it is not likely that the organization does this on purpose as a rational "best practice" for producing awareness. The fact the BorderLinks does this blending reminds us that experiential learning through travel is a distinct tool for awareness raising. As we have come to see, immersion travel enacts lots of experiential possibilities.

One of the most important conclusions that we arrive at by looking at the content of immersion travel is a better understanding of the form of liminality produced by this mode of travel. Classic writing about liminal experiences focuses on a dynamic tension between individuals, the community they leave, and the community to which they return.[34] The structure of that relationship is presented as a dyad: an individual's relation to a home community changing over time. The liminal experience functions as a space of separation to renegotiate the roles and responsibilities of that dyad. Other persons (strangers, messengers, antagonists) may inhabit the liminal space but they do not transform the structure of the dyad itself. When travelers of the generic liminal form reemerge, they may have a new social role, but it is a social role defined by a new way of relating to a social group that has been in existence all along.

The liminal form of immersion travel, however, is structured around a third relational pole from the outset: distant sufferers. In BorderLinks' case, these are undocumented immigrants who can be represented in various ways. In contrast to other liminal experiences, the structure of this relationality is a triad: travelers, their home social group, and distant sufferers.[35] Immersion travel differs from many forms of liminal experience by its focus on constructing a suffering object for travelers to engage with. The activities of immersion travel change the form of liminality in comparison with other liminal experiences. The sufferers, imagined at first, are made real through the activities of travel. The many immersion

[34] Turner and Turner, *Image and Pilgrimage*; Smelser, *The Odyssey Experience*.
[35] Georg Simmel, "The Number of Members as Determining the Sociological Form of the Group," *American Journal of Sociology* 8, 2 (1902).

trip activities solidify this relational structure. Talks, visits, and simulations all urge travelers to learn and feel about this third entity. For immersion travel, the potential of transformative experience is not found in just the cultural form or content, but at the intersection of the two.

In the next chapter, we look more closely at the activities that Border-Links prioritized for personalizing a relationship between travelers and distant persons. We will see how the emotional configurations discovered in this chapter help to explain the surprising results of these activities in practice.

5

Why It's Better to Walk than Talk

I wish I could go on the desert hike again. I mean, I feel solidarity in the other things we've done, but then we were *really* walking where immigrants walk.

Anne Marie, a BorderLinks traveler

The main difference between immersion travel and other forms of raising awareness about distant suffering is how immersion travel bridges geographic and cultural distance. Through this bridging, travelers can directly engage otherwise distant sufferers, what BorderLinks refers to as "real people." This simple distinction from other modes of transnational civic engagement is crucial, as it makes possible the sorts of personal interactions that travelers, and social theorists, expect to be meaningful, and around which, as we saw in the previous chapter, the itinerary is built.

Social theories about the power of direct contact, reaching all the way back through Gordon Allport's contact theory to Adam Smith, generally predict that these interactions can produce interpersonal understanding and connection.[1] With the right conditions, direct engagement should produce empathy. Civic organizations that promote transnational engagement have institutionalized this ideal about intercultural contact,

---

[1] Boltanksi, *Distant Suffering*; Thomas F. Pettigrew and Linda R. Tropp, "Does Intergroup Contact Reduce Prejudice? Recent Meta-Analytic Findings," in *Reducing Prejudice and Discrimination*, ed. Stuart Oskamp (Mahwah, NJ: Lawrence Erlbaum Associates, 2000).

turning it into a little-questioned assumption, what Bornstein has referred to as the liberal project of creating global empathy.[2]

Yet it is clear to social scientists and ethicists alike that travel across distance does not "naturally" cause an expansion in travelers' empathic concern for formerly distant others. To the contrary, travelers may treat the suffering they encounter as a spectacle to be viewed or ignored.[3] Privileged travelers may maintain a moral distance from the suffering they encounter, seeing it as exotic.[4] When partnership ideals and good relations exist, inequalities in power and resources still limit the meaning and results of engagement.[5] Even acclaimed sites of transnational engagement, like global social fora and transnational activist networks, are places where conflicts can occur.[6]

Given hopes and realities at the heart of transnational engagement, what are the prospects of empathic understanding to develop through immersion travel? In the previous chapter, we saw evidence for the complex palette of emotional outcomes that developed through Border-Links' immersion travel activities. What that chapter lacked was a sense of travelers' empathic response to those activities. In this chapter, I focus on the way that BorderLinks uses specific activities to personalize immigrant suffering and convey its depth, the most intimate goals of immersion travel.

As I go, I introduce a new concept for the sociological study of engagement with distant suffering: empathy strategies. Empathy strategies are interactive templates that organizations use to establish a relationship with suffering persons by producing an emotional understanding of suffering and the perspective taking of those who suffer. I illustrate two distinct ways of attempting to produce empathy, which we met in the last chapter, and which enable the core relationality of immersion travel. Both aim to personalize knowledge about social suffering, but through different modes of interaction. A *relational empathy strategy* uses face-to-face

[2] Erica Bornstein, *Disquieting Gifts.*   [3] Frenzel et al., *Slum Tourism.*

[4] John Hutnyk, *The Rumour of Calcutta: Tourism, Charity and the Poverty of Representation* (London: Zed Books, 1996).

[5] Adler Jr. and Offutt, "The Gift Economy of Direct Transnational Civic Action."; Probasco, "Prayer, Patronage, and Personal Agency in Nicaraguan Accounts of Receiving International Aid."

[6] Jackie Smith, "Bridging Global Divides? Strategic Framing and Solidarity in Transnational Social Movement Organizations," *International Sociology* 17, 4 (2002); Bandy, "Paradoxes."

interaction with suffering persons, while a *mimetic empathy strategy* uses simulated interaction with the conditions of suffering. At BorderLinks, the former ideally happens through conversations with immigrants, while the latter ideally occurs through a walk along desert trails that immigrants use in their desert crossing.

BorderLinks staff members saw these particular activities as central to their work. The previous chapter demonstrated that these two strategies resulted in similar emotional profiles, producing sorrow more than anger. By observing and contrasting these two empathy strategies, this chapter offers a detailed picture of what empathy production looks like in practice, providing surprising evidence about the diverse ways it is nurtured. In theory, these two empathy strategies were different routes to producing the same outcomes of understanding distant suffering. In reality, however, immersion travelers had different reactions to these empathy strategies. Direct, face-to-face engagement with immigrants often created a much weaker empathic connection when compared with a simulation of walking in immigrants' footsteps. Walking the paths that undocumented immigrants walked was more effective at producing empathy than talking to them in person.

This is a potentially disturbing finding for civil society organizations, like BorderLinks, that hold relational empathy strategies as ideologically and pragmatically central to producing understanding. These strategies are supposed to provide an occasion for the sort of interaction between "common people" that is central to a grassroots democratic imaginary. While such conversational interaction *can* be powerful, my observations of BorderLinks travelers show that relational empathy strategies are susceptible to interactional hurdles that can prevent identification, confuse emotion, and slow understanding. After examining why this is the case, I explore what this evidence means for the relational ideal at the heart of cross-cultural interaction like immersion travel.

EMPATHY AND ITS STRATEGIC USE

Empathy is a concept whose elements and meaning have been the object of philosophical debate for nearly two centuries, considered an aspect of moral behavior among psychologists, historians, and even novelists.[7] Empathy for distant others has been contrasted to the "natural" empathy

---

[7] Suzanne Keen, *Empathy and the Novel* (New York: Oxford Unversity Press, 2007); Stephen Turner, "The Strength of Weak Empathy," *Science in Context* 25, 3 (2012).

observed among fellow citizens or close relations.[8] For a founder of social science, empathy was a way of understanding social action through orientation to its "emotional context."[9]

A recent review of empathy described it as "a set of constructs that connects the responses of one individual to the experiences of another."[10] Empathy can help "advantaged groups" move toward identity, commitment, and action that benefits "disadvantaged" groups.[11] The role of empathy as part of other-directed concern and action is increasingly clear, but the sociological processes that establish, weaken, or destroy empathy have yet to be charted like moral concepts such as altruism, sympathy, or solidarity.[12]

Three characteristics of empathy suggest that it is a useful concept for understanding what organizations like BorderLinks are trying to accomplish with their activities. These characteristics provide the framework for observing and evaluating what organizations like BorderLinks do in practice to produce empathy.

First, empathy is a condition tied to specific social situations and contexts, not a generalizing outlook. It can entail "vicariously placing oneself 'in their [disadvantaged persons'] shoes' and experiencing the events *with* them."[13] Empathy involves both attitudinal and emotional alignment to understand situations of localized suffering.[14] Like sympathy, empathy is a social product, borne of a history of interactions.[15] In this light, organizations' empathy strategies should involve localized,

---

[8] Smith, *The Theory of Moral Sentiments*.

[9] See Max Weber as cited in Turner, "The Strength of Weak Empathy."

[10] Davis, "Empathy," p. 443.

[11] Thomas et al., "Transforming 'Apathy into Movement'."

[12] Batson and Powell, "Altruism and Prosocial Behavior."; Martin L. Hoffman, "Empathy and Prosocial Behavior," in *Handbook of Emotions*, ed. Michael Lewis, Jeannette M. Haviland-Jones, and Lisa Feldman Barrett (New York: The Guilford Press, 2008); Candace Clark, "Sympathy Biography and Sympathy Margin," *The American Journal of Sociology* 93, 2 (1987).

[13] Thomas et al., "Transforming 'Apathy into Movement'," p. 320, italics in original text; Stephanie D. Preston and Frans B.M. De Waal, "Empathy: Its Ultimate and Proximate Bases," *Behavioral and Brain Sciences* 25, 1 (2002); Frans B.M. De Waal, "Putting the Altruism Back into Altruism: The Evolution of Empathy," *Annual Review of Psychology* 59 (2008).

[14] Christopher J. Einolf, "Empathic Concern and Prosocial Behaviors: A Test of Experimental Results Using Survey Data," *Social Science Research* 37, 4 (2008).

[15] Clark, "Sympathy Biography and Sympathy Margin."; Candace Clark, *Misery and Company: Sympathy in Everyday Life* (Chicago: University of Chicago Press, 1997).

focused interactions that seek to produce emotional and attitudinal alignment that connects benefactors to beneficiaries.[16]

Second, empathy develops through various pathways. Mark H. Davis reports that the mimicry of others' bodily expressions, particularly at a preconscious level, can prompt empathy.[17] Conscious perspective-taking activity, a theoretical and empirical tradition linked to George Herbert Mead, can likewise influence empathy development.[18] The different ways to produce empathy are like the two modes of cognition articulated in the "dual-process model" of cognition.[19] These two modes of cognition – practical/embodied and symbolic/reflective – map onto two empathic processes of bodily mimicry and deliberate perspective taking.[20] Thus, organizations' empathy strategies can have different interaction patterns and activities that are based on distinct cognitive processes.

Third, empathy is variable, able to grow and to fade, with different intensity levels in between.[21] Thus, we should expect that organizational empathy strategies could produce varying intensities and lengths of empathy. Variance in these outcomes provides an evaluative basis for comparing how empathy strategies work.

TWO TYPES OF EMPATHY STRATEGY

Table 7 characterizes the two types of empathy strategy at BorderLinks by their logic of interaction, their cognitive bases, their representation of suffering, their emotional mechanisms, and their perspective-taking mechanisms.

The first, a relational empathy strategy, uses communicative interaction with foreign others.[22] The pure form of this is face-to-face

---

[16] Jasper, "The Emotions of Protest."; Davis, "Empathy."   [17] Davis, "Empathy."
[18] Ibid.
[19] Sarah K. Harkness and Steven Hitlin, "Morality and Emotions," in *Handbook of the Sociology of Emotions*, ed. Jan E. Stets and Jonathan H. Turner (New York: Springer, 2014); Lizardo et al., "What Are Dual Process Models? Implications for Cultural Analysis in Sociology."
[20] Davis, "Empathy."
[21] C. Daryl Cameron, Victoria L. Spring, and Andrew R. Todd, "The Empathy Impulse: A Multinomial Model of Intentional and Unintentional Empathy for Pain," *Emotion* 17, 3 (2017).
[22] Bornstein's analysis of empathy poses "relational empathy" as a possible step towards a kin-type humanitarian relationship. In her analysis, relational empathy refers to ongoing proximity and interaction that can take on the obligation structure of kin. In my usage, relational refers to a mode of communicative interaction that, in immersion travel, is brief.

TABLE 7 *Characteristics of empathy strategies*

	Relational	Mimetic
Interactive Logic	Connection through interactive discourse	Connection through embodied simulation
Cognitive Bases	Conceptual, implicit, slow, effortful	Practical, explicit, rapid, easy
Representation of Suffering	Autobiographical (I or we)	Third person (she/he; they)
Emotional Mechanism	Attunement	Bodily production
Perspective-Taking Mechanism	Hearing narrative	Having "authentic" experience

dialogue, though it could be achieved in nontravel contexts through mediated letters, emails, phone calls, or various forms of internet-based interaction. The logic of a relational empathy strategy is that communicative interaction provides the opportunity for understanding difference and finding commonality. Emotional connection is achieved through attunement, through the copresence of traveler and sufferer.[23] Descriptions of suffering or injustice are autobiographical, given by actual suffering persons. Their comments can construct a first-person narrative through their storytelling abilities or the *post hoc* framing work of brokers.

The second pattern, a mimetic empathy strategy, uses bodily movements, activities, or rituals that place persons into simulated conditions of sensory experience evocative of suffering. Mimetic strategies involve the simulation of the conditions of suffering as a way to produce an authentic sense of suffering. The logic of a mimetic empathy strategy is based on an ideal of human connection achieved through common sensation and embodied cognition that gives feeling-based knowledge of what suffering might be like.[24] Mimetic strategies need some minimal amount of information about the conditions of others so that simulations of those conditions can be realistically created. Perspective taking is achieved through

[23] The pure form of copresence would be simultaneously bodily and temporal, but these aspects of copresence can be constructed in different ways.

[24] Gabriel Ignatow, "Culture and Embodied Cognition: Moral Discourses in Internet Support Groups for Overeaters," *Social Forces* 88, 2 (2009).

the placement of one's self into new conditions and the projection of one's self into a narrative about what suffering might feel like when it "actually" occurs. The result is a version of the imagined connection that Benedict Anderson attributed to the practices of nationhood, despite immense geographical distance and internal identity differentiation.[25] Here, this imagined connection is between individuals, but still unites through shared feelings borne of mimicked contexts and behaviors.

Mimetic empathy strategies are a mode of awareness raising that has not drawn much theorization, despite the presence of such strategies in various social movement and educational settings.[26] When mimetic strategies have been a part of activist mobilization in the past, they were used as a way to bridge to distant suffering that was far removed. On US college campuses in the 1980s, "shantytowns" were built to resemble the impoverished communities of apartheid South Africa.[27] As Sarah Soule writes, "The shantytowns provided a graphic representation of the evils of apartheid, and thus helped to mobilize potential participants to act on behalf of people in a very distant land."[28] In civic engagement work, Oxfam America uses a "hunger banquet" exercise that randomly distributes unequal portions of food to participants to mimic the global distribution of food.[29] Like in other campaigns related to global poverty or refugees, this exercise is meant to generate temporary conditions that shift bodily sensations.[30]

With this theoretical construction in mind, I turn now to show what empathy strategies look like in practice.

---

[25] Benedict Anderson, *Imagined Communities: Reflections on the Origin and Spread of Nationalism*. Revised edn. (New York: Verso, 2006).

[26] Erin K. Wilson, "From Apathy to Action: Promoting Active Citizenship and Global Responsibility amongst Populations in the Global North," *Global Society* 24, 2 (2010); Sarah A. Soule, "The Student Divestment Movement in the United States and Tactical Diffusion: The Shanytown Protest," *Social Forces* 75, 3 (1997).

[27] Sarah A. Soule, "Situational Effects on Political Altruism: The Student Divestment Movement in the United States," in *Political Altruism? Solidarity Movements in International Perspective*, ed. Marco Giugni and Florence Passy (New York: Rowman & Littlefield Publishers Inc., 2001).

[28] Ibid., p. 172.   [29] Oxfam America. "Our Signature Event."

[30] Anke Schwittay and Kate Boocock, "Experiential and Empathetic Engagements with Global Poverty: 'Live Below the Line So That Others Can Rise above It'," *Third World Quarterly* 36, 2 (2015); Wilson, "From Apathy to Action: Promoting Active Citizenship and Global Responsibility amongst Populations in the Global North."

AN EXAMPLE OF RELATIONAL EMPATHY
AT BORDERLINKS

The main relational empathy strategy used by BorderLinks was the inter-action between immigrants and travelers. As we have seen, a BorderLinks trip itinerary made many such encounters possible. In monitored settings, such as immigrant feeding programs or overnight shelters, immigrants' presence was brokered by Mexican volunteers or officials providing immigrant services. In these settings, immigrants were expected to sit with BorderLinks travelers during dinner to share their stories. In nonmoni-tored public spaces, these interactions were less organized and often *sui generis*. The first example below is of a monitored exchange, the second of an unmonitored exchange, and the third a mix. These three vignettes were selected because they represent a dominant theme from field notes: that face-to-face interaction between travelers and immigrants was stilted, sometimes conflictual, and often confusing.

Eating Together and Filtering Incongruent Stories

After entering an immigrant service center in Mexico two miles from the border, the St. Michael's Church group was directed to sit at folding tables set with plastic plates and disposable silverware. The BorderLinks staff member, Janice, told us to situate ourselves so we could talk with immigrants during dinner. After a few minutes, five adult male immi-grants arrived for dinner and were directed to the empty seats near myself, Mary, and Roland. We quietly began eating boiled chicken, rice, and salad. It took time, but after five minutes a few questions were asked by the St. Michael's group to the immigrants, which I translated from Span-ish to English.[31] Do you have kids? What work do you do? Where are you going? Following the immigrants' responses to these questions, the con-versation trailed off as Mary, Roland, and I listened in on other conver-sations, ate our food, or talked in English among ourselves.

After dinner, once the immigrants left for their sleeping quarters, Mary commented that she noticed that one of the immigrants changed his answers, first saying he would work with family members in a printing business in Arizona, then saying he would look for landscaping work.

---

[31] My ability to translate was not made publicly known to travelers to avoid being viewed as a BorderLinks staff member. On a handful of occasions during fieldwork, such as this one, I translated.

Mary then asked her fellow group members, now gathered in a courtyard outside the dining area, to share stories they heard during dinner. Matt said that the men he talked with at his table claimed, "to be 18 and 20 years old, but Janice says that's 'not true' since they look much younger." Janice, the BorderLinks staff leader whose tone suggested irritation that the immigrants' accounts were being questioned, said in reply, "It [their small size] *could* be true, like from malnutrition. But they also lie so that there is no custody chain" if they are caught and deported. Otherwise, she explained, they would enter a juvenile detention system in the United States that was difficult to exit. A bit puzzled, Jeanne wondered aloud, is it "better for these two [immigrants] to lie?" Janice replied that "lies are natural, [for example] so that you are not deported to Guatemala," which would be a more costly place to attempt another crossing into the United States. After more questions from travelers spurred her frustration, Janice cut the conversation off, moving the group to another activity, a talk by the shelter's coordinator.

Group Conversation and Broken Norms

On a different trip, Sojourner University's travelers were invited to tour a for-profit "house of hospitality" in Ciudad de la Luz. This dimly lit, haphazardly furnished, three-floor building was one of the dozens that sprung up as the town's economy converted to supporting the immigration industry. We were told not to expect to meet immigrants while we were there. After passing through a darkened, empty sleeping area, our group emerged into an internal courtyard, where a group of seven male immigrants was standing off to the side. Our BorderLinks leader, Sarah, commented that the immigrants were probably passing the time in safety, waiting for directions from their *coyote*. The men were looking at us as we stood close together, surprised to encounter such a large group of immigrants. After a few awkward moments, Sarah asked the men whether they would like to talk with us.

With Sarah providing translation, we spent the next twenty minutes in a conversation about immigration policies, mistreatment in prisons, the election of President Obama (which had just occurred), and the racist behavior of Sherriff Joe Arpaio. At times, the conversation was driven by comments from immigrants to the BorderLinks group, which Sarah translated. These included a few comments from one immigrant about the attractiveness of female members in our group and questions about their marital status. In a dismissive response, the females crossed their arms over their bodies and turned away from the interaction, toward each other instead. One female blushed, but said quietly to the other female she was next to, "I have a boyfriend already." Shortly after, the conversation stalled and the group left the place.

Rejection

Interactions with immigrants could fall short in an even worse way: rejection. When Sojourner University visited the Grupos Beta immigration assistance shelter in Mexico, I observed that Julia and Jennifer, both fluent in Spanish, seemed to be having a difficult time speaking to an immigrant. Over fifteen minutes, there were many breaks in their exchange, with the woman often looking away from them. Later, during the group's reflection time, they reported that the woman quickly made known her opinion that "people in the United States hate us." She insisted to the travelers that "we [immigrants] are equal to you [Americans]." Julia and Jennifer recounted that they were taken aback and tried to explain what they were doing in Mexico to the immigrant, but to no avail.

Their trip leader, John, had a different experience of rejection during the trip, but he was the protagonist. At the end of the week, he recalled that he "had felt a strong connection to the guy who I ate dinner with" at an immigrant shelter. The immigrant "was warm and talkative," as they went back and forth in Spanish. At the end of the meal, the immigrant had asked for money, but John had declined, following the donation rules set out by BorderLinks and the shelter. He recounted that the immigrant left the shelter before he had a chance to say goodbye. But this wasn't the end of the story according to John. The next day, as he sat in the church located in the town square, someone "came over towards me and said in English, '[the immigrant from last night] needs a way to call his family to let them know where he is.'" As the group listened intently to John, he continued, "The night before, I had said, 'No.' Once again, I said, 'No.'" After hearing these two rejections of support for an immigrant whom each member of the group had personally met at the shelter dinner, the group members sat in still silence. John breathed deeply, and a tear dropped from his eye before the group discussion moved on to another topic.

Short-Term Results of a Relational Empathy Strategy

These relational empathy vignettes were characterized by the interaction of travelers and immigrants, but also by interactional hurdles that

TABLE 8 *Empathic outcomes at BorderLinks, by empathy strategy*

	Relational	Mimetic
Emotional Reaction	Pity; defensive	Shock; trust
Role-Taking Perspective	Distrust; confusion	Bodily; "authentic"
Moralization	Awareness	Urgency

fractured the idealized notion of a natural connection with immigrants. What effect did this experience of the relational empathy strategy have on travelers?

Table 8 provides an overview of the sorts of emotional, role-taking, and moralization outcomes that could arise from empathy strategies. The relational empathy strategies at BorderLinks were poorly received by travelers in the moment, appearing to produce a weak experience of empathy.

When an interaction hurdle like skepticism toward immigrants arose, travelers responded in many ways, each attempting to save face.[32] Across six trips, with dozens of traveler-immigrant interactions, I had no observations of travelers directly challenging immigrants over their "stories." This was likely due to BorderLinks' strong norms about "respect" that were relayed during orientation. In response to immigrants' narrative incongruities, travelers sometimes commiserated with other travelers, which provided an opportunity to relieve empathy expectations.[33] Travelers floated a variety of reasons: immigrants may have been momentarily intoxicated or traumatized by what happened in the desert, or innocently performing for an audience of travelers, or just lying to avoid discovery of their real selves during an uncertain journey. Each explanation avoided imputing duplicitous motives to immigrants and worked to rescue a sense of empathic connection. While travelers respected the ideal of a relationship built through the respectful narration of personal story, these efforts to save face slowed the development of emotional bonding and the establishment of role-taking perspective.[34]

In the vignette with free-flowing conversation, the uncomfortable content of the conversation and unwanted personal attention overlaid the

---

[32] Erving Goffman, *The Presentation of Self in Everyday Life* (New York: Doubleday, 1959).

[33] Clark, *Misery and Company.*   [34] Polletta, *It Was Like a Fever.*

interaction, producing emotional defensiveness instead of emotional connection. In situations like this, which lacked the discussion norms imposed by service providers in shelters, exchanges challenged travelers' discursive norms of nonjudgmental listening and mutual respect. The result, among travelers, could be embarrassment or silence. The rupture in relationality created in this exchange was difficult, and an empathy account toward immigrants was challenging to establish.[35] The best travelers could do was to spread the relational difficulty across their group by retelling and discussing difficult interactions after the exchange itself had ended.[36]

As these vignettes suggest, the experience of relating with immigrants was often unsettling. The complexity introduced by diverse stories, ruptured interactions, and motive questioning required interpretive processing, which was inefficient for solidifying concise, focused meanings.[37] Emotional connection and understanding were delayed and difficult to achieve. This evidence suggests that relational interactions did not readily produce an immediate sense of strong empathy through identification or moralization.

Longer-Term Outcomes of Relational Empathy Strategies

In follow-up interviews about six months after travel, I asked BorderLinks travelers to describe the interactions they had with immigrants in these settings. Despite the many hurdles I observed during the relational empathy strategies, travelers generally claimed that the opportunity to meet with immigrants was important, suggesting some minimal level of empathic connection and an expectation that such empathy should have emerged. Derek, an African-American male, and his group, Southern Seminary, talked with immigrants on two occasions, during a stop at a nightly feeding program and a stay at a shelter for immigrants. Derek commented during his posttrip interview:

I really felt, I really was aware of my own sense of privilege. Yeah, kind of an unwarranted sense of privilege that I certainly enjoy, on a global level ... [Immigrants] expressed a lot of the same qualities that I would hold in high regard: humility, hope, some type of faith, or a belief in God ... They were just very, very human.

---

[35] Clark, "Sympathy Biography and Sympathy Margin."
[36] Clark, *Misery and Company.*   [37] Dimaggio, "Culture and Cognition."

Derek's recollection about the interactions shows an underlying sense of emotional connection and identification. However, despite this evidence from Derek of a longer-term empathic outcome, interactions with immigrants were more frequently recalled with frustration. During follow-up interviews, I asked each traveler: "Was there an activity during the week that was particularly difficult at all?" Doris, a middle-aged female, fluent in Spanish, with a history of social justice work in Latin America, volunteered:

Yeah, I'd say that what was most difficult for me was approaching strangers and speaking with migrants who were clearly in very vulnerable positions, and feeling a little bit, you know, 'This is out of my comfort level.'

Later in the same interview, I asked Doris, "Could you describe the interactions with migrants? What sorts of things did you learn from them?" She replied that,

[the interactions] were extremely valuable ... For me, the human interaction was definitely an important part of the trip ... but it [immigrant interaction] is sort of like the seasoning – the salt and pepper. It's a horrible metaphor, sort of like nothing that I learned from the migrants themselves was particularly shocking, or revealing, or stayed with me. It was important to listen to them and hear different stories, but it wasn't the thing that, you know, stayed with me and captured my imagination.

For Doris, who was fluent in Spanish, the interactions were awkward beyond the constraints of language. Travelers like Doris heard stories of poverty, loss, and physical pain from immigrants. Also, like Doris, they valued the act of personalizing distant suffering. The most salient residual effect of these relational interactions appeared to be the memory of personal faces and stories encountered in interaction, which provided some memorable index of the suffering travelers encountered.[38]

During an interview, the trip leader, Janice, indirectly admitted the problems, and lingering benefits, of even difficult interactions. Recalling her experience, Janice said that, "even when their stories are not perfect, are not clean, are not rosy, you're still looking at this person [a deported immigrant] and seeing a person who is suddenly back in Mexico," in an unfamiliar place with no connections. She suggested that "it's suddenly much more difficult to dismiss ... [than] if you heard about in on TV."

---

[38] Emmanuel Levinas, *Totality and Infinity: An Essay on Exteriority* (Pittsburgh, PA: Duquesne University Press, 1969 [1961]).

This may be, but the intensity of moralization about the systemic problems of immigration does not appear strong. Travelers achieved a sense of personalization without a strong sense of understanding or feeling the emotions or perspectives of those they met. As we see next, this is quite different than what can happen with a mimetic empathy strategy.

A MIMETIC EMPATHY STRATEGY AT BORDERLINKS

One mimetic empathy strategy in particular – the desert hike – was a central part of BorderLinks' work.[39] The hikes were led by local activists who walked immigrant trails to deposit water and offer first aid. Since the desert was a different setting for most travelers, the hikes were introduced as opportunities to encounter the environment that immigrants inhabited. The passage below recounts one of these hikes.

On the day of the hike in late March, the Eastern College group left Tucson early to meet Cathy in the community of Arivaca.[40] Arivaca is located 20 miles off the Mexican border, a small town amid square miles of uninhabited desert that doubles as the grazing area for local ranchers. Our twelve-passenger van followed Cathy's SUV down a pock-marked dirt road for four miles. In the parking lot, as we ate our lunch, Cathy explained that she looked for immigrants who were struggling to offer food, water, and medical aid, but that we should not see any immigrants.

For ten minutes we walked in single file, chatting, bunched up on the trail. Small cacti inserted a variety of thorns into the path. Within the first 10 minutes, one of the travelers, Anne Marie, fell on the loose rock. Within an hour, I did the same, embarrassingly falling to my butt in a cloud of desert dust. Cathy said that "when someone is hurt, they'll [the *coyotes*] leave you behind. They're not completely heartless – they'll leave water." As the trail veered into a bone-dry wash, Cathy explained, "In some places, it's easy to lose the trail, especially at night."[41] Allison,

---

[39] As Shapira in his study of the Minutemen notes, movement through the desert is framed by groups in ways that reflect and impute meanings about immigration. For the Minuteman, such a walk would be called "recon." See Harel Shapira, *Waiting for José: The Minutemen's Pursuit of America* (Princeton University Press, 2017).

[40] Cathy's actions and comments are a composite of actions and comments by two activists on the same hike. These activists were Tucson community members with long, supportive ties to each other and the organization. The composite is used to protect anonymity.

[41] A wash is the bed of a stream or river, which, in an arid environment, is dry most of the year.

FIGURE 4 A migrant artifact found in the desert

one of the travelers, said to no one in particular, "I can't imagine what this would be like at night." Cathy explained the tough environment a few minutes later: "When the monsoon hits there can be a 40- to 50-degree temperature change in one day." Hearing this, Ronald replied, "Oh God!"

The bright background of the wash threw any unnatural object into bright relief. As we rounded a bend, there was a lone, black shoe resting in the wash about five feet off the side of the embankment. Our group abruptly stopped in the wash to have a close look at the shoe. There were no laces, the tongue had been pulled forward, and the fabric seemed to have baked in the sun. As Cathy walked up, she immediately began commenting on the shoe. "This is what they [the group] need to see ... and it's painted!" She said that immigrants, in addition to wearing all-black clothing, would use a marker or paint to black out any white on their shoes. Group members snapped pictures, but no one touched the shoe.

Twenty minutes later we came to a makeshift shrine tucked into the wall of a gorge. The shrine was a natural cutout in the rock. In the cutout, there were dozens of prayer cards. A dirty "tortilla towel" served as a rudimentary altar cloth. Crucifixes leaned against the back wall. A few rosaries and prayer cards had tumbled out of the front of the cutout alongside a scattering of water bottles and food wrappers. There were also many pictures of humans, the types of small photos someone might pass out to friends. The travelers walked around in silence, snapping pictures. One traveler, Allison, collected some prayers cards, but only from the ground. We stood in a loose semicircle around the shrine.

Cathy stood under a mesquite tree that was leaning from the gorge wall to the middle of the wash. She said, "This seems like a good time to tell about Josseline."[42] Over the next few minutes, in quiet tones blurred by the breeze, Cathy told the story of a girl left in the desert to die. Cathy continued, "Close your eyes and imagine the silence out here if you were by yourself." Every member of the group closed their eyes. I heard someone take a deep, meditative breath. Cathy explained that local humanitarian aid activists found her body "by chance."

The travelers reopened their eyes after two minutes of silence. All kept their heads lowered and their eyes down. Cathy summarized: "That's why we do this, to try and prevent that from happening. As we walk, think of the people of faith who do this journey." After a few minutes of quiet reflection, we filed behind Cathy and began the return trip, reaching the parking lot about thirty minutes later. As we drove away, we saw a Border Patrol vehicle on a nearby hilltop, using the camera mounted on a towering pole on its roof to monitor the desert.

Short-Term Results of a Mimetic Empathy Strategy

Immediately after the hike, I stood with two of the travelers in the dusty parking lot and asked what they thought of the experience. Jonathan quietly said, with a sad face, "It was emotional." Anne Marie mentioned feeling guilty. Jonathan responded to that theme, saying in a soft voice, "I could do this 100 times and never really know what it's like. But people *really* experience this reality, here in the desert." A few days later, Anne Marie commented to me, "I wish I could go on the desert hike again. I mean, I feel solidarity in the other things we've done, but then we were *really* walking where immigrants walk."

---

[42] The story of Josseline was prominent among activists, later becoming the title of a book on immigrant suffering. Margaret Regan, *The Death of Josseline: Immigration Stories from the Arizona Borderlands* (Boston: Beacon Press, 2010).

FIGURE 5 A discarded water bottle in the desert, with the border wall in the distance

These brief comments differ markedly from the postactivity comments of the relational empathy strategy discussed above. After the desert hike, travelers' comments suggest a strong emotional element and a less problematic entry into a role-taking perspective. The immediate use of terms like guilt and solidarity suggest the beginnings of a moralized connection. As Table 8 shows, this mimetic strategy at BorderLinks was well received.

Longer-Term Empathic Outcomes of a Mimetic Empathy Strategy

During the interview with Derek mentioned above, I asked him about his group's hike: "One of the other events of the week was when we stopped, and we had that hike in the desert. What was that like for you?" Derek replied:

Two things that I remember. One, it's kind of comical, but only comical because we were a group in broad daylight, that was very much being guided. . . . I remember getting a very, very small little cactus ball stuck into my shoe. When I looked down and saw it, I was going to just kind of swat it away with my hand. And, I reached down and Adelia [the Mexican BorderLinks staff member] grabbed my hand."

[Derek laughs as he recalls the scene.]

She's [Adelia's] like, 'You're going to bleed.' She picked up a stick and knocked it away. I picked it up very gently [off the ground], and I kind of pricked my finger anyways. It was unbelievably sharp! Here I am, with a guide, we'd just eaten [so we had energy], with a large group, it's broad daylight, and I'm still making bonehead mistakes! How much more, if I really had something on the line, you know like life and death was hanging in the balance with my ability to navigate the desert, and it's dark, and I get separated, you know . . . The desert was no joke, even though we were in a very controlled, safe environment.

In Derek's recollection, the desert hike introduced him to the physical sensation of what immigration might be like. He transitioned from recalling the experience to imagining what it might be like in "reality" for an immigrant, someone who "really had something on the line." The transition from his recollection to the imaginative extension of real experience was relatively seamless. While not every traveler articulated the same quality of empathic connection, desert hikes rarely "failed" in the sense that no traveler reported a negative, emotionally fractured experience in the desert.

In contrast to the relational empathy strategy discussed above, this mimetic empathy strategy was able to bypass interactional awkwardness and engage a range of emotions. Desert hikes evoked a range of emotional terms from interviewees; they were "haunting" or "shocking." In contrast to relational conversations with immigrants during the week, the meanings taken from the desert hike were more definitive, often evoking a sense of authentically understanding immigration. An interview with Jonathan, a college-aged white male, shows that sort of outcome:

I thought it [the desert hike] was a haunting experience, mostly because we were, like, physically walking in the tracks of these people, a matter of hours or days before they had been there. . . . Overall I thought the experience was great to be in that physical place where migrants were . . . [The hike was] physically exerting, even though we went a very small portion of what migrants actually do . . . It was cool to not just read about it or hear someone, but to physically use your body. . . . I think about what or who those objects represent. These people who are leaving their homes, leaving their families, to go and pursue a better life in the US.

Jonathan's comments demonstrated all three elements of empathic connection: emotional tenor, role taking, and incipient moralization. This is not to say that a simulation like this is accurate about others' lives, but that it is useful for producing empathy.[43]

SORTING THROUGH EMPATHY

Empathy is making a comeback in social science, with the concept used to help account for variations in prosocial action. Empathy is also an oft-used folk concept, an ideal that articulates the type of concerned connection people can have with others, particularly those whose lives are beyond immediate reach. Here, I have taken advantage of empathy's familiarity to argue for its utility as a "thick" concept that brings together learning and motivational processes that are experienced together.[44] Empathy provides a way to understand and compare the activities that organizations use to create a moralized connection, something often seen as a building block of awareness raising in civic organizations and social movements.

Empathy strategies are interactive routines used by organizations to establish an emotional relationship with distant persons, a perspective of those who suffer, and a moralized view of the need for ameliorative

---

[43] Schwittay and Boocock, "Experiential and Empathetic Engagements with Global Poverty."

[44] Gabriel Abend, "Thick Concepts and the Moral Brain," *European Journal of Sociology* 52, 1 (2011).

action. For immersion travel producers like BorderLinks, empathy strategies are a means toward an end. If immersion travel is a distance-bridging form of awareness raising, then empathy strategies are a prime organizational mechanism that may unite information, emotion, and perspective into moral transformation.

The construction of empathy entails numerous processes familiar to scholars of collective action.[45] The empathy strategy concept draws together emotional and evaluative processes into one process, uniting them in a way that comes close to how actual people experience them.[46] By tying the accomplishment of empathy to distinct activities, the empathy strategy concept makes clear that empathy is a social production, the result of organized interaction with objects of concern. Organizations elaborate emotions and promote role taking, while also providing interpretations that moralize, and potentially politicize, empathy's meaning. Thus, empathy strategies help to round out an account of how organizations develop and deploy cultural aspects of prosocial and collective action, especially across distance.[47]

The case of BorderLinks has been especially fruitful for revealing multiple ways that an organization can go about creating empathy, each of which taps into different cognitive pathways and different portrayals of human relationship. As we have seen, different empathy strategies can also have a different influence on how immersion travelers understand their moral relationship with the humans whose life conditions they are concerned about. This makes them especially useful for understanding variation in immersion traveler experience. In the case of BorderLinks, interactional difficulty and untrustworthy stories were hurdles during face-to-face interaction. The relational empathy strategy was valued, but it produced little connective emotion, a weak sense of moral evaluation, and some minimal role-taking perspective. In contrast, the mimetic strategy of a desert hike appeared to generate a longer-lasting, strong emotion in addition to an embodied sense of immigrant perspective and a felt sense

[45] Jeff Goodwin, James M. Jasper, and Francesca Polletta, "Introduction: Why Emotions Matter," in *Passionate Politics: Emotions and Social Movements*, ed. Jeff Goodwin, James M. Jasper, and Francesca Polletta (Chicago: The University of Chicago Press, 2001); Jasper, "The Emotions of Protest."

[46] Goodwin et al., "Introduction."; Nepstad, "Oppositional Consciousness among the Privileged."

[47] Florence Passy, "Political Altruism and the Solidarity Movement," in *Political Altruism? Solidarity Movements in International Perspective*, ed. Marco Giugni and Florence Passy (New York: Rowman & Littlefield, Inc., 2001).

TABLE 9 *Empathy strategy examples, by physical separation*

Empathy Strategy	Physical Separation	
	Proximate	Distant
Relational	Empowerment projects (Eliasoph); Worker testimonials (Briscoe et al.)	Child sponsorship letters (Bornstein); Microcelebrity activist networks (Tufekci)
Mimetic	Urban plunge (Gehm); Prison tour (Meisel)	Apartheid shantytown (Soule); Hunger banquet (Oxfam)

of moral urgency. The contingent physical setting of the desert, the brokering activity of guides, and the embodied sensations of walking worked together to achieve this.

These results should point researchers toward a more comparative analysis of how organizations attempt to generate a connection between advantaged and disadvantaged people.[48] While I have been focused on empathy strategies in immersion travel, there is no reason to think that empathy strategies are only used in immersion travel. Table 9 suggests an array of empathy strategy examples. Empirical examples from research literature are listed in parentheses. For example, both "adopt-a-child" charity tactics and social-media-based networks, like that which emerged at Tahrir Square, can generate empathy through relational connection.[49] Empathy strategies are also important locally, when the empathic targets are proximate to listeners.[50] Many "tours" used by educators and advocacy groups are proximate mimetic strategies, such as "urban plunges" or

---

[48] Though I do not theorize them here, *informational* empathy strategies are likely the broadest and most well-known attempts at generating empathy for distant suffering. An informational empathy strategy is characterized by the use of symbolic media like writing, film, photography, or art to portray distant suffering. The interaction involved in this strategy is stretched out diachronically through mediated representation processes, with limited or no synchronic reciprocity between those who suffer and those who discover suffering.

[49] Bornstein, "Child Sponsorship, Evangelism, and Belonging in the World of World Vision Zimbabwe"; Zeynep Tufekci, ""Not This One": Social Movements, the Attention Economy, and Microcelebrity Networked Activism," *American Behavioral Scientist* 57, 7 (2013).

[50] Forrest Briscoe, Abhinav Gupta, and Mark S. Anner, "Social Activism and Practice Diffusion: How Activist Tactics Affect Non-Targeted Organizations," *Administrative Science Quarterly* 60, 2 (2015).

"prison tours," placing travelers in spatial contexts that produce a new bodily sensation.[51]

What do these results reveal for our understanding of immersion travel activities and their effects? The insights of this chapter suggest the need to look carefully at how immersion activities that mean one thing on paper, with similar evaluation scores and emotional configurations, can mean something very different in practice. The opportunity to "meet immigrants" was often held up by BorderLinks, group leaders, and travelers themselves as one of the most exciting parts of travel. Why else go all the way to Mexico and the Mexican border except to meet people? The observational evidence presented here, though, shows that the rhetoric about that activity does not match the sense of relationship that ensues.

None of this is meant to say that face-to-face dialogue is hopeless or unimportant in immersion travel. In theory, and under the best circumstances, relational interactions could be structured in such a way to be more successful.[52] Nor is this meant to say the simulation always work better, as many of BorderLinks' other simulations did not work as well as the desert hike.

What is noteworthy is that BorderLinks has brought these distinct ways of solving a basic problem in transnational relationships together, part of its approach to generating awareness and inspiring action. The next chapter turns the focus from activities and individual travelers' reactions to the group processes that shape those reactions. By doing so, we understand one more factor that patterns immersion travel experience and that, surprisingly, ties the power of the experience together for travelers.

---

[51] John Gehm, "Urban Plunge: An Intensive Experience in Criminal Justice Education," *Journal of Criminal Justice Education* 10, 1 (1999); Joshua S. Meisel, "The Ethics of Observing: Confronting the Harm of Experiential Learning," *Teaching Sociology* 36, 3 (2008).
[52] Elizabeth Levy Paluck, Seth Green, and Donald P. Green, "The Contact Hypothesis Reevaluated," *Social Science Research Network (SSRN)* (2017).

PART III

PATTERNS OF EXPERIENCE
AND TRANSFORMATION

6

Guided Unsettledness: How Groups Safely Shape Travel

Over the last two chapters, we have seen the importance of observing variation within the immersion travel produced by BorderLinks, whether in the emotions or the empathy prompted by activities. In this chapter, we look at one more source of variation in the experience of immersion travel: group affiliations.

As I traveled with different groups during immersion travel, I observed striking differences in the ways they made sense of the experience. Some groups accepted immigrants' testimonies as authentic representations of their suffering. Other groups intensively questioned the testimonies off-stage, suggesting that they were one voice among many in a crowded field of discourse. For some groups, public emotional displays in response to what they encountered indicated deepening personal awareness. For other groups, emotions were treated with suspicion, a challenge to be overcome to understand reality. Why did groups differ so drastically when partaking of the same travel itinerary and what does this difference mean? The answer to this question brings "the group" into a topic that often revolves around the traveler and the trip. The answer also reveals a cultural trick at the heart of experiences like immersion travel: a traveler's subjective feeling of unexpected transformation during an experience that, to outside observers, appears stable, predictable, even predetermined.

The fact that travelers from very different groups can go on a Border-Links trip and report fulfilling experiences suggests that immersion travel prompts an aspect of group life to emerge that implicitly structures the travel experience. I call this feature of immersion travel "guided unsettledness." As we have seen, the cultural form and activities of immersion travel generate a subjectively felt sense of *unsettledness* that enables the surprising facets of the experience to arise. However, immersion travelers are *guided* through this unsettledness by tacit group processes of which they are only partially aware. The unsettledness allows for discovery, while the guidance of group processes helps that discovery to become meaningful. Group styles provide stability by orienting the practices, boundaries, emotional rules, and speech norms as travelers gather in information from new experience. Instead of being thrown off by new experience, the styles of travelers' groups provide a reliable guide into the new experience.

I reconstruct two different styles, using observations from two different groups. The two styles differed in the epistemological weight they gave to testimonials and the utility of emotions for understanding reality. Southern Seminary interacted with immigrants gingerly, emphasizing the power of individual stories that they heard during the week. These travelers inquired about activists' motivations and spiritual beliefs. For Southern Seminary, emotions connected them with what they learned and signaled their openness to the experience. This *story-building style* focused on the authority of personal stories, motives, and emotions. In contrast, Eastern College travelers collected information through continual questioning, as if they were piecing together a puzzle. Through talking with anyone they met, they gathered the outlines of a larger drama that contained multiple, conflicting voices. They tried to emotionally distance themselves from the stories as a way to keep their analysis of perspectives and discourse clear. This *sleuthing style* saw the borderlands as a mystery, questioning the authority of stories and emotions while piecing together clues of power and suffering.

The findings presented in this chapter help to explain why feeder organizations value and trust liminal experiences like immersion travel to begin with. Feeder organizations believe in the power of unsettledness through immersion travel. They trust that travelers' group-based identities will grow instead of being overly challenged or negated. Guided unsettledness is the mechanism that makes liminal experiences attractive: it creates continuity for travelers as they move from their day-to-day organizational lives, through a new experience, and back again. In this light, immersion travel is a conservative strategy of awareness raising: it occurs through group membership in preexisting organizations, and organizations' group styles stabilize it. To understand why group styles would work this way, we first need to think about how culture works during immersion travel. Cultural sociologists have recently focused on unsettledness as a social condition in which culture may have a clear influence on behavior. If immersion travel involves unsettledness, then it also offers an opportunity to provide insight into how culture works.

UNSETTLEDNESS AND LIMINALITY

Settledness is a relatively unarticulated scope condition in theories of culture that assume stability in the material structure and action patterns of social life.[1] Beginning with Swidler's influential statement on culture in action, the condition of *un*settledness became increasingly central to sociological distinctions of how and why culture "works."[2] In Swidler's theory, culture is not a coherent whole. Instead, it is a resource that individuals can deploy to accomplish social action.[3] Swidler pointed out that the settledness of social life made it possible for cultural repertoires (vocabularies, ideas, metaphors) to be causally disconnected from the day-to-day behaviors of most people. She argued that commonsense repertoires of daily life are "more disjointed and less seamless" than the systemic portrayals of culture that sociologists inherited from Clifford Geertz and Talcott Parsons.[4]

Her argument implied that culture in settled times is characterized by a loose connection between ideas and action. Individuals have many cultural "toolkits" available to them at any given time and live in a rather predictable social world. During settled times, individuals live within institutions that constrain meanings and actions, linking them through recurring, habituated patterns.[5] As a result, much social behavior does not require the overt, conscious application of ideas and meanings. In settled times, culture exists more in the background. In the evocative words of Swidler, "For most people most of the time culture is mobilized

[1] Pierre Bourdieu, *The Logic of Practice*, trans. Richard Nice (Redwood City, CA: Stanford University Press, 1990 [1980]); Swidler, *Talk of Love*; Stephen Vaisey, "Motivation and Justification: A Dual-Process Model of Culture in Action," *American Journal of Sociology* 114, 6 (2009).

[2] Ann Swidler, "Culture in Action: Symbols and Strategies," *American Sociological Review* 51, 2 (1986); Ann Swidler, "Cultural Power and Social Movements," in *Social Movements and Culture*, ed. Hank Johnston and Bert Klandermans, Social Movements, Protest, and Contention (Minneapolis: University of Minnesota Press, 1995); Swidler, *Talk of Love*.

[3] John Levi Martin, "Life's a Beach, but You're an Ant, and Other Unwelcome News for the Sociology of Culture," *Poetics* 38, 2 (2010).

[4] Swidler, *Talk of Love*, p. 96.   [5] Abramson, "From 'Either-Or'."

piecemeal, to tinker at the edges or to defend their existing patterns of life."[6] In settled times especially, there is a harmless disconnect between what individuals do and what they say about what they do.[7]

Under conditions of unsettledness, however, the way culture works changes. In unsettled times, such as political crises, economic collapses, or massive military defeats, "culture takes a more explicit, coherent form when people are reorganizing their strategies of action or developing new ones."[8] Unsettled conditions make old behaviors problematic because they fail when called upon to answer new problems. This sort of failure provides the pragmatic motivation for humans to explore new strategies of action since the old ones no longer work.[9]

Unsettled times are opportune moments for ideological work, for meaning-making that problematizes reality.[10] Where settled times involve the unseen unity of theory and practice, unsettled times involve a conscious reconstruction of ideas, behavior, meaning, and practice.[11] During unsettled times, cultural repertoires can be dismantled and rearranged, animating a new course of action. New ideas and understandings of reality can prompt new ways of acting in the world.[12]

One problem with this line of research on culture and unsettledness has been the implicit focus on "objectively" unsettled times. Research has tended to focus on drastic change, situations that are seen as "large" enough to produce dramatic effects, such as Bourdieu's well-known "Don Quixote" effect.[13] Society can be unsettled, by economic transformation or terrorism, and so can individual lives, by illness or relationship transitions.[14] The problem is that this objectivist approach to unsettledness,

---

[6] Swidler, "Cultural Power and Social Movements," p. 30

[7] Vaisey, "Motivation and Justification."   [8] Swidler, *Talk of Love,* p. 93.

[9] Hans Joas, *The Creativity of Action,* trans. Jeremy Gaines and Paul Keast (Chicago: University of Chicago Press, 1997).

[10] Berger, *The Survival of a Counterculture.*   [11] Bourdieu, *The Logic of Practice.*

[12] Doug McAdam, *Freedom Summer* (New York: Oxford University Press, 1988); Robert Wuthnow, *Communities of Discourse: Ideology and Social Structure in the Reformation, the Enlightenment, and European Socialism* (Cambridge, MA: Harvard University Press, 1989).

[13] Christopher Bail, *Terrified: How Anti-Muslim Organizations Became Mainstream* (Princeton University Press, 2014); Pierre Bourdieu, *Pascalian Meditations* (Redwood City, CA: Stanford University Press, 2000).

[14] Bail, *Terrified: How Anti-Muslim Organizations Became Mainstream;* Wuthnow, *Communities of Discourse;* Corey M. Abramson, *The End Game* (Cambridge, MA: Harvard University Press, 2015).

while accurate, misses situations of unsettledness that are intentionally constructed and subjectively experienced as unsettling. Far from being a rare occurrence, intentionally produced unsettledness is common. The long line of research about liminal experiences is only one example, with a connotation of unsettledness even showing up in the etymological roots of liminality (*limen*: threshold; margin).[15]

How can the concept of unsettledness be reconfigured to understand such intentionally produced experiences like immersion travel? In an attempt to clarify the role of unsettledness in cultural theory, Omar Lizardo and Michael Strand have argued for differentiating between social "contexts in which actors can rely on externalized, stable cultural scaffoldings ... and contexts in which this externalized scaffolding is absent or non-existent."[16] The former contexts parallel Swidler's idea of settledness and the latter contexts her idea of unsettledness. Between these two is a continuum of more-or-less unsettledness. The middle of the continuum is occupied by contexts in which institutional structuration is weak. Lizardo and Strand term this crossover point between unsettled and settled contexts as "gaps in the institutional order."[17] These are crevices in which taken-for-granted behaviors of normal life may not be useful, crevices in which other cultural components can emerge to orient individuals.

The authors argue that during gaps in the institutional order, the practical consciousness of habit and routine that was formed through institutions will continue to produce "regulated improvisation." Lizardo and Strand are distinguishing between types of consciousness that function during unsettledness, noting that Swidler's theory focused on the strong role of discursive culture in moments of social unsettledness and the strong role of practical culture in moments of settledness. By contrast, Lizardo and Strand expect that, in moments of *mixed* unsettledness, culture that is practical will continue to be important for orienting action, but will require improvisation to deal with new social conditions. Discursive culture, like ways of talking, will also be important as individuals make sense of the patterned improvisation they are doing.[18]

[15] Turner, *The Forest.* [16] Lizardo and Strand, "Skills, Toolkits," p. 216.
[17] Ibid., p. 213.
[18] Omar Lizardo, "Improving Cultural Analysis: Considering Personal Culture in Its Declarative and Nondeclarative Modes," *American Sociological Review* 82, 1 (2017).

This theoretical clarification of unsettledness and culture is an important reformulation that is useful for understanding how immersion travel works. The image of gaps in the institutional order is relatable to the phenomenology of immersion travel, which involves temporal, geographical, and social separation of travelers from their institutional roots (family, work, church, and/or college). One of the few referents to selfhood that are left during immersion travel is a traveler's affiliation to a group based in a feeder organization. If immersion travel is indeed a gap in the institutional order, then we would expect that the culture of the organization that someone is traveling with will be important during travel. Preexisting practices and organizational ways of doing things will be especially important, with travelers' discussions helping to tie these to the new experiences of a liminal period.

One theme that Lizardo and Strand do not conceptualize is how this middle-of-the-continuum version of unsettledness can be *subjectively* produced. At one point they argue against the social constructionist (subjective) nature of unsettledness. This is not because they think it does not exist but because they are interested in how the unsettledness of objective social conditions affects culture. By extension, their theoretical work accidentally ignores the purposeful way that many social institutions attempt to produce unsettledness for organizational goals. The unsettledness of liminal periods like immersion travel is "subjective" in its origin. It is done intentionally, out of an understanding that contingency and liminality can have powerful influences on individual identity and organizational life. One only needs to think of vision quests or boot camps to understand why. Travelers on immersion trips subjectively know unsettledness is coming and even seek it. However, even when expected, just enough newness and contingency remain that the unsettledness that travelers feel appears as external to themselves. The key is that immersion travel unsettles travelers *just* enough to allow culture to work in a creatively shaping way.

THE GROUP BASIS OF TRAVEL STABILITY

Once travelers in immersion travel are unsettled, how does culture work? The groups that carry people on immersion travel are embedded in the institutional logics that undergird the identities and rationales of their feeder organizations. Institutional logics are sets of legitimated practices and meanings used and perpetuated by actors (individuals and organizations) residing within a specific field of social action. Institutional logics are broad boundaries that shape how people and groups within an institution think, relate, and act.

The small groups on BorderLinks trips come from organizations in two distinct institutional realms: religion and education.[19] When college students go on an immersion trip, they come from an organization in the field of higher education. When seminarians and congregation members go on an immersion trip, they come from an organization in the field of religion. What institutional logics do for immersion travel groups is provide an essential coherence around the group's purpose as an extension of a feeder organization. Institutional logics set the boundaries for what can happen, what a group can draw on and improvise with. In immersion travel, group styles work as a mediating cultural structure between individual travelers and the institutional roots of their feeder organizations.

The concept of group style was developed as a way to understand the aspects of culture that emerge and guide interaction among individuals. Group styles are "recurrent patterns of interaction that arise from a group's shared assumptions about what constitutes good or adequate participation in the group setting."[20] Group styles tie social identity, boundaries, shared meaning, and patterns of communication together, making them a local-level instantiation of institutional logics. They are not predictable from institutional logics, but draw from the meanings and practices embedded in institutional logics. Because of their tie to organizational socialization, group styles can operate as an element of practical institutional consciousness, providing guidance even when activated without decision.[21]

In the context of immersion travel, group styles help us to make sense of patterns that arise that noticeably shape travelers' experiences. However, this requires some theoretical extension from the mainstream of group style research. First, the groups of immersion travel are ephemeral enough that they do not have long, recurrent patterns of interaction. Second, the groups that go on immersion travel have incredibly strong mutual attention during a short time period. These conditions limit the possibilities of how groups behave as the appropriate way to "do"

---

[19] Thornton et al., *The Institutional Logics Perspective.*
[20] Eliasoph and Lichterman, "Culture in Interaction," p. 737.
[21] Lizardo and Strand, "Skills, Toolkits."

TABLE 10 *Group styles at BorderLinks*

Group Style	Components		
	Approach to Immigrants' Stories	Relation to Speaker Motives as a Source	Emotion Handling
Story Building	Passive listening	Eliciting	Probing
Sleuthing	Active questioning	Complex doubting	Overcoming

immersion travel. Traveling individuals are familiar with many institutional logics and group styles before travel.[22] Potentially, then, any given traveler could have multiple logics to engage when entering the new experience of immersion travel. Yet the unsettledness of immersion travel and the presence of fellow travelers that share a common affiliation prompt a particular group style for use in immersion travel.[23] Since group styles are products of shared affiliation and pragmatic context, both of which are tightly wound together during immersion travel, feeder organizations are not concerned that "anything goes" on trips. Instead, they have a good idea of what will go on: travelers will go forth into unsettledness under the pull of familiar group processes. This taken-for-granted aspect gives a sense of why feeder organizations so readily send their members on immersion trips.

Stability through Two Group Styles

Each of the six groups I traveled with can be categorized in Table 10 according to the way they gathered in the new experience. In this section, I use examples from two groups, Southern Seminary and Eastern College, to show how these style elements work. I compare the behaviors of these groups as they confront nearly identical situations during their Border-Links trip. I show three components of group style that characterize groups and create different group experiences: how they navigate boundaries with immigrants, the treatment of personal motivations, and the handling of emotions.

---

[22] Andrew J. Perrin, *Citizen Speak: The Democratic Imagination in American Life* (Chicago: University of Chicago Press, 2006); Mische, *Partisan Publics*.

[23] Thornton et al., *The Institutional Logics Perspective: A New Approach to Culture, Structure, and Process*.

TWO GROUPS

Southern Seminary

The Southern Seminary group was a collection of seminary students and their professor, with participants ranging in age from midtwenties to second-career ministers in their fifties. The seminary was affiliated with Mainline Protestant denominations and was located in a midsize city in the southern part of the United States. This experiential education was part of the seminary's curriculum to expose students to social justice issues as they learned to be religious leaders. Before coming to Arizona, the class met a handful of times to discuss books that they read in preparation for the trip. The books were used to introduce issues surrounding immigration from a theological point of view. This group had two female members and five male members; three of the seven were African American. Over half the members of this group had never left the country before the trip. When we approached the US-Mexico border crossing for the first time, some excitedly showed off the brand-new passports they had acquired for the trip. Most of the travelers had some anxiety about traveling to Mexico, due to images that friends and family had about safety and sanitation in Mexico.

The group cohered by drawing a boundary against conservative religious groups. Both the professor and the students repeatedly drew contrasts as a way of distinguishing their unique understanding and practice of religion.[24] On the first night that I was with the group, seated in the back of the twelve-passenger van on the way back from the airport, I asked some members about their seminary and the types of people who go there. As part of his response, Dan, the group leader, said that some of the people in the seminary, and many religious people, were influenced by the efforts of nationally known evangelist Joel Olsteen. According to Dan, Osteen's message was about "praising versus the cross" as the centerpiece of faith. The problem with this approach, according to Dan, was that "you might as well just take the cross down and preach prosperity," a reference to the "prosperity gospel" movement. One of the students, Robert, sarcastically followed this by saying that those students should quit wasting their time at seminary and just go on television, sell oils, and lead a megachurch – all things that connoted Joel

---

[24] Paul Lichterman, "Religion and the Construction of Civic Identity," *American Sociological Review* 73, 1 (2008).

Osteen and other prosperity preachers like him. Those behaviors were all signs of "success" in the world of feel-good theology that these students were resisting. Later during the week while traveling in Mexico, we passed a Seventh Day Adventist Church, a religious group whose sectarian tendencies are at odds with the public theology approach of this group. Another student, Paul, made an aside that "it's nice to see they're screwing up Mexico too." On the final day of the trip, the group engaged in a short discussion during a meal about "fundamentalists." According to their comments during this discussion, fundamentalists had no joy, no understanding of the role of doubt in faith, and no connection with the suffering of social injustice. These were all aspects different from the group's approach to being religious.

Travelers from this group lacked some of the progressive behaviors familiar to most BorderLinks staff and many travelers from nonreligious organizations. The construction of progressive food boundaries that has become quite common within American discourse was absent with this group. No one in the group was a vegetarian, and only one member regularly ate organic food. While the group members willingly ate according to the BorderLinks-enforced vegetarian diet during the week, they longed for meat. When meat was served during our homestay in Mexico, it was met with enthusiasm, as well as a sense of thankfulness for having had "real" Mexican food.

Throughout the week, the travelers from Southern Seminary made humor a central part of the experience, whether about other members of the group, the anxieties of border crossings, funny incidents, or retelling of favorite movies. Everyone laughed at the jokes and rolled their eyes as they came, particularly since the two travelers cracking many of the jokes were well known for doing so back at the seminary. Lines from Adam Sandler's "The Waterboy" were oft-quoted, as were various pulpit-friendly jokes about religion. The seminary professor's familiarity and accessibility with the students encouraged a relaxed environment.

Eastern College

Eastern College was a group of twenty-something college students and two professors from an East Coast liberal arts college. Both professors were teaching classes connected to issues of economics and politics in Mexico, Central America, and South America. Among the ten people on the trip were two men and eight women. Two of the students were from racial minority groups, and the vast majority of the students had traveled or studied abroad. The two professors were archetypal examples of public scholars who connect their academic work with the political struggles of oppressed communities. The first evening together at BorderLinks began with "oohs" and "ahhs" over the homemade hummus and organic bread that were laid out for snacking. Taking in the posters, sleeping arrangements, and communal kitchen, Doris, the group's leader, commented that "this place reminds me of the cooperative I lived in college." Those group members still in college smiled, with one joking, "You mean the *commune* you lived in?"

The students considered the class a unique opportunity to learn in the close company of professors that they looked up to. The bonds within the group centered on a shared connection from their collegiate context. Some of the students knew each other well, while all the students at least knew of each other. At various points, discussions turned to academic majors and dorm life. Students discussed the clubs that took up the majority of their time and talked about the research projects they were doing as part of the immersion trip.

In contrast to some other collegiate groups I traveled with, there was not as much role leveling within this group. The professors tended to take leading roles in cleaning or loading the van. Most of the students reciprocated this continuance of well-established roles by using the professors' last names. The professors at one point took a break from the group, going for a walk in a neighborhood in Tucson to get away from the demands of such intensive group activity. Realizing their professors had walked away without publicizing their exit, two students commented that they were not invited to participate: "Professors only," one said. The presence of status roles did not mean a lack of group bonding, but a bonding that was premised on preexisting roles in the collegiate environment.

Key Differences between Groups

These two groups, which never knew of each other's presence a few months apart at BorderLinks, differed in significant ways. Southern Seminary's travelers were older and had less international travel experience when compared to the college-age students with extensive international travel from Eastern College. These demographic and experiential differences indicate the different types of feeder organizations they came from. The more significant differences have to do with the boundaries and meanings the groups displayed, which were rooted to their feeder organizations' institutional bases.

THE STORY-BUILDING STYLE OF SOUTHERN SEMINARY

Southern Seminary Meets Immigrants

A typical stop on a BorderLinks trip was at a for-profit "house of hospitality" in Mexico. Immigrants usually stayed at these places for a hefty fee, sequestered in them while their *coyote* finalized plans for transportation to the border. The house of hospitality that BorderLinks visited was always the same, based on a personal connection between a local immigrant shelter worker and the owners. The rooms were over-crowded, the walls were dirty, and there was no personal space. The only symbols in the rooms were improvised drawings by immigrants sketched onto the walls.

As Southern Seminary entered the darkened outer room of the house, the BorderLinks delegation leader provided no introduction to what the group was about to see or hear. Walking through the darkened first room in single file, the seven group members noticed the dirty walls behind a bunk bed wide enough to hold five or more adult men on each level. After a few more steps, we passed a makeshift kitchen with a well-worn open gas burner and a few unmatched pans. We turned a corner in the hallway and entered a courtyard that was open to the sky. The courtyard was surrounded on three sides by two floors of small bedrooms, each with a window and a door. The place had the feel of an old, Southwestern cinderblock motel. As we paused in the courtyard, our eyes adjusting back to the bright light, our delegation leader relayed what the owner had said to her upon entering: the place was empty today. Just as the group took in this information with an air of disappointment, a young man exited a room upstairs, walked downstairs, and passed our group on the way to the bathroom. The place was not empty after all. The young man was dressed in a pair of worn pants and a long-sleeve shirt. As he passed, the on-site manager standing next to our delegation leader asked the weary (and wary) young man to speak to us.

Our BorderLinks staff leader said to him (in Spanish), "These people are students, you can talk to us." The man appeared uncertain. He began to speak quietly, saying (through interpretation) that he crossed into the United States through the desert in the past month, but was caught and deported. If his next crossing attempt was successful, he would head to an urban area, which happened to be in the same state in which the group's seminary was located. As this was translated, some of the group members expressed surprise, verbally exclaiming "Oh!" Beyond this brief exclamation, the group remained quiet, arranged in a semicircle around the man, staring. One of our group members finally ventured a question: "What type of work do you want?" There were no other follow-up questions. The entire interaction lasted about two minutes. As it closed, we each shook his hand.

This unscheduled interaction with an immigrant was emblematic of how Southern Seminary related to immigrants throughout the week. The group refrained from asking many questions, particularly at the beginning of each interaction. When questions were asked, they were usually few and directed at individual experiences, such as where immigrants were headed or what type of work they sought.

On another day we stopped at La Corazon, a program that fed immigrants. The space was open for mealtimes in the evening when up to 100 immigrants came through for food and a chance to sit. Tables and chairs projected a comfortable, welcoming environment not far off a well-traveled road. On the wall was a picture of the Virgin of Guadalupe and a small crucifix. At the time we arrived, the place was crowded with dozens of men sitting around, finishing generous plates of food. The director ushered us in and invited us to mingle among the immigrants.

As might be expected among a group of people not fluent in Spanish, most travelers were shy about trying to interact with immigrants. At this location though, with so many immigrants that were recently deported, English was not uncommon. After our group's poor Spanish-speaking ability became obvious, two immigrants walked up to talk with myself and two other group members. The ensuing conversations were driven by the immigrants, for example, asking if we knew a particular town. As I stood with the group, quietly watching the immigrants talk, few words came from the travelers as they took in the stories the men shared.

In these examples, travelers absorbed the story unfolding in front of them when interacting with immigrants. Travelers did not have a roster of questions to probe with. They watched the elements unfold and took in the accounts that were provided by the immigrants. Travelers seemed reluctant to probe the immigrants for information, preferring to let a "natural" telling occur. Immigrants were treated as story givers while travelers were story receivers.

Southern Seminary Seeks Motivation

Much of a week with BorderLinks included talks by activists and service providers along the border. After an informal presentation by an activist or service provider that ranged from ten to forty-five minutes, travelers had a chance to ask questions. Southern Seminary and other groups with a story-building style prioritized discovering the motivations of speakers that they met. On four different occasions the question of motivation was the first question, and sometimes the only question, asked by travelers of Southern Seminary toward a speaker. The special access that a speaker might have to information about immigration was not as important as the story of why and how the speaker had come to be doing the work.

After the meal service was done and the immigrants were gone from an immigrant shelter in Mexico, we sat down with one of the on-site organizers. She described that the work she did was done in the name of Jesus and God. With so many immigrants coming through each day, she said they were always in need of resources. She claimed that, as with the story of loaves and fishes, enough food always seemed to arrive so that no one went away hungry. She talked about her work as an alternative version of evangelism, through tending immigrants' hunger and supporting them in their journey.

After ten minutes listening to this energetic woman, the first question from a group member was: "Who inspires you, besides Jesus?" The organizer laughed at the idea that something else besides Jesus would fill that role, then said she was inspired by the interest and responsibility shown by North Americans that visit. The next question from the group, though, did not leave the motivation theme behind, asking: "How important is daily prayer [to your work]?" She chuckled again before stating that it was indispensable for her work, infusing a normal activity with deep meaning. Otherwise, the danger was to lose contact with the presence of God in the work.

This story-building process occurred somewhat differently with activists and clergy than with immigrants. Immigrants' stories were helpful for providing a narrative that, as a form of metonymy, could stand in for a much larger story about the personal details of immigration.[25] With this intense focus on an unsolicited individual story, though, the particular person of the immigrant could recede. The result of this distance was both

---

[25] Francesca Polletta, "Culture in and Outside Institutions," *Research in Social Movements, Conflicts and Change* 25 (2004).

clarity about a particular immigrant's story and the ability for the *particular* story to stand in for other immigrants' stories. It posed immigrants as incapable of revealing other information, viewpoints, or attitudes. Spiritual motivations that could be useful to these travelers came from activists, not the realm of suffering and material deprivation inhabited by immigrants.

Where immigrants' stories were left as relatively untouched narrative objects, activists' stories were elicited and prodded by the groups. Among groups with a story-building style, interactions like this had a beneficent tunnel vision that left other parts of the work blurry. The questions of travelers turned activists into storytellers, directing attention toward the content of the story that was most useful for the group. When travelers from Central College sat with the leader of an immigrant shelter in Mexico, they asked a few questions about immigrants, but focused on the surroundings and her. They asked, "Who is the [saint on the wall]?" "What is the most difficult part of your work?"

Travelers wanted to know why they were involved. By a collective focus, the group displaced the speaker from a larger picture, in effect creating a personal storyteller out of a person who was attempting to represent a larger organization. The speaker's usefulness for the group was as a storyteller of a personal narrative, not of a system of unjust immigration. Even when the speaker tried to make it different, these groups were less inclined to engage. With the Central College group, the woman answering their questions ended by saying: "In your government, you can change laws. [Tell them] we aren't terrorists or criminals, especially since you take advantage of their [immigrant's] work. I hope this motivates you. If you can't do anything else, at least pray." Most of the group simply nodded, then the interaction was cut off when Susan said, "Can we take your photo?"

In both of these types of interactions, travelers were building stories. What immigrants and activists could provide to this story building differed, but the group was attuned to information that highlighted personal information and motivational processes over a bird's-eye view of the borderlands.

Southern Seminary and Emotions of Commitment

A part of story building was how travelers' own stories began to interweave with those that were being told to them. As the week wore on, the group sought to understand their link to immigrants and their stories. For these groups, strong emotions were that link.

During the week with Southern Seminary, emotional life was on display through reactions of anger, frustration, or disgust that were shared among the group. On the morning after Southern Seminary arrived at BorderLinks, as a way to provide an overview of the situation on the borderlands, we watched the documentary movie "Crossing Arizona" at BorderLinks. The video was edited in such a way as to be emotionally compelling, with stark images of immigrant suffering and mournful music. My field notes record that I wanted to cry during a long stretch of the movie that followed Mike Wilson, a member of the local Tohono O'odham tribe. In the movie, Mike explained that a large percentage of border-crossing deaths happened on Native American land. Border enforcement agencies were allowed on the tribe's land, but humanitarian aid groups were not. Because of this, only members of the tribe could do humanitarian aid on the reservation. The reality, though, was that most would not. The video followed Mike on his solitary runs to put out water in a geographical area the size of Connecticut. During one water drop on the video, Mike met an immigrant on a dusty, rocky road, under the sweltering sun on a 100+ degree day. The immigrant told Mike he was lost from his group of fellow crossers, then explained that the only reason he came north was to raise money for his wife's lifesaving surgical operation. She was in Mexico with their children; he was lost in the Arizona desert. As they stood at the tailgate of Mike's pickup truck on the side of the road, Mike gave the immigrant water. He watched while the immigrant gulped it down. Then, Mike gently told him to walk the road until he encountered the Border Patrol. After all, it was better to be deported than to be dead.

During our viewing, the group paid close attention to the video, especially since this was an introduction to the borderlands and issues that they did not know well. Immediately after the video, Paul said he was "pissed off." He sat on the edge of the sofa with a tensed body. He said he understood "both sides" to the issue, but, since he was in the ministry, this understanding made him emotional. The group did not probe this emotional response at this point, but also did not censor it either.

At breakfast the next morning, Paul apologized to a few of us as we sat eating cereal and yogurt. His apology, though, led us back into a discussion of the film. It was a way to reengage the topic and clarify his emotional connection to what he was seeing. He explained that when he saw the dead body shown lying in the desert on the film, he was irritated that the US government could know about the deadly impact of channeling immigrants into the desert but still allow it to happen. He said to us, in a serious joke: "Why do people [in the United States] love Mexican restaurants but not the actual people?"

Other pieces of public emotion came up during the week with Southern Seminary. During a reflection midway through the week at the Albergue de Fe y Asistencia, Kate said she had "anger at people at home" for their ignorance and nativism. Paul followed on this a few minutes later, saying "I have a lot of anger at the government ... I just keep thinking of those 'red dots' on the map" of Southern Arizona provided by Humane Borders that signified where dead bodies were found in the desert. By the end of the week, Jason shared with the group that he was frustrated and confused about how he was going to bring this experience home.

These emotions did not become the foci of a group attempt to explain them away or suppress them. The emotion rules of this group were expression and consideration.[26] As they were expressed, the emotions were connected with comments about the suffering of immigrants along the border, the problems of border policies, and ignorance among the people they know back home. Emotions for this group were a way to signal to themselves and group members that they were allowing the experience to affect them.

HOW THE STORY-BUILDING STYLE WORKS

Group styles, such as the story-building style, simplified the process of gathering experience, providing a tacit filter of what the group should pay attention to and how to begin responding to what they were seeing. For Southern Seminary, this meant a focus on story, particularly the uniqueness of individual stories as authoritative and generalizable. Stories they gathered could provide characters to help think through action, surface surprising conclusions that drove home more significant points, or introduce ambivalence to be revisited at a later time.[27]

But how did this style become the preferred way to gather in a new experience for Southern Seminary? This style has roots to the practices and ideals of the group's institutional background, expressing a distinct way of approaching the world. Southern Seminary was within the institutional field of American religion, a field oriented to story as revelatory,

---

[26] Hochschild, *The Managed Heart: Commercialization of Human Feeling*.

[27] Francesca Polletta and Pang Ching Bobby Chen, "Narrative and Social Movements," in *The Oxford Handbook of Cultural Sociology*, ed. Jeffrey Alexander, Ronald N. Jacobs, and Philip Smith (New York: Oxford University press, 2012).

not only of the workings of the divine but also of individual lives.[28] Southern Seminary was also located within a Mainline Protestant part of the religious field that used biblical stories to understand contemporary social inequality, not just to restate character lessons or history.[29]

All four of the groups I traveled with that expressed this group style were from mainstream Protestant religious settings, whether a seminary, a theology class at a religious college, or a church. These locations in the broader field of liberal religiosity exposed them to similar institutional forces that made story authoritative, both as a revelation of truth found in scripture and also as a mode of understanding the world and human action within the world. Ruth Braunstein has argued that religiously liberal advocacy groups use stories strategically, part of a religious social justice repertoire that can be deployed for a variety of reasons, including internal identity and external authority.[30] At BorderLinks, liberal religious groups used stories more implicitly. Story building was an epistemological practice for making sense of the world. In line with Braunstein's argument, story *telling* was important for a liberal religious group such as Southern Seminary in settled times. But in unsettled times this orientation toward the pragmatic power of story made story *building* the tacit group style to understand immersion experience. In doing so, the group was not being overtly strategic but doing what felt natural, a sign of its engagement of shared practical consciousness to creatively engage new experience.

This evidence of the multiple ways that stories constitute liberal, religious groups suggests the importance of attending to the uses and outcomes of story processes. In describing the variety of ways that story in activism can be viewed, Francesca Polletta and Pang Ching Bobby Chen list a series of binaries about how stories might be viewed: "as normatively powerful but politically unserious, as authentic but also deceptive, and as universal in their implications but also dangerously idiosyncratic."[31] Southern Seminary and other story-building groups would land squarely on the positive side of each binary, seeing immigrant stories as powerful, authentic, and universal.

---

[28] Andrew Greeley, *Religion as Poetry* (New Brunswick, NJ: Transaction Publishers, 1995).
[29] Edles, "Contemporary Progressive Christianity and Its Symbolic Ramifications."
[30] Ruth Braunstein, "Storytelling in Liberal Religious Advocacy," *Journal for the Scientific Study of Religion* 51, 1 (2012).
[31] Polletta and Chen, "Narrative and Social Movements," p. 499.

During follow-up interviews, I tried to understand this aspect of group style. After asking a series of questions about different interlocutors during the week – immigrants, activists, service providers, and government authorities – I asked each interviewee: "Would you say that you trusted any of them more than others?" This meant asking them to give a discursive explanation of a group style that had been implicit. As these travelers replied overwhelmingly with preferential trust of immigrants, the theme of story as metonymy recurred. One member of Southern Seminary, Derek, replied:

Yeah. I would say definitely I trusted the migrant voice. I tended to trust the migrant voices a little more because I think the entire issue, for me, is centered in their story. In terms of research, they are the primary source. In terms of information gathering, they would be the primary source. Everybody else is kind of secondary – important secondary sources in some cases – but for me, the real interest was, 'What is this issue doing to the people?' At least it's how it was focused. I was really encouraged to ask the question, 'What does this issue mean to the people who are crossing the border?' ... In the class prior to the trip, our readings, really [focused on that]. One of the things, as we thought about it theologically, was to just remember that migration stories at least in the history of Western religions are about the movement of God's people. God's people are moving usually for life-sustaining reasons. Yeah. Everything else would just sort of be secondary. It comes from that theological perspective.

Derek's response clearly articulates the roots of the story-building style as well as how that style affected his experience of the BorderLinks trip. Derek referred to the way that the immigrant perspective was prioritized in the lead-up to the trip. At the end of his response, the archetypal story of immigration from religious texts has been connected to meaning – finding new life. As Derek and other Southern Seminary travelers traveled to the US-Mexico border, they arrived with an orientation toward story as a primary way of knowing for themselves what this experience meant.

An interview with the group leader from Central College, Betsy, shows the explicit, expert logic behind the story-building style. I asked her, "Would you say that you trust any of them more than others, in terms of what they can share about immigration or the border?" Betsy replied, "Are you asking me personally?" She chuckled, shifting from speaking about the students she had led to talking about her own experience and view as a theologian. She continued:

I have a deep value in what is called the epistemological privilege of the oppressed. This is a term from liberation theology. . . . The way it's unpacked is as follows.

People who are on the receiving end of oppressive systems and practices are going to be much more reliable about being able to be truthful about the reality than people who are in other places. So, my tendency would be to trust the voices of the people who are at the receiving end. That would be the migrants. Secondarily would be the providers because they hear the stories and because they have commitment.

GARY: Is it possible immigrants may distort what they portray?
BETSY: That's always true. Not only may there be a kind of . . . shifting, but
        I think there are certain things that don't lie. Somebody's blistered feet
        don't lie. Someone who is hungry and who has no money to get home,
        that's pretty hard to lie about. Somebody who's standing in shackles
        in front of a courtroom. That's what I mean about truthfulness about
        that kind of experience.

For religious groups, the truth-making referent in a story refers to personal, firsthand experience. This is one reason why immigrant stories were heard without interruption by these groups – they were interacting with something that expressed the deepest level of truth. Betsy articulated this well, noting the priority of suffering as a source of knowledge, a theme familiar to the liberation theology she taught. By contrast, stories that lacked the first-person referent to suffering were treated dubiously. The evening after listening to the PR manager of a *maquila*, Paul simply said that it sounded like she had done this before and you couldn't trust what she said.

The story-building style could loop back around to its roots, particularly as travelers from congregations and seminaries considered how their feeder organizations might respond to stories they had gathered. They were strategically attempting to build a new story with their feeder organizations. Paul, a seminary student, exemplified this during a final reflection of his trip in December. The previous day we had stood on the grounds of BorderLinks' "Casa" center at night. The Casa was perched on a hilltop in the middle of a Nogales neighborhood that sprawled up the unpaved hillsides. Across the surrounding hills we saw the twinkle of electric Christmas lights. Paul, zeroing in on one house whose roofline was strung with lights, said he had not expected to see that here, given the impoverished conditions of the homes and the lack of public infrastructure. During the reflection the next day, he said, with a look of excitement, that "I have a sermon [idea]: Christmas lights in the slums of Nogales." He felt sure this topic would speak to his congregation about what he had seen. Other members of the group nodded their heads at the power of the image, with Dan commenting offhand, using a Christian allusion, "Light in the dark, Christ in the world."

In other words, personal story of suffering as universal truth.

THE SLEUTHING STYLE OF EASTERN COLLEGE

Eastern College Meets Immigrants

As Eastern College entered the house of hospitality, we were told that all immigrants were gone for the day. In the courtyard, the group spent a few minutes looking around, then decided to explore upstairs, something that no other group did. In the back corner of the balcony walkway, the travelers found several rooms, one of which still had immigrants, some dozing and some awake. This surprised both the immigrants and the group members. It was an awkward interaction at first; the group members apologized for disturbing the immigrants.

After the apology, the group members began to ask questions of the men. Other members of the group, who had not been upstairs, gravitated toward the interaction. By this time, the walkway was so crowded that the latecomers could barely see in the doorway to the room. Some of the students moved further into the room, taking up the three feet between the walls and the beds. The interaction became a back-and-forth conversation, carried by the students' questions. Why did you decide to migrate? What sort of work were you looking for? What were deportation conditions like? What will you do now? The interaction lasted ten minutes, to the point that the BorderLinks delegation leader, who was not actively involved in translating, was showing impatience. She walked with a few remaining members of the group outside the house to wait on the sidewalk.

This is a good example of the sleuthing style. The interaction was driven by questions from travelers, who sought the interaction out. The group was literally sleuthing through the courtyard and, once the interaction began, turned the conversation into another clue. The travelers took the initiative in asking questions, directed toward various aspects of the immigrants' experience. The probing of immigrants' accounts with new questions allowed the travelers to fill their notebooks with many voices and pieces of information. At the end of the interaction, despite the thanks and the wishes of good luck, there were no physical interactions with the immigrants, such as a handshake or a hug.

Interactions like this one recurred throughout the week, providing material for travelers to reflect on with each other. The sleuthing style did not stop with one story but sought multiple stories to be gathered in multiple ways. The data points for sleuthing information about the border seemed endless: the accounts of immigrants, physical data, traveler's reactions, and the reactions of fellow travelers. Instead of preferring particular sources as authentic, and first-person accounts as coherent packages to be accepted, the sleuthing style treated everything as a source of data.

The sleuthing process was visibly aided by various tools. Most travelers on a BorderLinks trip bring a pen, a notebook, and a camera. However, with Eastern College, these sleuthing tools were regularly visible and continuously used. When we approached the border wall in Nogales for the first time, at a spot that nearly every BorderLinks trips visited, every member of Eastern College had a sleuthing tool at the ready, either a notebook to record their observations, a camera to snap a picture, or a video camera to document the scene. While standing near the wall, two students working with the video camera interviewed other members of the group, collecting their reactions as they looked at the wall.

Questioning Motives

In a sleuthing style, travelers related to the stories they heard during the trip as a form of data with a history and a position in a larger field of narratives about immigration and the border. The group respected all stories publicly but intensely questioned them with other group members to reveal their social and positional biases.

This was brought into focus one day in Nogales when the group had lunch with male immigrants at a local shelter. During lunch, an immigrant at our table recounted his personal story but, in doing so, shared a narrative with details and dates that were out of joint with each other. The veracity of the account was challenged by the shelter supervisor directly to the immigrant. The travelers did not question the story at that moment. After we left the shelter, the group discussed their discomfort with the shelter manager's approach. Their discomfort was not about the critical questioning, but its publicity. As it turns out, the group agreed with the manager, as it *did* examine this particular immigrant's story, just not to his face. When they examined this story, they explained any discontinuities by reflecting on the constructed, purposeful nature of all accounts that humans give of their behavior. Doris commented that the supervisor "kept pressuring the guy we were talking to, to see what was the story. We're aware that these are stories: they have the subjectivity of informants!" During this discussion the group mentioned the controversy over the "factuality" of Rigoberta Menchu's autobiography as an example of how *all* autobiographical accounts are constructed and received according to different criteria.

This style was encouraged by the presence of professors during the week, as I was told numerous times by the student travelers how glad they were to be able to "do research" alongside their professors. But the style was also one that the students had embodied and would use of their own volition. In the middle of our trip, we arrived about an hour early at the immigrant shelter in Ciudad de la Luz, leaving us with time to pass. The entry table to the shelter was littered with information for immigrants, including a comic book meant as a popular education tool for those immigrants unfamiliar with the dangers of the desert. I was sitting in the courtyard, chatting with Jonathan and Ronald about what trips "like this" were like. They had both traveled before with religious service groups, so they were comparing their past experiences with the current one. Jonathan said that on a trip like this, compared to others, it is more "analytical, we use categories like 'cultural production' to understand what is going on." Jonathan proceeded to demonstrate what that looked like, pulling out a comic book made to educate immigrants about the danger of the desert, which he had picked up from the table. He flipped through it to show how the desert was represented, how strangers were portrayed to be dangerous, how the arc of the story ran from hope to tragedy. His sleuthing was on display as he uncovered the positionality of the messages and their symbolic meanings.

One result of Eastern College's view of all testimonies as discursive constructions was that they required hearing multiple voices to distill truth. Trusting any one account was problematic. All stories from the week were data points that needed sifting and exposure to reveal a hidden structure and hidden truths. In this way, travelers from Eastern College trusted accounts both less *and* more than story-building groups. They were more likely to doubt immigrant accounts, but also more likely to hear out the accounts of governmental authorities than travelers in story-building groups. Immigrants' vulnerability and inability to provide coherent narratives made their accounts a problem. They were unable able to present a story that escaped the trap of overly personal viewpoints, which emphasized their particularity over their generalizability. In contrast, government authorities' ability to present a clarified position statement that delved into structural processes made them potentially more useful for a process of sleuthing. When I spoke with Ronald about his interactions and whom he trusted, he replied:

I didn't really relate on a personal basis with the activities [of hearing speakers]. There were some that did make that [personal] impression, [but] on the whole it was an opportunity to learn more about statistics, the history, the context within which these things were going on.

GARY: How would you describe your interactions with government authorities, such as the agent from Customs?
RONALD: The same sort of thing. It was informational, like seeing the situation from a different perspective. And definitely an important one, a perspective that is much [more] different than the activist perspective. It's one that takes into account multiple political factors, much more objective than subjective ...
GARY: Which group or speaker would you say you trusted the most?
RONALD: I think people are as honest as they could be, but [there are] certain aspects of their perspective and situation that makes them view certain things in a certain way. I wouldn't say I trusted one more than another. I might've been able to relate to one more than other. In terms of trust, it was all the same.

Ronald's comments reveal core aspects of the sleuthing style that were shared among the group, like reflecting on perspectivity and seeking multiple perspectives. I continued our conversation by asking:

GARY: You said you felt like you related with one more than another. Could you tell me more about that?
RONALD: Yeah, I related more on a personal basis with the migrants ... it's because, that was more of a way of their role in those situations, their presentation of self. The activists, the government workers, came into specific situations to talk to our group in specific roles, and not a personal, one-to-one level. Immigrants didn't come into a certain situation and think, "Oh, I'm an immigrant, I need to talk like one."

For Ronald, the immigrants' situations meant they were not presenting any viewpoint except their own. It might have made them relatable, but it did not make them more trustworthy. It made immigrants less trustworthy for revealing reality about immigration as a whole. Terry, a fellow traveler, explained this in my interview with her.

GARY: Which group or speaker from the week did you trust the most?
TERRY: I think it would have to be the activists and the government workers. Obviously, government workers aren't going to lie to you because they're not supposed to. Obviously, their information is framed

in a certain way, but it's not like they're going to flat-out lie to
you ... It's not like I felt the migrants were ever lying to us, or that
we couldn't trust them, but they weren't necessarily completely
aware of all the laws and what was going on in their case, and why
they were sent certain places, and maybe they were confused about
their situation.

Continuing, Terry explained that, with immigrants, "it was confusing for
us to piece together a story, a timeline, because maybe they didn't remember the timeline exactly correct ... The way they remember it is true
for them."

In my interview with Doris, she articulated that a sense of complexity
should guide the evaluation of testimonies. Lack of complexity, like what
Ronald or Terry encountered among immigrants, made these accounts
less useful for sleuths trying to build a bigger picture. Accounts that could
be trusted as appropriate data points were those with, "enough complexity for me to feel completed, that I was coming away with a deeper, more
complex understanding of what was at stake." She continued:

With performances like [the CBP] there was a sense of not [being totally] one-
dimensional, but almost. It was reductive in a way in which the narrative was
being constructed ... to gesture towards some complexity, but the purpose of the
narrative itself, the performance itself, was to present a unified, finished, tied up
with a nice little bow of narrative for us to digest, as opposed to opening up the
complexity of something and saying "I don't know what to do with it."

Notably, Doris' view of the CBP agent's account was different from
that of Terry, her student. Sleuthing groups were more likely to have
this sort of variance in trust for the accounts they heard. The variance
was at least partially the result of the group's ongoing suspicion about
any one account being true. Sleuthing groups heard stories as discourse,
each a part of a complex picture in which all were needed to see that
picture.

Putting Emotions in the Proper Place

In the process of sleuthing, emotions were an acknowledged but trouble-
some piece of the experience. For some travelers, emotions connoted
religious experience, a problematic public boundary for a group from a
secular college. On the last night of the Eastern College trip, I was talking
with two travelers about what made their trip unique for them. They
asked me about the other groups I was studying. Ronald said to me that

a "BorderLinks [delegation] with another group might make it more religious, like emotional reflections that are touchy-feely." Following this, Allison suggested that other groups would focus "more on what's inside, and why to be involved." Comparing this with the approach they tried to take during their trip, Ronald said that, we're "more on the [objective side of the] objective-subjective continuum or the cognitive-emotional continuum." He said that he had previously done work with Habitat for Humanity and their "reflections were emotional, about what 'memory' or 'image' from the day stuck out."

As Ronald's and Allison's comments suggest, these travelers were familiar with different group styles from their experience in other organizations. When they were with Eastern College, though, emotions were a problem to be avoided or overcome, mainly because of their association with subjectivity and religion. This was spectacularly displayed when Anne Marie spoke after lunch one day with the group about how she was feeling. The day had included a visit to a town square, bordered with vendors hawking wares for a desert crossing and migrants passing the time. In the middle of the square, the students visited an old, small Catholic church, which had a prayer for migrant safety on the wall. Anne Marie reflected,

I have a lot of thoughts. I had an intense experience in the church [in Ciudad de la Luz]. I'm not religious. Sitting reading the prayer [of the migrants on the wall], I wished I was religious so I could say the prayer and mean something. I wish I believed so I could appeal to a higher power for help. I wished it would make it better. It was very emotional for me ... I have nothing analytic to say.

She started tearing up but pulled the tears back as silence settled on the room. No one engaged her comment, or the emotion. Most members looked away from Anne Marie; they were shifting uneasily as she worked to stop the tears. A few minutes later, as the group talked, Ronald appeared to engage her comments, but did so in a way that was reductive toward religion (even using sociological terminology to do so): "I was in the church too [watching the migrants]. With all the boredom, the immigrants go to church to get power from the collective effervescence."

The discomfort with religious experience had consequences for how group members related to immigrants emotionally. During the same reflection, Terry recalled a conversation she and others had had with an immigrant during lunch at a shelter. She related that, "Our guy at lunch was religious. He said that 'God knows the injustice done to me.'" Terry explained that while she was eating and talking with the immigrant at lunch, "there was a lull and he asked me if I was religious. I was raised Catholic, so I felt I wanted to say 'Yes,' because it would be more troubling to him to say, 'No.' I wasn't going to deny his God. I felt like I was not being upfront [when I said 'Yes'], but I'm kind of okay with it. It's hard to reconcile." The connection of religion to emotions made the sleuthing activity more difficult to accomplish.

Emotions had a way of resisting bracketing; they kept coming up during the week. When travelers expressed sadness or frustration at what they were experiencing, the emotions themselves became objects of analysis for the travelers to identify and overcome. Emotions became useful for revealing the difficulties of doing their course research during the trip. Emotions might signal when the research process was not working well. For example, some Eastern College students felt that their analysis was suffering because their note-taking was degenerating into personal reflection or personal concerns for people they had met. The ideal proposed by the professors leading the trip was to acknowledge the presence of emotions but to let them reenergize a commitment to the sleuthing process. Their strategy, in effect, was to redouble the sleuthing but to incorporate the emotions as a data point that recommitted them to the style. The issue of emotions may have been difficult to answer but part of it was just a matter of practicing the group style.

This came up in group discussion midway through the week. The group was tired as we stayed in Albergue de Fe y Asistencia one night. Terry was worried: "I don't know how to do the analytical part [of my project] ... it feels more descriptive." Dana, her professor, became animated and said to her, "You're in the field. You are where you need to be. You have no analytical distance at this point, so your comments now do *not* have to be analytical – you can't be." Doris followed by saying that, "You're responding more strongly to experience and reactions than information ... You're figuring out where you are standing." Lisa reflected on what she had seen during her interactions. She explained that the various activists and service providers they had spoken with all "talk about their emotions. [So] there's also an emotional labor for all of us, trying to match up to their emotional labor in what they do." Bridget followed, "It seems like everyone is really emotional when they are talking to us ... This trip is emotionally exhausting. When you talk to people, you have to act, too, with an engaging expression." The conversation wound down, but then one of the students (I did not catch who it was) asked if we could do yoga. Some travelers practiced it regularly, and everyone in the group knew their leader led yoga sessions back home.

There was a general encouraging murmur at this idea, after which Dana reluctantly agreed. Bridget offered to help.

We spread out through the room and were warned that yoga was meant to be done on mats. A few of us considered attempting this on the sleeping pads that the shelter provided for us to sleep on the floor, but they were too cushy. I was standing near Doris, at the far end of the line of Eastern College members. Julia, the BorderLinks staff leader, looked over at me, shook her head, and smiled; she told me later that she had never done anything like this with a group before. It was a bonding activity *par excellence*, as we were all in comfortable sleeping clothes, having just shared our thoughts, and were aware that it was the end of a long day. But it was also a crystallization of how sleuthing dealt with emotions: by overcoming the confusing nature of them.

As she led us, Dana said to "let go of something. You can have an intention if you want when you do this. A common one is 'let light shine from my heart.'" She took us through some low-skill moves. Everyone in the group tried the various poses. After ten minutes the group activity came to an end. We all prepared ourselves for sleeping; some people journaled, some people showered, others read a book. The yoga seemed to settle the confusion that the group had been sharing. The yoga itself had nothing overtly to do with the immigration. It was, however, a way to safely overcome emotions that might have prevented the group's sleuthing work the following day.

HOW THE SLEUTHING STYLE WORKS

The sleuthing style is primarily an orientation about the proper and trustworthy way to gain information. The sleuthing style uses a sampling method to accrue many points of data, seeks to construct a model of objective reality with these data, and brackets out contaminating elements, such as emotions. For sleuthing groups, accounts are seen as products of discursive positions in a field of multiple discourses and viewpoints about the border.[32] At first glance, this is reminiscent of the scholastic gaze that Pierre Bourdieu used to characterize an objectivist form of science.[33] This style seeks to interrogate experience, looking for generalizability over specificity. However, this style is not merely the deployed product of a scholastic vision of the world. This group was attuned to the

[32] Bourdieu, *The Logic of Practice*.
[33] Pierre Bourdieu and Loïc J. D. Wacquant, *An Invitation to Reflexive Sociology* (Chicago: University of Chicago Press, 1992).

use of body and personal experience for gathering information about the borderlands. For example, they included as data their walk along immigrant trails in the desert and the reactions of their classmates to the experience. Even if emotions might clog their ability to sleuth, emotions themselves became an object of study. The curious fact that a group like Eastern College would even be at the border suggests that the sleuthing style is less a gaze, more an engagement with practical reality. The leaders of the group were using immersion travel as a tool of resistance from standard modes of academic inquiry that sleuth from afar, often silencing the voices of victims of injustice or the implications for researchers.

This group style imagines religion as primarily a source of emotionality or personal knowledge, not itself a tradition that provided resources for this group to engage. Religion is a way of knowing that, despite its presence in American society, is considered an illegitimate way of knowing in many locations of higher education. Individual travelers of a group like Eastern College were religious, and they may have even thought about the trip in religious terms, but the ability to do so within the group context was constrained. Sleuthing groups like Eastern included individual members that were personally religious. In side conversations with me during travel, or after the trip, they noted that they had wanted to reflect on their own spiritual story, use religious language, or share more emotions, all reminiscent of a story-building style they were familiar with from their participation in religious congregations. However, they felt they could not because of the boundaries defining their group's shared approach to the trip. This did not mean that the group was antireligious: far from it. They were respectful enough of their interactions with religious organizations and persons along the border that they worried about being irreverent of their beliefs.

Sleuthing with Sojourner University

Most groups that made their way to BorderLinks did not display the sleuthing style, but one other group I traveled with did: Sojourner University. A few observations from that trip help to corroborate the patterns and roots of this style. Composed of college-aged students, half of whom were not white, the group was led by the college's chaplain, part of an alternative break program. Most students knew of each other, but the group did not preexist the BorderLinks trip.

Like Eastern College, the group approached immigrants' accounts as a source of information for big themes, not for the intrinsic power of story. During one interaction with immigrants, which lasted about half an hour, the travelers asked questions like: "Do people who have been deported come back angry?," "Why aren't there any jobs [in Mexico]?," "Shouldn't there be lawyers prosecuting all this?," and even, "Why isn't there a revolution [in Mexico]?" They filtered this information alongside other information, getting into multiple discussions about whether capitalism or border policies were causing the suffering they were seeing.

When they talked in this way, personal stories were not the focus. Instead, they displayed a seminar style – making coherent points, engaging those points, and developing opinions based on new data. When sleuthing, new data were always needed, and new data could make a difference. During a follow-up interview, Jennifer said that she and her fellow travelers approached the trip "like academics ... [who] challenge everything." During my interview with her fellow traveler, Daniel, he mentioned he had "felt comfortable to disagree" during the week as he and the other students were used to being encouraged to "listen to another perspective." On the first day of the trip, during a discussion, Daniel had suggested that the group pay attention to everything, since "hidden power has the same results everywhere." After the trip was done, the BorderLinks staff member Sarah mentioned that she was surprised by the group's willingness to discuss everything and its attention to power and privilege.

Like Eastern College, Sojourner University was attuned to the positionality of the voices it encountered. In a follow-up interview with Daniel, he mentioned that "all speakers were putting on a mask to present their best side." Likewise, Jennifer mentioned that "facts and stories" were important during immersion travel, both of which aided "critical thinking" about what was seen. Julie recalled that "you'd miss something if you never talked to a migrant," but that there were limits to their authority because "migrants could only talk about their story," not the structural aspects of immigration.

Finally, similar to Eastern College, this group recognized emotions but was on guard against becoming too emotional. Martina recalled the emotions of the week but had resisted becoming too emotional, since that would lead to a "martyrs from Mexico, monsters from America" mindset. She worried that the emotions, though natural given what they saw, could deceive about what was happening. Ironically, the chaplain leader of the trip was ordained in a Mainline Protestant denomination. He said in a follow-up interview that he assumed the personal stories and emotions of the trip were the most powerful for the students. But he also observed that, among the group, there was an inability to "touch the emotional side." Though he and at least two of the students were religious, that mode of understanding was not part of the group's public experience, and neither was extensive emotional processing.

CONCLUSION

It is no great surprise that groups would differ in their experience of immersion travel. Until now, though, we have known little about the sources of that difference and the implications for understanding how immersion travel works. Part of this is due to past research strategies that have examined similar types of groups. In this chapter, I leveraged the diversity of groups that traveled through BorderLinks to examine how they gather in the experience of immersion travel.

One insight from this approach was that immersion travel regularly produces both a feeling of surprising discovery and stable conditions that support travelers to make meaning about the experience. Guided unsettledness helps us appreciate why travelers can find immersion travel so appealing and why feeder organizations may embrace it is an awareness-raising mechanism. This brought us into a current debate in cultural sociology about how culture works. Cultural sociologists have shown how unsettledness can be crucial for changing the way that individuals think and act. As we saw, though, there has been little attempt at connecting this aspect of cultural theory to phenomena that are unsettling, in an intentional way. Immersion travel lies on a continuum of unsettledness, at a point where travelers are both objectively unsettled by the liminal aspects of the experience and subjectively interested in being so. As theorists predict, that point is where both practical and discursive elements of culture can be influential, which makes immersion travel a rather exciting moment of cultural activity.

During moments of intentionally produced unsettledness, group styles emerged. Shared membership cued these styles, which provided tacit, pragmatic guidance for travelers. By tracing different styles, we saw how groups encountered new realities in patterned, but different, ways. This sort of variability has usually been assumed to operate at the level of individual travelers. My analysis points to group styles as a source of difference as well.

The *story-building* style encountered the complexity of immigration through individual stories, which were accepted as evidence of systemic processes occurring at the US-Mexico border. The story-building groups were more likely to trust the accounts of immigrants or activists instead of government authorities, whose personal story was inaccessible and possibly duplicitous. Story-building groups experienced emotions as a tool of understanding during immersion travel, an essential source of knowledge to probe alongside others.

The *sleuthing* style oriented groups to gather information by piecing together individual stories into a systemic understanding of the border. Immigrant testimonies did not contain the truth of the system; they were pieces of a system. When interacting with immigrants, sleuthing groups processed the accounts they heard as data points that revealed portions of more extensive, transpersonal forces structuring immigration. The sleuthing style was more likely to see all accounts as problematic, *including* those from immigrants and activists, not just governmental authorities. Accounts were performances that provided evidence of the interests and ideologies of the account maker, pushing travelers past personal details to a puzzle picture that emerged from the system of accounts. Emotions were part of the experience for sleuthing groups but were seen as problematic to the extent that they clouded travelers' ability to competently analyze the numerous accounts that they encountered.

In this chapter I have focused on how styles worked to stabilize experience and noted that the styles I observed were not the product of long interaction patterns between travelers. These observations help to recognize the strength of the group style concept, since some of the patterns I saw were quite similar to those discovered by other researchers. For example, the story-building style is similar to the personalized politics that Paul Lichterman has written about, especially how the style assumes the importance of individual inspiration for involvement.[34]

Is the concept of group style the only way to account for the evidence presented in this chapter? An obvious alternative would focus on demographic characteristics, but the difference in group style between these groups was not likely due to these. Differences in age, gender, and race were scattered across the groups in this research. Eastern College and Southern Seminary were both mixed-gender and mixed-racial groups. While some groups, such as St. Michael's Church, had older travelers, they shared a storytelling style with a group that was much younger: Central College.

Another possibility is that the extent of travel experience among travelers produced differences. Groups did vary in travel experience, with

---

[34] Paul Lichterman, "Religion in Public Action: From Actors to Settings," *Sociological Theory* 30, 1 (2012).

one-third of Southern Seminary's travelers having never left the country, in comparison to a group like Sojourner University in which all but one member had left the country before. This alternative explanation does not work, though, since groups sharing the same style had different levels of immersion travel experience. We are left, instead, with the importance of group styles.

It is not surprising that the experience of an immersion travel itinerary should vary from group to group. What is surprising, however, is what this variance helps to reveal about how immersion travel works. Through paying attention to the patterned styles that groups deployed, we can see how feeder organizations structure the experience of travelers, an effect that is predicated on a group's origin but magnifies in a moment of cultural unsettledness. This insight made visible the special trick of immersion travel: a traveler's subjective sense of entering unsettled space and time while being tacitly guided by the very organizational structures that define settled space and time. With this understanding of open, but stabilized, unsettledness as the backdrop, we can now turn to the question of what happens when that unsettled time ends, when travelers come back home again.

7

What Changes and Why?

We know that most participants in our programs come away transformed by the experience.

BorderLinks fund-raising letter

The official understanding of how a BorderLinks trip changes travelers comes from a story. The biblical conversion story of Paul on the road to Damascus was presented by the organization as the way that immersion travel works. According to Gill, Paul's conversion was a "complete realignment; it was truly a 'transformative experience'."[1] Gill argues that,

It is precisely this type of experience that many BorderLinks participants testify to having had as a result of their involvement with our programs. It's not just the direct confrontation with the poverty on the border that triggers this response, but it is even more their interaction with the genuine and faithful people living the border reality. These folks are so full of grace, hope, and love that, even though (or perhaps because) they do not have all the 'toys' people on this side of the border have, they make the very best experiential education teachers.

This template, like Rick's story, builds up the expectation of transformation for travelers. It even suggests how this transformation occurs, as the result of seeing poverty and interacting with "real people" at the border. And it occurs to "many."

Imagine my surprise, then, when I asked BorderLinks staff members what they knew about travelers after they left Arizona. It was an off-the-cuff question that I asked just after my last immersion trip. I wanted to

---

[1] Gill, *Borderlinks II*, pp. 148–9.

compare notes between what I was finding out and what the organization already knew. It turns out that the organization did not track travelers in any systematic way. Instead, when a trip ended, staff members moved on to the details of producing the next immersion trip. They would send thank-you letters to travelers, add them to the organizational mailing list, and invite them to connect on Facebook. Occasionally, Janice told me, she or other staff members received a letter or an email from a traveler who had been transformed.

Looking back, this loose coupling between an ideal end and practical knowledge about that end should not have surprised me. As we saw in Chapter 3, the organization was vague about its encouragement of post-trip actions, emphasizing personal discernment of emotions, increased awareness, and storytelling, while shying from specific political possibilities. Not surprisingly, when I asked staff members, directly, what they wanted travelers to do, their answers followed this pattern. Molly, the longest-serving delegation leader at the time, answered, "It's hard to generalize, but what we want them to walk away with is that they've thought critically about their role in these systems that they've been exposed to. Like the food system, the immigration system, our country's policy." Patricia struck a similar chord, emphasizing storytelling. She hoped that,

First, that they don't stay silent, that it doesn't become an experience of a trip. [I hope] that they go, take it back home, and they speak with their schools, with their churches, with their families, with their communities. That they write their local newspapers. That they do reports.

The organization's stance toward the open-ended possibility of action, with an emphasis on personal development and story sharing, comported with an image of civic engagement familiar to travelers through their feeder organizations.[2]

The organization had hopes for more, but a problem was that these hopes stayed below the surface of the organization's public identity. Molly, the long-serving delegation leader, admitted that "most people on the staff have certain ideas about immigration or immigration policy" and are themselves involved in social movement organizations and advocacy groups. But they were not advertising these to travelers given the

---

[2] It also comports with the model of the non-partisan "informed voter" that evolved in the twentieth century. See Michael Schudson, *The Good Citizen: A History of American Civic Life* (New York: Free Press, 1998).

organization's formal neutrality. The organization seemed to rely on the faith implicit in the story of Saul, in effect stating: "How could someone *not* be changed by a BorderLinks trip and then act in new ways?"

This expectation of change introduces the most significant difficulty for thinking about individual change in immersion travel. The logic of travel has an expectation of transformation so deeply woven into its fabric that disentangling the evidence of change is difficult. Should change be seen in travelers' attitudes, emotions, or behavior? All three? Something else? Is change best understood in relation to travelers or undocumented immigration? In practice, the organization punted on nearly all of these questions, hoping that the inspiration of immersion travel would be enough.

But some of us want to know more, suspicious of the brief or self-centered nature of personal change through experience. Even immersion travelers had this concern. On the second-to-last day of my trip with Sojourner University, I asked John, the group's leader, what he expected a trip to do to his students. He explained that he hoped they would find "presence in the present," which they might carry for years to come, but he also worried about the "gluttony of experience" for his privileged students. And most scholars of travel carry this same concern. In one of the earliest sociological studies of experiential journeys, to the alpine heights of Europe, Georg Simmel observed this about travelers' immediate reactions: "Strangely this excitement and euphoria, which drive the emotions to a level more intense than normal, subside remarkably quickly."[3] With this warning, there is every reason to be suspicious that effervescence from the travel phase of social life need not flow into the next. Yet, as Doug McAdam recounted about the "freedom high" experienced by activists during the Mississippi Freedom Summer, the embodied memory of an ephemeral, experiential high *could* become part of a radical personal change toward action.[4] Might immersion travel do the same?

I have found it difficult to think about change through immersion travel. On my very last research trip for this book, my fellow traveler (and research subject) turned the question toward me. Lucie, the professor guiding her students on the trip, asked me, "How has this changed you?" That was and is a good question. Lucie's trust that something had changed in me, and the feeling I had of needing to produce evidence in response, suggested to me that an understanding of change through

---

[3] Georg Simmel, "The Alpine Journey," [Alpenreisen.] *Theory, Culture & Society* 8 (1991), p. 220.

[4] McAdam, *Freedom Summer*.

immersion travel needed to be both inclusive and incisive. It needed multiple levels, addressing evidence of discursive, behavioral, and identity change while retaining a healthy skepticism about it all.

This chapter analyzes indicators of change drawn from traveler surveys, as well as travelers' accounts of the feel of transformation. We begin by arriving "back home" with Jonathan, Roland, and Kate, the three travelers we met in the first chapter. Their experiences of being misunderstood at home show how difficult reentry could be for Border-Links travelers. The emotions and stories of immersion travel clung to them, at least for a while, confirming for travelers that something powerful had happened. But, as the first few days back home stretched into weeks, and the liminal period receded, whether the experience translated into something new was an open question.

The chapter continues by reviewing longitudinal evidence of change in travelers' attitudes, emotions, and behaviors, drawn from a survey done about six months after the end of travel. Change in any of these could indicate micromobilization, the personal shift that, if connected to networks, affiliations, or action opportunities, could channel the Border-Links experience in a new direction.[5] Finally, I focus on travelers' accounts of how immersion travel influenced them.[6] *All* travelers make sense of immersion travel somehow, displaying baseline reflexivity about experience. This discursive level of change is the most common and well documented, and less directly reliable, for tracing the meaning of change.[7] By parsing out discursive motifs of change, and connecting those accounts to behavioral evidence, we can observe how the BorderLinks experience may enter an autobiographical narrative to shift identity over time.[8] There are some ways of talking about the experience that indicate an autobiographical effect of disorienting discovery, around which travelers

---

[5] Summers-Effler, "The Micro Potential for Social Change."; Klandermans and Oegema, "Potentials, Networks, Motivations, and Barriers."

[6] Lofland and Skonovd, "Conversion Motifs."; Francesca Polletta et al., "The Sociology of Storytelling," *Annual Review of Sociology* 37 (2011); Robert Wuthnow, "Taking Talk Seriously: Religious Discourse as Social Practice," *Journal for the Scientific Study of Religion* 50, 1 (2011).

[7] Colin Jerolmack and Shamus Khan, "Talk Is Cheap: Ethnography and the Attitudinal Fallacy," *Sociological Methods & Research* 43, 2 (2014).

[8] Peter S. Bearman and Katherine Stovel, "Becoming a Nazi: A Model for Narrative Networks," *Poetics* 27, 2–3 (2000); Michèle Lamont and Ann Swidler, "Methodological Pluralism and the Possibilities and Limits of Interviewing," *Qualitative Sociology* 37, 2 (2014).

may reorganize their sense of self and professional vocation.[9] I pay particular attention to the conditions that generate this pathway, showing how the *critical reflexivity* that is produced among some traveling groups provides a critical element of discursive reorientation.

The arc of this penultimate chapter, then, is to sort through what change means by hearing what change feels like, measuring what change looks like, and delineating the conditions that pattern both.

COMING HOME

When travelers recounted their experience of returning home, they usually spoke of emotional fatigue. I asked Kate how she felt when she first came home. She explained,

I guess the sense of [feeling] overwhelming. I don't know if exhaustion is an emotion but drained. Emotionally drained. . . . Just even on the plane ride back, feeling, like, tired. Not just tired from being busy, but overwhelmed I guess. Emotionally overwhelmed.

Jonathan also reported feeling exhausted, but mixed in a new feeling as well: "I was [also] really impassioned." Most travelers reported a similar mix of fatigue and excitement, prompting them to share their experience with people back home. As they did so, they quickly bumped into boundaries between their felt authenticity and what others were willing to hear. For Jonathan, one of the boundaries he bumped into was the political nature of undocumented immigration. Jonathan talked with his family, giving them a day-by-day recounting of the trip. He explained,

My family is very traditional and very religious and very conservative. So, they had never thought about migration or what the US's role is in why these people are coming to the US. They just think of a foreigner who is here using resources that their tax dollars paid for.

As he talked with his family, he felt pulled into a debate that was not of his own making. He and most other travelers took BorderLinks' advice seriously to share stories about immigration, to be respectful, and to avoid conflict. But, even if they wanted to spread the word about immigration this way, some people did not want to listen. Jonathan continued,

Immigration is very politicized. So when you want to talk about migrant rights, it's all of a sudden this political debate. But that's not what I was interested in . . .

---

[9] Joas, *The Genesis of Values.*

I wanted to appeal to their humanity ... it was hard to distinguish that from the political debate of red and blue.

Another boundary that came up quickly for many travelers was a sense of confusion about their responsibility. Roland explained that his return home,

was confusing because I was very rapidly getting yanked back into my normal life and priorities and stresses. I felt like I was not following up on the moving experience that I had had [at BorderLinks]. It was confusing of whether or not I was spending my time wisely [back at home].

While trying to figure out what to do, Roland shared his trip experience with family and friends, particularly during the first few weeks after returning. Like Jonathan, though, he ran into misunderstanding and opposition as he ventured beyond speaking with like-minded friends:

I was finding that a lot of people wanted to have simple answers. It was difficult because I knew there weren't simple answers. [I tried] to not argue but to recognize that they didn't have the experience. I found myself trying to educate more than convince because I wanted them to understand what I saw and what I felt about the inhumanity of what I saw. And that it wasn't just economics, jobs; it wasn't people that were stealing. Just all the nasty comments that happen and are spread in the US are fairly rampant. And I was surprised at how strong it was.

Kate had a similar confusion that involved her own decisions about what to do. I asked her to explain why the trip felt overwhelming as she returned home. She replied,

Just seeing so much that needed to be done and not knowing how to do it. Not knowing how to start. . . . I remember writing [a course paper] about wanting to talk to people, to talk to someone like my dad who doesn't think that immigration is important and that "those people" shouldn't be here [in the United States]. I remember writing about maybe not being able to change someone's mind by talking to them, but maybe if they see how I respond and how I react, that maybe that will influence them. . . . [I was] having the emotion of wanting to change the world but not knowing where to start.

Survey evidence confirms the resistance that all three of these travelers mentioned. While almost one-fifth reported a friend or family member disapproved of their participation *before* travel, after the trip conflict increased: nearly 60 percent of travelers reported having a conflict with a family member or friend about immigration-related issues.

Besides the emotional challenges of getting back into the regular routines of settled life, returned travelers appear to have been confused about what to do with the expectations they had for themselves. When they actually took the step that BorderLinks suggested – sharing the story – a majority of them ran into disinterest or even outright conflict. They were encountering new pressures that did not exist during the experience of immersion travel. These new pressures for travelers and for those who study them are the first inkling that the big transformation expected by BorderLinks might play out differently in practice.

THE PROBLEMS OF MEASURING CHANGE AMONG IMMERSION TRAVELERS

Measuring change related to immersion travel is difficult for many reasons. First, the process of self-selection into a BorderLinks trip through feeder organizations produces a group of people that are distinctly different from the "average" US population. Before their trips, BorderLinks travelers were *already* more politically liberal than average Americans, more accepting of immigrants, more active in civic and political life, more educated, and more religious (see Methodological Appendix). Such self-selection meant travelers had comparatively little room to change in their attitudes and behaviors. If they already supported immigrant rights compared to the US population, was it possible to support them *even more* after their trip?

A second hurdle to measuring change in BorderLinks travelers is that changes can occur on different timelines. Due to my own limits, I only surveyed BorderLinks travelers up to six months after travel. This short amount of time between trip and survey may have been too limited for some changes to occur. This is less of a problem for evidence about attitudes and emotions, which might appear more changed ("nudged") closer to an experience. It is more of a problem for the sort of behavioral outcomes that collective action scholars seek. It is possible that certain behavioral changes that require initiative and time – like joining an immigrant-rights organization or developing contacts with other activists – could have taken longer than six months. Certainly, the long-term consequences of civic behavior and activism that unfold over a life course would be undetectable at the six-month mark.[10] The possible benefit of the six-month measurement mark is that it may have allowed

---

[10] Doug McAdam, "The Biographical Consequences of Activism," *American Sociological Review* 54, 5 (1989); Darren E. Sherkat and T. Jean Blocker, "Explaining the Political and Personal Consequences of Protest," *Social Forces* 75, 3 (1997).

just enough time to pass by, avoiding the period after the trip when a "travel high" was present.

A third hurdle to determining change through immersion travel comes from the difficulty of designing a rigorous methodological design. In an ideal world, this research would have included a control group of non-travelers from feeder organizations, but this proved too difficult. It required knowing who was coming from an organization, a piece of information that many organizations did not communicate until a few days before the trip. Furthermore, some feeder organizations, such as universities, presented a massive challenge when attempting to create a control group. Without control groups, evaluating change is still possible, but comes with specific weaknesses. The longitudinal method used here, given the lack of a control group, is a one-sample pretest/posttest. Participation in a BorderLinks trip was the common "experimental condition" present for all travelers. This approach assumes that any differences between pre- and posttest are due to participation in BorderLinks. This is a very liberal assumption since many other unmeasured factors could produce change regardless of immersion travel. This liberal assumption is tempered somewhat by my focus on changes that would logically follow from BorderLinks' immersion travel: attitudinal and behavioral changes related to immigrants and immigration. The most defensible interpretation is that the data here are suggestive of short-term traveler changes, providing an opportunity to consider the mechanisms of those changes.[11]

WHAT CHANGED?

Table 11 shows binary (yes/no) variables from the survey for which significant evidence of longitudinal change exists among BorderLinks travelers. The final column in the table shows the percentage increase from the pretrip baseline level. The table shows that the BorderLinks trip may have increased basic understanding about immigration. There was a significant increase in the number of travelers that had heard the term *maquila*, as well as heard about the School of the Americas, a high-profile concern among progressive, religious groups that dates back to the Central American wars of the 1980s.

---

[11] The relative strength of my methodological design appears when contrasted to other research on immersion travel, most of which lacks a longitudinal design, relies on a single data source, and usually does not report response rates to help diagnose nonresponse bias (see Methodological Appendix).

TABLE 11 *Longitudinal change (binary variables)*

| | % | | *p* | % change |
	Pretrip	Posttrip	(one-tail test)	over pretrip
R reports sorrow for immigrants crossing	47	59	0.08	26
R reports despair for immigrants crossing	13	30	0.01	131
R reports compassion for local immigrants	72	85	0.04	18
R reports anger toward Border Patrol	19	30	0.06	58
R reports frustration toward Border Patrol	48	64	0.04	33
R reports anger toward politicians advocating immigration enforcement	36	73	0.00	103
R reports sorrow toward politicians advocating immigration enforcement	8	20	0.02	150
R has anger	40	79	0.00	98
R has head the term *maquila*	79	89	0.06	13
R has heard of the School of the Americas	45	58	0.06	29
R reports that a specific policy causes immigration	15	28	0.07	87
R reports that a general cause causes immigration	73	84	0.06	15
R has donated to BorderLinks	3	15	0.01	400
R has contacted politician about immigration at some time	28	40	0.07	43
R has been part of an immigration advocacy group at some time	35	51	0.03	46

R = respondent.
Excludes "don't know" answers.
Comparison of proportions using a binomial distribution.

There was also a significant change in how travelers described the causes of immigration. Travelers were asked an open-ended question regarding what they saw as the cause of immigration along the US-Mexico border. These answers were coded according to three types of answers: immigration caused by a general force (e.g., economics, poverty), immigration caused by a particular policy (e.g., NAFTA, agricultural trade, peso devaluation), or immigration caused by individual decision-making of immigrants. Travelers could list one, two, or all three of these explanations in their answer. Posttrip answers would indicate whether travelers had a more structural understanding of the social forces causing undocumented immigration. In fact, after travel, travelers were more likely to say that a general force and/or a specific policy caused immigration. BorderLinks travelers had an increasingly structural way of thinking about immigration. The talks by activists, the visits to agencies, and the simulations during the trip appeared to shift some travelers' interpretations of immigration toward political-economic explanations.

Despite this evidence, we should keep in mind that the *absolute* level of BorderLinks travelers reporting policy as the cause of immigration was still quite low: less than one-third of travelers used such an explanation *after travel.* By comparison, about 40 percent of travelers both before and after the trip still mentioned individual decision-making by immigrants. These results suggest that BorderLinks' immersion trips did not shift most travelers away from individualistic explanations of undocumented immigration. This may be partially the result of so much attention during immersion travel given to hearing the testimonials of individual immigrants. Those testimonies articulate proximate reasons for immigration but provide little if any insight into the political and economic forces behind that decision. Immigrant testimonies may reconfirm BorderLinks' view about the "complexity" of immigration, without producing a clear diagnostic frame that can be conducive to collective action.[12]

Table 12 shows other evidence of change in attitudes among travelers. There was a marked increase in the salience of the border and immigration among travelers. Before the trip, about 60 percent of travelers paid attention to the border and immigration. After the trip, over 90 percent claimed that border and immigration issues were important to them. The remaining attitudinal items show that a significantly different proportion of travelers thought that the United States was too strict in border

[12] David A. Snow et al., "Frame Alignment Processes, Micromobilization, and Movement Participation," *American Sociological Review* 51, 4 (1986).

TABLE 12 *Longitudinal change (categorical variables)*

	%		*p*
	Pretrip	Posttrip	(two-tail test)
R frequency of shopping at farmer's market in a typical month			
More than once a week	7	18	0.00
Once a week	18	29	
Several times a month	18	12	
Once or twice a month	28	26	
Never	28	15	
R frequency of consuming Fair Trade products in a typical month			
Daily	16	32	0.01
A few times a week	16	6	
Once a week	9	13	
Several times a month	13	24	
Once a month	18	12	
Never	27	13	
R frequency of attending religious services			
Weekly or more	47	46	0.07
Occasionally	32	25	
Never	21	29	
How important have border and immigration issues been to you?			
Don't know	1	0	0.00
The most important issue	6	7	
One issue among a number	53	84	
Somewhat important	32	7	
Not important at all	7	1	
The United States is too strict in enforcing immigration laws along the US-Mexico border			
Don't know	22	10	0.05
Strongly disagree	6	5	
Somewhat disagree	19	17	
Somewhat agree	31	43	
Strongly agree	22	25	
One can rely on the government to do the right thing			
Don't know	5	7	0.01
Strongly disagree	17	24	
Somewhat disagree	33	42	
Somewhat agree	44	27	
Strongly agree	2	0	
The growing number of immigrants will improve US culture with new ideas and customs			
Don't know	13	6	0.03
Strongly disagree	0	0	
Somewhat disagree	2	3	

	%		*p*
	Pretrip	Posttrip	(two-tail test)
Somewhat agree	37	32	
Strongly agree	49	59	
An amnesty program for undocumented immigrants already in the United States?			
Don't know	11	3	0.01
Somewhat oppose	2	3	
Support	42	34	
Strongly support	45	60	
Greater federal spending for tighter border security to prevent immigration			
Don't know	6	5	0.02
Strongly oppose	48	77	
Somewhat oppose	41	14	
Support	5	5	
Strongly support	0	0	

Note: Statistical tests are Wilcoxon matched pairs signed-rank tests.

enforcement, that the US government was untrustworthy, that immigrants improved the United States, that amnesty for immigrants in the United States should be declared, and that increased federal spending on border security was not a good idea.

In the study of social movements, numerous studies show how these sorts of changes in ideas can influence changes in behavior.[13] The beliefs and opinions of eventual activists – before they are activists – can be quite incoherent or illogical.[14] BorderLinks appears to be somewhat successful in framing the structural causes of immigration, bringing more coherency to where it may not have been before.

Returning to the binary indicators in Table 11, we see a significant change among travelers in emotions toward local immigrants, immigrants crossing the desert, border control authorities, and politicians involved with immigration issues. After travel, more travelers had the classic motivational emotion of anger, now connected to politicians and border control authorities. Other emotions increased as well, such as sorrow for

[13] Jane Mansbridge, "The Making of Oppositional Consciousness," in *Oppositional Consciousness: The Subjective Roots of Social Protest*, ed. Jane Mansbridge and Aldon Morris (Chicago: University of Chicago Press, 2001); Doug McAdam, *Political Process and the Development of Black Insurgency, 1930–1970* (Chicago: University of Chicago Press, 1982); Nepstad, "Oppositional Consciousness among the Privileged."

[14] Ziad W. Munson, *The Making of Pro-Life Activists: How Social Movement Mobilization Works* (Chicago: University of Chicago Press, 2009).

immigrants crossing the desert and immigrants in travelers' local communities. The emotions with the highest level of increase were anger toward politicians and despair for crossing immigrants. In both cases, more than twice as many BorderLinks travelers reported these emotions after the trip compared to before the trip.

These changes provide substantial evidence that BorderLinks serves as a producer of targeted emotions. BorderLinks appears to generate what Jasper has called "context-specific emotions," but focused them on specific targets of approbation (immigrants) and targets of opposition (border authorities and politicians).[15] These emotional changes constructed crossing immigrants as suffering and border authorities and politicians as agents that created that suffering. Travelers acquired an emotionally grounded sense of injustice that appears as strong or even stronger than the new understanding they gained. This sort of emotional change that links to specific targets is crucial to collective action, since these sorts of emotions can persevere over time.

To briefly summarize: at six months after travel, immersion travel through BorderLinks appears to have produced some informational and emotional change in travelers. The emotional work that BorderLinks did in connecting travelers to immigrants and prodding the emotional awareness of travelers showed some evidence of success. Likewise, but to a slightly lesser magnitude, the informational work that BorderLinks did through expert talks speakers showed some evidence of success.

What about behavioral outcomes? The bottom rows in Table 11 document the proportion of travelers who had ever done a particular civic or activist behavior. These rows indicate whether the BorderLinks trip was associated with new behaviors among those who had never done the behavior before. As an example, focus for a moment on the item "R[espondent] has contacted politician about immigration at some time." The mean in the pretrip column shows that 28 percent of travelers had done this before the BorderLinks trip. After the trip, 40 percent of travelers had done such an activity. The mean listed in the posttrip column does not indicate that 40 percent of travelers had done the activity *since* the trip. Instead, it shows that the number of travelers who have *ever* done the activity was 12 percent higher after the trip. Similarly, there was a significant increase in the proportion of travelers who were a part of an immigration-specific advocacy group after travel.

---

[15] Jasper, "The Emotions of Protest."

Together, these results suggest some important change in behavior among travelers who had not previously been actively involved. To date, research on immersion travel has shown its effects on general civic behavior but has not connected the unique themes of immersion trips to political behaviors.[16] Here, we have evidence that some political behaviors directly connected with the thematic issues of an immersion trip may emerge after travel.

Table 12 shows behavioral change in consumption patterns, drawn from ordinal questions on the survey. Travelers showed significantly increased frequency of shopping at a farmer's market and consuming Fair Trade products in a typical month. Before the trip, 25 percent of travelers shopped at a farmer's market once a week or more, but after the trip 47 percent reported doing so. Similarly, 41 percent of travelers consumed Fair Trade items once a week or more before the trip, but 51 percent reported doing so after the trip. As we have seen in BorderLinks' attention to food practices and economic-focused visits, one type of change the organization proposes is in consumption. It appears the trip may have spurred such change, whether the consumption activities are intentionally connected to immigration or unintentionally the result of picking up progressive identity behavior.

In summary, the most unambiguous evidence of change from these tables, statistically speaking, is for the development of new knowledge, targeted emotions, proimmigrant attitudes, some political behavior, and some consumption behavior. Change in political activity, like contacting a politician or joining an immigration advocacy group, is known as a higher-cost political behavior that demands time, energy, and focus. The BorderLinks trip may have been a motivating experience that prompted travelers to seek out this new engagement and made them more available for recruitment into immigration-focused civic activity and activism.[17]

There is one behavior in Table 12 that changed in a *negative* direction among the sample of travelers – attendance at worship services. After a BorderLinks trip, fewer travelers reported worship attendance than before the trip. The table shows a substantial increase in the percentage of travelers that reported *never* attending worship services. This shift was due to travelers who had only occasionally attended worship before the

[16] Beyerlein et al., "The Effect of Religious Mission Trips."
[17] Klandermans and Oegema, "Potentials, Networks, Motivations, and Barriers"; Munson, *The Making of Pro-Life Activists.*

trip not reporting religious attendance after the trip. The six-month period may have unintentionally caused this result, as there was less time to "occasionally" attend. But this result may have also been due to actual, conscious shifts in religious behavior. A follow-up question on the post-trip survey provides some insight as to why this might have happened. One traveler mentioned an increasingly busy lifestyle, while another simply reported not having "the interest or the time." But one respondent's answer appears directly related to the BorderLinks experience, suggesting the potential reorientation of religious practice through immersion travel. A participant from a seminary reported: "I could no longer attend a church that believed things that were so contradictory to what I believed. I couldn't continue to worship in such a conservative setting." This finding, though rare, comports with a pattern detected in past studies of religious activists, which showed that new moral commitments and behaviors could cause them to disengage from their religious roots while increasing in their activism.[18]

Longitudinal Changes by Group Type

Given the group style patterns discussed in Chapter 6, it is possible that travelers from different feeder organizations differed in how they changed after the trips. The sample sizes were quite small for such an analysis, so caution is needed when interpreting these data. Secular college groups displayed the most emotional development, with significant, positive change in sorrow for crossing immigrants ($p < 0.05$) and compassion for local immigrants ($p < 0.10$). The emotional levels toward immigrants of travelers from secular college groups were relatively low before travel. By the end of travel, though, these travelers' emotional levels were like those from other feeder organizations.

Travelers from congregations and those from secular colleges had significant shifts in their attention to immigration as an important issue ($p < 0.10$). While travelers from the different feeder organizations presented similar levels of contacting politicians about immigration *after* travel, for congregational group members this was achieved through a significant upward shift ($p < 0.10$). The BorderLinks trip may be particularly important for politicizing the behaviors of congregational members,

[18] Michael P. Young and Stephen M. Cherry, "The Secularization of Confessional Protests: The Role of Religious Processes of Rationalization and Differentiation," *Journal for the Scientific Study of Religion* 44, 4 (2005).

who are embedded in organizational environments that provide opportunity and skills for increased political engagement.[19]

One of the most interesting group-related patterns involved religious behaviors. For travelers from seminaries or congregations, there was a marked increase in some religious behaviors: reading the Bible for congregational group members ($p < 0.05$), praying among seminarians ($p < 0.10$), and valuing the Virgin of Guadalupe by congregational members ($p < 0.05$). As we have seen, these groups tended to orient toward the religious aspects of story and personal relationships in travel, an orientation that appears to have prompted reengagement with travelers' preexisting religious resources.

One notable group-based contrast was how travelers from different feeder organizations responded to the politicizing aspects of the trip. In the case of travelers from secular colleges, travelers were significantly less likely after the trip to see voting as the only way to have a say ($p < 0.05$) and significantly less likely to see politics as too complicated to participate in ($p < 0.05$). These travelers appear to have walked away from immersion travel with a new sense of the value of noninstitutionalized political engagement, like activism. In the case of travelers from congregations, they were significantly more likely to value the contributions of immigrants ($p < 0.05$) and to think that the United States was too strict in keeping immigrants away ($p < 0.05$). These travelers appear to have solidified their moral concern around stronger opinions toward immigration. These sorts of outcomes suggest that the organizational type of the group a participant travels with oriented the way the participant experienced change, if at all, through immersion travel.

Other Posttrip Activities

While our focus has been on a clear set of attitudinal, emotional, and behavioral outcomes across time, immersion travel can also produce new behaviors that travelers could not have done before travel. Table 13 shows other behaviors that BorderLinks travelers reported on the posttrip survey.

Nearly every BorderLinks traveler reported talking to a family member and at least one other friend about the US-Mexico border or immigration issues. Three-quarters of travelers reported having a blog or social

---

[19] Kraig Beyerlein and Mark Chaves, "The Political Activities of Religious Congregations in the United States," *Journal for the Scientific Study of Religion* 42, 3 (2003).

TABLE 13 *Reported posttrip activities*

	%
Talked to a friend about the US-Mexico border or immigration	100
Talked to a family member about the US-Mexico border or immigration	99
Mentioned trip experience and/or posted pictures on web in previous four months	71
Gave *group* presentation/talk about trip experience	68
Showed pictures of the trip in public as a *group*	54
Read a book about the US-Mexico border or immigration	50
Showed pictures of the trip in public as an *individual*	43
Gave *individual* presentation/talk about trip experience	36
Volunteered to help immigrants from Mexico, Central America, or South America in the local community	30
Wrote article as *individual* about trip experience	25
Made video or podcast with *group* to show publicly	12
Communicated with someone from Mexico who was met during the BorderLinks delegation	12

n = 68

networking site, of which 71 percent had mentioned their trip experience and/or posted pictures. The solidarity provided by being part of a group during immersion travel carried over to how travelers publicized their trips: 36 percent of travelers reported giving an individual presentation about the US-Mexico border upon return, but nearly twice as many (68 percent) reported giving a presentation as part of a group. Just under half (43 percent) of travelers reported showing pictures of the trip as an individual, but more than half (54 percent) reported doing so as a group. Video or podcast sharing of the experience was less common, but 12 percent of travelers reported doing this activity as part of a group. All of these actions appear to be in line with BorderLinks' request for travelers to "tell the story." This storytelling was most frequent with travelers' close networks (family and friends), decreasing as the storytelling reached a larger and more anonymous audience (writing an article for an organizational magazine or newsletter).

In contrast, new posttrip civic actions were less frequent. Less than 10 percent of travelers reported participating in a group-based fundraising or donation drive for immigrants in their local community. Only 30 percent of travelers had volunteered since their trip with a local community organization regarding immigration. The urgency of immigrant needs at the US-Mexico border did not translate to massive engagement with immigrant needs in travelers' home communities within six months. Even though travelers' emotions and attitudes appear to have been receptive, it is likely that most lacked preexisting organizational outlets for such behavior.

The evidence from BorderLinks supports the conclusion that transnational, personal relationships are unlikely to emerge after short-term interaction. Despite the binational partnership rhetoric of BorderLinks and the homestays during travel, only 12 percent of travelers had been in touch with anyone that they had met in Mexico. Furthermore, more than three-quarters *unsuccessfully* reported the names of the Mexican family whose home they had stayed in for a homestay (most could not remember any name). This low amount of transnational attention and connection seriously challenges immersion travel ideals about the personalizing nature of connections between trip-goers and those they meet during travel.

In summary, there is evidence of change among BorderLinks travelers. Given methodological limits and a short window of time, it appears that travelers after a BorderLinks trip were most likely to report attitudinal and emotional changes, with some behavioral changes related to consumption and, even less, to political engagement. Even if we attribute *all* of these new changes to the motivating effect of the BorderLinks experience (which is probably unreasonable), we are still left with evidence of the trip's limited effect. A BorderLinks trip prompted behavioral change for some travelers, not for all. It is far from clear that the trip experience encouraged connection with immigrants in travelers' local communities or produced a tangible connection to people in Mexico. Only a minority of travelers ended up involved in civic or political action targeted explicitly at immigration.

These results suggest a conclusion that may not be too surprising given what we have seen about the practices of BorderLinks' immersion travel and the difficulties of generating empathy. BorderLinks has produced awareness, but the inspiration to action is more hoped for than realized in practice. This type of outcome is functionally similar to the work of movement halfway houses, which nourish a seed of social awareness, often without seeing how that seed grows. For some, this could be a frustrating portion of transnational awareness raising, because it could be read as inefficient and ineffective.

But maybe this outcome is surprising in a good way. The organization, most travelers, and travelers' feeder organizations are seeking something altogether vaguer: an experience that is moralizing but open-ended in its interpretation and fulfillment. So, before closing the book on

BorderLinks' efficacy, there is one more portion of the experience that could continue to bear fruit over time: travelers' understanding of what the trip has done to them. This forces us to understand how the experience of mobilization in social action is an identity-shaping process that can slowly reconfigure goals and desires in disruptive and productive ways.[20]

THE FEEL OF IMMERSION TRAVEL AFTER IT IS OVER

After travel, BorderLinks travelers talked about their experience in three different ways. Travelers either talked about the trip as an enlightening experience of awareness, as an experience of identity recommitment, or as a radical reorientation of life. Only the last of these three themes falls within BorderLinks' preferred model of drastic transformation, but each of them accomplishes something for travelers, allowing them to talk about what the experience means. Here, I provide examples of each of these themes, categorizing Jonathan, Roland, and Kate alongside other travelers.

Theme One: Awareness

Eight months after traveling with Sojourner University, I was able to speak with Jessica about her experience. Jessica was a white female, halfway through college. She had been excited to attend the BorderLinks trip with a group of fellow students she did not know well. BorderLinks was a chance to develop new awareness about immigration, an issue she knew little about. She explained that the BorderLinks trip,

feeds into a lot of other interests. I'm continually thinking, in general terms, how to improve the world. Right before you called, I'm on page eight of something I started writing last night to figure things out. I never stop thinking about what I care about, what I want to do about it in general terms. . . . But, I don't know, I'm always thinking about stuff. . . . I'm less of a protestor. Fair Trade to me is really important. The way I buy things. I've always bought organic food. Those are daily practices I valued before [the trip], and I value even more now. [I have] renewed reasoning behind that.

---

[20] Jocelyn S. Viterna, "Pulled, Pushed, and Persuaded: Explaining Women's Mobilization into the Salvadoran Guerrilla Army," *American Journal of Sociology* 112, 1 (2006); Munson, *The Making of Pro-Life Activists*; Bearman and Stovel, "Becoming a Nazi."

As Jessica explained, the BorderLinks trip connected to behaviors and self-reflection patterns that preexisted the BorderLinks trip. She fit rather seamlessly with BorderLinks' desire to encourage growth in "awareness." Evidence from her posttrip survey shows she had increased knowledge about immigration and had also made it a priority issue to be concerned about. She increased in Bible reading and prayer. She was discerning personal behaviors that were right for her as an individual. She had increased her shopping at farmer's markets and had gone from not purchasing Fair Trade items at all to doing so regularly. According to her posttrip survey, she had also signed an immigration-related petition and joined an immigration advocacy group, though she made no mention of this activity or its meaning in our interview. Coming from a socially engaged liberal arts college, that joining may have been easily fulfilled with a student group. Either way, the survey provides some evidence that the trip may have had a crucial motivating impact on her. Did she see it this way?

During our interview, I mentioned to Jessica that I occasionally heard people describe a BorderLinks trip as changing their lives. "Would this be an accurate description for your experience?" I asked. She replied,

Changed my life? No. It has to somehow be integrated into your daily life. You can't just wake up and be different, unless you change your job. As a student, I'm still an English major. [Laughs] . . . Saying an experience changed my life is a very big thing to say for me. To me, I take that quite literally.

Jessica recalled the experience with fondness. But she gave no sign that she thought of the BorderLinks trip as anything more than an experience that provided new insight into an issue she did not know much about. As she said, the trip had given her new "reasoning" for how to connect her preexisting interests to immigration.

Ten months after the trip with St. Michael's Church, I was able to catch up with Mary. Mary was a middle-aged, white female who worked as a professional administrator for a municipal government. During the trip, Mary had asked detailed questions about particular economic and political policies along the US-Mexico border. She had known relatively little about immigration, though she was aware of how globalization had affected the manufacturing industries in her hometown. As we talked, Mary said,

I came back [home] having had my eyes opened to an issue, the issue being "illegal immigration" (that's how I'm phrasing it), that really I had paid very little attention to. I guess I came back with a heightened awareness of something that is important locally as well as in terms of federal policy. But I didn't find it a deeply emotional experience or anything like that. So [I] didn't feel any sense of, I don't know, it wasn't an emotional thing. It was much more of an intellectual realization. . . . In our own group, one of our individuals described this as a life-changing experience, so different people respond to it in different ways.

Mary used well-known phrases that other BorderLinks travelers, and other immersion travelers in general, deploy. As used by Mary, "eyes opened" is a passive metaphor, suggesting events outside herself as the source of change. It seems to be true in her case: she had been minimally aware of undocumented immigration before the trip, but that was not the case anymore. Mary seems to fit the part of BorderLinks' organizational expectation well. She had become aware of the complex connections between federal policy, undocumented immigration, and the economic condition of her hometown. But she still used a turn of phrase (illegal immigration) that was not preferred at BorderLinks. Further, she deliber- ately noted, the trip experience wasn't an "emotional thing." It did not seem to inspire her any further. Mary clearly learned a lot during her trip, but her overt reference to lack of an emotional experience signaled that it had a constrained impact on her identity and life. At the end of the interview passage, she even compared herself to someone else on her trip who seemed to have had a life-changing experience. That individual was Roland, whom we met at the beginning of the book.

Soon after I talked with Mary, I was able to interview Roland about his experience with BorderLinks. During the BorderLinks trip, I had observed Roland becoming visibly emotional, crying when talking about the extent of immigrant suffering he saw. He was also deeply bothered by evidence that his company, a multinational corporation, was exporting jobs to Mexico, jobs that might not be safe or union protected. It seemed accurate to think of Roland's trip experience as more transformative than Mary's, but did he see it that way?

When Roland described his initial return to the United States, he explained that he was confused because he had a "moving experience" but did not know how to respond to it. Roland explained that the initial feeling had subsided:

What I rationalized, I'll say rationalized, is that what I do for a living does do a lot of good things for a lot of people in the world. . . . [Recently] I felt a similar [question to what I had felt just after the trip about] "am I doing the right thing?" I haven't been to Mexico to check my company's treatment of workers when that is one of the things I said I'd do within the first three months of being back. I still haven't done that yet.

Roland's admission of having had a "moving" experience confirms what both Mary and I saw during the immersion trip. The emotional experience connected to struggle about the moral meaning of the trip appeared to make him a prime example of how immersion travel could change a traveler, similar to Saul's drastic transformational story. Yet, by the time we talked, Roland was describing how he had deliberately rationalized his return to normality. He was doing the same job but had not looked into his company's connection to factories in Mexico. By the end of the interview, Roland had shared a couple of examples of things he had tried – joining the church mission committee, attending a prayer vigil for immigrants held by a local Catholic church – but mostly he had let go of pursuing the implications of the experience in a more intensive direction.

From the longitudinal survey, we know that after the trip Roland was seeking more news about immigration, saw immigration as a more important issue, and was talking about immigration more often with friends and family. But he appears to have struggled with the ethical implication of the experience, offhandedly commenting during the interview that, "I really should be doing something more." Near the end of our interview, he simply said, "I find it way too easy to go back to my regular life and regular things." What may have begun as something more transformative had become something less so.

Theme Two: Recommitment

Between the majority of travelers that experienced a BorderLinks trip as an experience of awareness and the minority that reported a sense of radical change, there was a sizeable portion for whom the BorderLinks trip was a deepening of previous commitments. The trip refocused them as part of a lifetime commitment to social justice.

On the trip with Midwestern Theological, Barbara was a black female of middle age, pursuing a second career in ministry. She had had a lifetime of work with oppressed communities and had even traveled to Mexico for a ten-day study of politics before going with BorderLinks. During our interview ten months after her trip, Barbara commented that,

The BorderLinks trip was a continuation of my own development and understanding of people and issues and situations that we take for granted in this
country. . . . It heightened my awareness to basically how we as US citizens in
this country exploit others in regard to resources and so forth and we don't really
think about it. For me, BorderLinks was an addition to my knowledge and
understanding [on top of an earlier Mexico immersion trip] in opening my mind
up to continue those thought processes.

For Barbara, the trip provided an opportunity for some new knowledge,
but more importantly a space to recall personal priorities and discern
plans. Her posttrip survey showed she had increased in her political
liberalism and Fair Trade consumption, as well as her prayers for the
poor and her feeling of being one with the universe. Immersion travel for
Barbara appeared almost to be a spiritual practice of reconfirming a
preexisting identity. During our conversation, Barbara noted how vital
the BorderLinks trip was in this particular stage of life as she became a
new minister. She said,

The trip helped to maintain that groundedness, for me, that God has called me to
do a work. And the only way that I can respond to that call is I have to be in tune
with the realities of people. . . . For me, it's that continuous reminder, especially at
this time in my life. I'm taking a different role in ministry. It's my reminder that
I still have to reach out to meet people where they are. It's not about me imposing
my will on other people, it's about us working together to figure it out. . . . I felt
like I needed to go on the BorderLinks trip because I was still trying to find my
voice. . . . The impact wasn't that the voice wasn't there, but I needed that
confirmation that what I was hearing my voice say was where, you know, I'm
in ministry. It was like a reaffirmation for me.

This feeling of recommitment arising from a BorderLinks trip was particularly present for group leaders. A BorderLinks trip was a special time
to introduce their trip members, particularly students, to a way of life they
valued. It recommitted leaders to their own lifelong identity. Seeing the
power of the experience on their trip members also helped to rekindle
motivation for work that was often hard to sustain in unfriendly institutions or geographical places.

Eastern College's group leader, Dana, reflected on the recommitting
impact of the trip on herself. She said,

A lot of the effect of the trip for me, personally, came into sort of a larger sense
of an approach to work, approach to my scholarship, approach to broader
questions about what I want to do with the rest of my career. . . . It got me excited
about teaching again. It definitely reenergized me in terms of, I don't care what
the university thinks this [immersion learning] stuff is. I don't care that it's not
valued or that it's not the stuff you're supposed to do. You're supposed to get

peer-reviewed publications – that's how you're supposed to spend your time. Or you're supposed to get good teaching evaluations. . . . I don't care that this [immersion learning through BorderLinks] is outside of that. This is the kind of thing I *want* to do.

Jonathan, one of Dana's students, first related his BorderLinks experience as something transformative. During our interview nine months after his trip, he recalled that when he returned home from the trip,

I really felt like I had been through a very transformative experience. . . . I think it was transformative in the fact that I feel like I went through a significant experience in my week there. I felt like my eyes were opened to a lot of different things that I had never really been exposed to before.

This sounded similar to BorderLinks' ideal goal of transformation and even seemed to be backed up by some evidence from his survey that he had joined an immigration advocacy organization, had become more politically liberal, and shopped at farmer's markets more often. But these increases have to be seen against the background of his preexisting attitudes, behaviors, and interests, which were already strongly oriented toward immigration. Later in the interview he explained,

I think [the trip] kind of reaffirmed my conviction to pursue some career or volunteer work, I don't know. I'm a senior this year, so thinking about this and how I want to incorporate migrant rights and immigration and law, or whatever, incorporate that into my life trajectory.

For Jonathan, the BorderLinks experience had a confirmatory effect, making a path he had taken initial steps down become a more valued way of life. During our interview, he explained that "the trip was another subversive act from my family," as he kept piecing together a more progressive self that he had been doing ever since leaving for college. His posttrip survey showed the intensification of religious activities, as he reported more prayer, more Bible reading, more religious attendance, more belief in God, and even a sense of being "called" since the trip. For him, the recommitment achieved through immersion travel included a reconfiguration of his religious identity, away from his family's more religiously conservative roots associated with opposition to immigrants.

For these travelers, the BorderLinks trip fit into an ongoing identity project that was already well underway, sometimes for decades. The experience along the US-Mexico border reaffirmed previous life decisions but also reenergized value and lifestyle commitments. Just going on a BorderLinks trip was a way for these travelers to establish recommitment.

Theme Three: Radical Transformation

For a minority of travelers, BorderLinks' theme of radical transformation was how they understood their experience. In this interpretive theme, the BorderLinks trip was described as a profound break that shifted not only their awareness but the importance they gave to immigration-related issues. These travelers continued to consider their present and future behavior, with the moralizing character of the BorderLinks experience as a reference point.

Ten months after traveling with Midwestern Theological, I spoke with Eve about her life since BorderLinks. Eve was a white woman in her early twenties who traveled as a first-year seminary student. Before the trip, she had no involvement with immigration issues, did not speak Spanish, and was beginning to discern her future professional pathway. Eve commented to me about the trip:

The message of BorderLinks was to be aware. I think it's just made me more aware of, you know, the things I go out and buy or the positions I hold politically or faith-wise. I'm a lot more aware of the repercussions of everything that I choose to do, and it doesn't just affect me, or my family, or my friends. It affects a large range of people.

At first, it seems that Eve's case was one of raised awareness. She said so herself. Yet her words also show that the implications of the trip had become generalized within her own life, affecting her consumption, her political views, even her understanding of her faith. She envisioned how her actions affected a range of people, both near and far. And the posttrip survey she completed suggests the same: she reported increased knowledge of immigration issues, increased information-seeking about immigration, and increased saliency of immigration as important. Before the trip, she had never purchased Fair Trade goods, but she did so regularly afterward. Her anger toward politicians had increased, and she had begun to include "the poor" in her prayers regularly.

In response to what she had said about the change in her life, I asked, "Did you expect this to happen? Did you expect to be changed in this way?" Eve replied,

Not at all. I thought it would be like every other [domestic immersion] trip that I had taken. That I would experience it and come back and there would be pieces of it that I would hold onto or be passionate about, but not on such a large scale [like how I feel now]. . . . Not to come back and analyze every single aspect of my life.

The immersion trip with BorderLinks had affected her enough that she thought quite a bit about her continued response to it, even considering going to the border to become involved. Eve commented,

I definitely want to be involved in the work that is going on at the border in some way. I'm not really sure what that is or how it looks, but even if it's just in the life I choose to lead and the lifestyle choices I make if that's all I'm able to do. I do want to go back to the border and do work for a while if possible.

Eve had not relinquished a focus on the border itself, even if she felt that she did not know what to do. It is possible that the meaning of this change for Eve would eventually slow down and come to resemble Roland's. However, what is striking is that Eve continued to assert the relevance of the trip to all aspects of her life. In this case, the theme of radical transformation articulated a shift from relative ignorance toward a mode of thinking in which the border had become central.

For some travelers that reported a radical transformation, the feeling was less of confirmation but one of confusion. Kate was a white woman in her middle twenties. She was halfway through her education at Southern Seminary. Kate knew no Spanish and was reserved during much of the BorderLinks trip itself. She was, however, deeply affected by her immersion trip. She struggled to respond to the ethical, and even divine, call she heard in the experience. She recalled with me,

It's been hard to live up to how I felt like I needed to change my life [since the BorderLinks trip]. Right now I took a class [about social justice] with [the professor who was also the BorderLinks trip leader]. When he first told me about [the class] last semester when I asked him what it was . . . he said it's about looking at people who have done and heard things, and let it change their life. [These are people] who couldn't just live a normal life, but had to go on to fight for justice for others. He said the class would help us decide what area you need to work on justice for [in your life]. That's how I feel, I guess. Now that you know the things you do, you can't *not* fight for justice for other people who can't fight for themselves.

Kate had become engaged in a purposeful examination of the meaning of her life through the BorderLinks experience and a later class. But the newness of the immigration issue made this feeling of commitment scary. Our conversation continued,

KATE: I felt a loss at what to do while we were on the trip. Like, I really didn't know what to do when I got back. I thought, "Well, move to Arizona!"

GARY: Really? Why did that feel like the right thing to do for you?

KATE: I mean there's lots of things to look at doing, just wanting to be involved. Like the activism thing is all there, and it seems like you have to go to somewhere like Arizona to make a difference. To be around other people that are already caring. I guess it's easier to get on the cause of someone else than to try and start it yourself.

In Kate's description, we hear the confusion that can emerge from the experience. Without a connection to "other people that are already caring" for immigrants near the border, Kate was finding it difficult to connect the trip experience to her posttrip life. Yet, in her recounting, there was a moral imperative that kept echoing from experience. Near the end of the conversation, she commented that she was,

Trying to see how all this knowledge is going to work into my ministry and what God is calling me to do. I don't know what that looks like. . . . [I've been] asking God to show me how my concern for the border and for Hispanic immigrants can work.

Even if the direction was unclear, there was a sense of significant personal change being demanded of her.

THE CONDITIONS THAT PROMPT NARRATIVE THEMES

The three themes explored above are similar in function to the various "conversion motifs" that religious people use to understand religious change.[21] Like conversion motifs, they do not provide objective accounts of precisely *what* travelers have been doing since their trip or *how* specific behaviors have changed. Instead, these themes express how a traveler processes the meaning of an experience given the particular conditions under which the experience occurred. These themes help us to understand how differently travelers experience the meaning of an immersion experience. They also show how the same behavioral or emotional evidence from surveys can align with different types of motifs. This is not to say that the themes of change do not matter, but that they tell us something about the place of an immersion trip in a life narrative. The presence of diverse themes invites the question of why BorderLinks travelers use one theme and not another.

[21] Ines Jindra, "How Religious Content Matters in Conversion Narratives to Various Religious Groups," *Sociology of Religion* 72, 3 (2011); Lofland and Skonovd, "Conversion Motifs."

TABLE 14 *Transformation motifs and their conditions*

| Critical Reflexivity? | Previous Experience/Attention to Immigration? | |
	Yes	No
Yes	Recommitment	Awareness or Radical (if at turning point)
No	Awareness or Recommitment	Awareness

Research on both religious conversion and social movement recruitment has used the overlap between subjective accounts and objective behaviors to understand the meaning of change to individual people.[22] From my analysis of survey information, interview transcripts, and trip observations, three conditions appeared to be critical factors in influencing which motif a traveler used to make sense of an immersion travel experience. The three conditions were the traveler's previous experience with immigration issues, whether the traveler was at a biographical turning point, and whether the traveler traveled with a group leader that promoted reflexivity. Table 14 displays how the motifs of change relate to these conditions.

Some travelers may have known very little about immigration, coming to BorderLinks to learn and to have an "experience." Alternatively, travelers may have known quite a bit about immigration. Travelers that already had engaged with undocumented immigration in some way had less reason to use a narrative about radical change since they already were involved in immigration-related activities.

The second condition that influenced how travelers recalled their BorderLinks experience was a biographical turning point.[23] Biographical turning points are defined as moments of autobiographical ambiguity in which individuals must make major decisions about future courses of action. Among BorderLinks travelers, biographical turning points included the impending completion of undergraduate or seminary education, both occasions for significant decision-making about one's future life course. From interviews with travelers, and as displayed in Table 14, an

[22] David Smilde, *Reason to Believe: Cultural Agency in Latin American Evangelism* (Berkeley: University of California Press, 2007); Viterna, "Pulled, Pushed, and Persuaded."

[23] Munson, *The Making of Pro-Life Activists*.; McAdam, "Recruitment to High-Risk Activism."

identifiable turning point appeared to be necessary for a traveler to articulate a theme of radical transformation, though it was not a sufficient condition for doing so.

The feeder organizations that sent travelers to BorderLinks united these two conditions – previous experience and turning points – in different ways. For example, many congregational groups included travelers with little knowledge of immigration issues. Congregational groups were also dominated by people *not* at turning points, such as teenagers in the midst of secondary schooling and middle-aged adults in professional careers. In contrast, travelers with secular college groups tended to be quite involved with immigration before the trip, appearing to self-select into college courses that had a BorderLinks trip as part of the curriculum. Many college students were also near a graduation turning point, with the BorderLinks experience providing a taste of what life could involve as they left their schooling. Seminary and religious college groups mixed these two conditions: they tended to contain individuals with less experience regarding immigration, but, unlike the congregational groups, these travelers were often at a turning point.

The various ways these conditions came together through different types of feeder organizations suggests why some thematic accounts of the BorderLinks experience are more prevalent among some travelers than others. Travelers from secular college groups tended to be in the left column of Table 14, those from congregations, seminaries, and religious colleges in the right-hand column.

WHAT CRITICAL REFLEXIVITY DOES
AND DOES NOT LOOK LIKE

The third condition that influenced travelers' thematic recall, shown as the rows in Table 14, is what I call critical reflexivity. This is a condition of immersion travel that is only noticeable through observation. Three of the six trips I traveled with displayed this. On these trips, leaders pushed travelers to confront what they were seeing, urging them to do so by using ideological resources that problematized reality. This is the element of immersion travel that comes closest to the ideal of radical consciousness raising, which interprets reality through principles that allow for both judgment and motivation. During these moments, groups were doing two things that the BorderLinks organization itself avoided: travelers were overtly judging the moral nature of undocumented immigration and group leaders were overtly prompting this activity. This practice of questioning appeared to stretch the impact of the BorderLinks immersion experience into the future and deepen its potential meaning.

The work of critical reflexivity occurred in the spaces between official activities on the BorderLinks itinerary. It was not part of the face-to-face interactions with speakers or immigrants during immersion travel. Group leaders promoted it as a way to question the social reality at the border, not as a way to provide simple answers about it. In these groups, travelers "switched scenes," pausing the flow of immersion travel experience to analyze the experience through a shared moral framework.[24]

A short exchange, emblematic of many during Eastern College's trip, provides a good example of critical reflexivity. Toward the end of the week, the group paused to discuss the people they had interacted with in Mexico. They had spent some time talking with artists who worked along the border. One student, Terry, was contrasting that interaction with an earlier interaction she had had with an immigrant who had been deported. Terry was wondering about the efficacy of art (or anything) in the face of suffering: "I thought the art studio was depressing ... these guys are doing great things, but the immigrant we met [earlier], who was crying, is still out there. He's still there. I didn't want to move on [from him]. What can we do to help [him]?"

One of the group leaders, Dana, refused to let that tension hang silently in the air, pushing it along instead. Dana said in reply: "Isn't that what you're studying?" Terry answered Dana with some frustration: "Yes, but what we're studying is long term!" The long-term focus was becoming too much to bear for Terry. Another student, Kelly, chimed in with agreement, "It's frustrating."

These responses did not deter Dana. She reached back to themes that she had set throughout the week for the group:

You're seeing how organizations look at this [immigration issue], and individuals are the heart of organizations. You're studying how collective actors are putting in place practices to hit this question [of immigration injustice]. You know that the immediate problem is part of the [longer-term] structure. How can you resist the inside/outside feeling? What about the difference between short and long term? What is the theory and praxis [here]?

The other leader of the group, Doris, picked up where Dana left off to keep the students engaging the tensions in the trip. Doris explained that "it's a double frustration. To be one person in a huge system is paralyzing.

[24] Lichterman and Eliasoph, "Civic Action."

An organization can do this one certain thing," but that does not take away, or completely solve, the responsibility of individual actions. Tag-teaming now, Dana pushed the point further. She said, "Take the [immigrant feeding shelter we observed]. [It was helpful, but] the kids are still hungry. Is that social change? The feminist [analysis] thing is that change occurs in daily life, it's not revolution. This is one vision of 'the personal is political.'"

This sort of exchange represented how the Eastern College group leaders pushed students during the week. They not only suggested that students think about the feminist resources that they had learned; they actively engaged those methods. Notably, they did not offer simple opinions to solve the moral ambiguity the students were feeling. In fact, the responses of Dana and Doris equipped the students to treat that moral ambiguity more deeply. The professors admonished their students to "stay confused" as a way to avoid concluding prematurely.

At another point in the week, after they had observed Operation Streamline, these travelers heatedly discussed what they had just seen. They noted how Border Patrol agents thinly veiled their physical power while handling detained immigrants. They noted how gendered the courtroom was through the division of immigrants into sex groups, with the dominant presence of men in the roles of judge, lawyer, and security. As the discussion wound down, Doris connected all of the group's insights to their emerging questions about the moral meaning of what they saw:

Within spectacles [at the courthouse deportation proceedings, there] are little ways of resisting. The judge saying "have a good trip" [to migrants about to be deported] was [both] perverse and humanizing. The lawyers, many of them, shook hands and said good luck [to the migrants as the marshals took them away]. Within the horrible structure there are little efforts to resist, to be humane.

Dana reflected to the group the value of their discussion: "I'm pleased to hear you [are] engaged, as 'researchers of life.' I'm proud of you all. You're where you're supposed to be. You're like a vitamin injection [for me in my work]. I'm glad this is not another service trip [for you as you ask hard questions about what this means for your lives]." She stopped for a moment, having caught the meaning of her words, which both verified her group's approach and reinforced its orientation away from noncritical approaches. She wrapped up by saying, "It *is* great to build houses, but *this* is different. I'm glad you're here."

Southern Seminary, though from a different type of feeder organization, also displayed striking critical reflexivity. Dan, the professor leading the group, modeled to students how to use theological tools for judging what they saw during the week. A moment early in the week displayed how the group's identity, and particularly its vision of biblically rooted justice, could become part of the experience. As the group ended its short, awkward interaction with an immigrant in a house of hospitality in Mexico, Dan asked if we could say a prayer. We stared at the immigrant expectantly; he looked unsure. Our BorderLinks leader appeared caught off-guard and uncomfortable as she translated this request to the immigrant. He replied with a shy nod. We bowed our heads and Dan began,

God, bless him on his journey, that he is safe and strong, that he feels your presence and finds welcome and compassion from all. That he be treated like a guest and welcomed. May all his friends find the same hospitality. In Jesus' name, we pray. Amen.

As we drove through Mexico later that day, Dan took a moment in the van to guide discussion about what the group had just seen at the house of hospitality. He said it was "like a place to store bodies." Beyond providing such a jolting description, Dan tied the scene to some group members' prior experiences volunteering at a homeless shelter in their hometown, using the theological theme of hospitality. Dan explained that the house of hospitality was equivalent to those conservative Christian homeless shelters which charged people for the basic right to shelter and provided disgusting conditions. He called the house of hospitality, a "desecration of hospitality." In other comments throughout the week, he referred students to the idea of hospitality, pointing to the work of Dorothy Day. Many of his comments to the group urged resistance to dominant ways of dealing with immigrants. In urging resistance to systems that perpetuated social ills, he noted that, after all, "Jesus resisted borders."

Dan was not only modeling reflexivity for the students; he pushed the students to begin a personal process of reflexivity. On the last day of the BorderLinks trip, the group headed to the federal courthouse in Tucson to observe the mass processing and deportation of immigrants through Operation Streamline. Before we went inside, Dan told the group to think of what they had seen in theological terms that they could expand in their course paper:

Reflect, *think*, write theologically. You'll need to explore three theological themes to reflect on story and experience. What have you learned about the border in relation to Christian life and faith? The wall, migration, art, food, crossing borders? How have poor or marginalized people been your teachers this week? Bring theology in here, what you've been taught about regarding God, Jesus

Christ, spirit, creation, sin, redemption, Pauline themes of faith, hope, life. How have you participated in sacraments all week? What about models of ministry? Use scripture, experience ... look at creation themes like "the land belongs to all people" or "made in the image of God."

He concluded his encouragement by reminding them that "writing isn't the end of questions or concerns." Indeed, after we left the jarring scene inside the courthouse, we sat for an hour in a park discussing what we had seen. The group engaged the theological themes Dan had mentioned earlier and actively probed the ambiguity and concern they were feeling. Dan had successfully set up a pattern of reflexivity and successfully led the members in thinking through the experience using theological themes.

Missing Reflexivity

Notably, half of the groups I traveled with did *not* establish this sort of intensive questioning practice. It was not necessarily for lack of trying. In Central College's case, the lead professor tried to introduce themes of anticolonialism into the trip. The group comprised students who had been studying the theological and historical relations of the Christian religious tradition to Mexico. She encouraged the group members to use these themes as they encountered churches, paintings, monuments, and people in the course of their travel. These themes, however, did not successfully become a part of the group's interpretive experience, as the following examples suggest.

Early in the trip, we stopped in the small Mexican town of Magdalena de Kino. I walked around with a group of the students who stopped to view a memorial to the Jesuit missionary Eusebio Kino. On the walls of a small rotunda that housed his bones was a mural depicting the area in the late 1600s. The students were without their professors and jokingly pointed out the ridiculousness of indigenous people represented as naked dependents in the mural. When the group reconvened an hour later, the group leader asked the students: "What did you see?" One of the students, Jim, replied with a smile: "Colonization at its best!" The other students chuckled. There was no further discussion. The statement closed off further interpretation by providing a simple answer to what they had encountered.

The group established a distance between themselves and the ideological resources of anticolonial thinking during the week, often using short bursts of humor as a way to short-circuit more in-depth discussion. The next day, while driving into Mexico, the students were joking with each other in the van. Bob at one point simply stated, "I'd like to have an island" to live on. Other students chuckled at the silliness of the statement and one student, Susan, tried to refocus the group. She said, "On a trip like this, one of the things is to learn to live simpler." Another student, Tricia, picked up on Bob's comment and shot back: "*You* want to be the *emperor* of an island." Susan, now entering into the jocular give and take, said, "That's the colonial mentality all right!" Displaying the unease they had with the ideological resources of anticolonial criticism, Tricia looked at Bob and simply blurted out: "Colonial!" They had been doing this joking with different words during the trip and had found a new one to do it with. The students all laughed and smiled – and no reflexivity emerged.

WHAT CRITICAL REFLEXIVITY DOES FOR TRAVELERS

The pattern of reflexivity that existed with Eastern College and Southern Seminary, but not Central College, differentiated how the groups could talk, think about, and moralize the experience. The unsettledness of travel made this aspect of group culture possible, but not automatic. Groups that successfully developed a pattern of critical reflexivity engaged a coherent set of ideas and deep meanings to judge social reality and consider action.[25] This was deliberate engagement with experience through discursive resources to understand answers and imagine pathways of action.[26] The leaders of reflexive BorderLinks groups were in effect telling travelers: "Use this *system* of ideas to think about this trip." This was different from telling travelers: "Think with this *particular* interpretation for this *particular* action." The description that Pamela Oliver and Hank Johnston give of ideological thinking in social movement groups echoes this process. They write,

When people are thinking ideologically, they are explicitly concerned with a theory of society, values, and norms, and with creating a comprehensive and consistent understanding of the world. Not everyone thinks this way, and no one thinks this way all the time. But some people do some of the time, and especially in social movements.[27]

[25] Rhys H. Williams, "Religion and Political Resource: Culture or Ideology?," *Journal for the Scientific Study of Religion* 35, 4 (1996).

[26] Vanina Leschziner and Adam Isaiah Green, "Thinking about Food and Sex: Deliberate Cognition in the Routine Practices of a Field," *Sociological Theory* 31, 2 (2013).

[27] Pamela Oliver and Hank Johnston, "What a Good Idea! Ideologies and Frames in Social Movement Research," *Mobilization* 5, 1 (2000).

For Southern Seminary, biblical stories about the themes of hospitality and liberation mattered. For Eastern College, critical, feminist consciousness and analysis of power mattered. Despite very different content, one based in progressive theology and one in critical social science, both group leaders introduced guiding principles and standards of evaluation. These helped travelers to question reality and to question their responsibility to that reality.

During immersion travel, the practice of critical reflexivity gave travelers the chance to try out moral meanings that could be used *after* travel to extend the meaningful power of the trip into the future.[28] A half year or more after their immersion trip, as I interviewed travelers from groups like Eastern College and Southern Seminary, they sounded markedly engaged with the immersion trip experience compared to travelers from other groups. They expressed a commitment to allowing the experience to continue affecting their views and behaviors. They tended to recall their trips with more moral urgency concerning their current and future life courses.

In my interview with Eve, she recalled the role of her leader in pushing questions and urging her to use theological content to make sense of the experience. She recalled that during the trip,

There was a lot of reflection about God, the nature of God and the theology of the border. There was [*sic*] a lot of discussions with that type of conversation, or that mentality of trying to understand theologically what was going on and trying to explain what we were seeing.

GARY: Was that important that that happened?

EVE: Definitely. The longer I was there, the more questions I had about the nature of God and how God was working through the border and what my response should be. To be able to be in conversation with other people who were doing the same and had the same kind of questions really allowed me to express what I was feeling as well. . . . A lot of it had to do with [the trip leader], her openness in allowing us to have conversations but also to not lead us towards those conversations, but ask us the hard questions. To really make us think as well.

Jonathan's comments also suggested how his group's reflexivity process had embedded itself. He recalled that for his group,

[28] Luc Boltanksi and Laurent Thevenot, "The Sociology of Critical Capacity," *European Journal of Social Theory* 2, 3 (1999).

Our mission was to go and better understand what is happening at the border, then from that go back to our home communities and share the information with our community. I felt like we were not being passive recipients, internalizing it, but that we were also reproducing it and becoming advocates ourselves, to become better advocates for social injustices going on at the border. . . . In the first couple of days we were there, it was still very unclear, "What are we doing here? How can we legitimate our presence?" We are a bunch of privileged white people.

GARY: Was there a moment where it turned for you? Where this tension cleared up?

JONATHAN: I can't point to a moment. I feel like this was a topic we discussed extensively in our reflection time every night. Like, "What are we doing here?" How can we not just see what is happening but also bring positive change to these people's lives? And if we can't do that how can we inform the public back in [home]. . . . It was always students and professors, analyzing our role as advocates but also as academics, trying to see how those two can work together.

In contrast, Roland, the traveler from St. Michael's Church who *seemed* to be having a radically transformative experience during the trip, recalled his group's approach very differently. He appreciated the group's prayers and discussions, but,

I think [we experienced the week] fairly individually. There was a group dynamic, but I didn't feel like the group influenced a great deal the experience. I felt like each person was having an individual experience.

CONCLUSION

Change was in the air at BorderLinks. The inevitability of change was promoted by BorderLinks, and the feeder organizations that sent groups expected it. This bias toward change, which is baked into the cultural form of travel to begin with, makes it difficult to conceptualize what changes *should* occur through immersion travel and how to measure them. Detecting change among travelers is made even more difficult when immersion travel producers, like BorderLinks, suggest a range of possible changes in travelers' lives but provide little direction about the exact behavioral outcomes they expect.

In this chapter, I used different types of information to understand possible outcomes of immersion travel. As we conclude, I should recall the weakness of the data so as not to overstate the possibilities of immersion travel. The survey data only extended six months after travel; the interview data a few months beyond that. It is possible that other immigration-related behaviors emerged after travel, or it is possible any immigration-related behaviors all came to a screeching halt. We cannot know for sure. With the recent upsurge in audit studies in sociology, future research might use the multiple modes used here, for a longer period, with additional, unobtrusive ways to check on the behaviors of travelers.

Using evidence from a longitudinal survey of travelers, I observed some attitudinal and emotional shifts among BorderLinks travelers that, together, indicated the increased presence of an empathic orientation toward undocumented immigrants. The immersion travel experience of BorderLinks appeared most influential for consolidating emotions around targets of opposition and victims of injustice, for introducing new knowledge, and for prompting attitudinal liberalization about the social benefits of immigration. These results echo patterns found in other research on transnational civic engagement.[29] But, whereas previous research has often focused on generic developments in cultural tolerance or transnational concern, the most salient aspect of BorderLinks' work is its specificity. The organization has produced emotional and attitudinal outcomes tied to the specific place (the US-Mexico border) and persons (undocumented immigrants), moving transnational engagement away from abstraction.

These types of changes were in accord with BorderLinks overall goal of raising awareness through the processes we detailed in the past few chapters. The roster of talks, visits, and simulations, which produced a complex emotional palette by the end of an immersion trip, appears to have sustained that palette among many travelers a half year later.

The other half of BorderLinks' overt, but vague, goal was to inspire action. On this score, the linkage between immersion travel and immigration-oriented civic or political behaviors is weaker. We saw some evidence of new civic and political behaviors.

Some of these results varied by the origins of traveling groups. Most studies of immersion travel ignore group-level differences, making it difficult to understand how organizational processes shape the travel experience and its effects. As we have seen, changes among travelers were not evenly distributed across the diverse range of feeder organizations that sent groups to BorderLinks. One reason is that feeder organizations

---

[29] Lough et al., "The Impact of International Service on the Development of Volunteers' Intercultural Relations."; McBride et al., "International Service."

produce different group profiles, with travelers arriving with different levels of emotion and understanding. Another reason is that the feeder organizations elicit and focus on select behaviors for returned travelers. Thus, immersion travel research that fails to account for group diversity may underestimate the effect of immersion travel within a population of travelers.

Where BorderLinks travelers most excelled was in the realm of storytelling. A vast majority of travelers shared their experiences upon return, in a variety of ways. For most scholars of civic engagement and activism, this storytelling outcome might be negligible, an ephemeral side effect of travel that is too obvious to deserve much attention. The transnational terrain of distant suffering is different, however. Story, according to Boltanski, is a central element of relating to distant suffering, a mechanism for communicating information, emotion, and moral concern about people from afar that others may never meet. If we think of story as critical to transnational engagement and civil society, then BorderLinks has excelled. It has extended stories of undocumented immigration far beyond Arizona.

Of course, travelers also had their personal narratives. *All* travelers reflect on immersion travel in relation to their identity, with different levels of confusion or conclusion about the moral implications of their trips. The three thematic motifs of awareness, recommitment, and radical transformation provided diverse ways for travelers to articulate the place of immersion travel in their construction of moral selves.[30] By connecting travelers' narratives with evidence from surveys they completed, I pointed out a loose connection between talking about transformation and longitudinal evidence of change in behavior. In short, transformation talk was revealing, but not in a straightforward way. A traveler using a theme, like awareness, may have had very different posttrip changes than another traveler using the same theme. Some changes detected by the longitudinal survey did not show up during interviews. This warns us against using travelers' testimonies as the sole way to understand change through immersion travel. By the same token, survey evidence alone cannot articulate what the meaning of immersion travel experience is for travelers' lives.

A final contribution of this chapter came from evidence about the importance, and unequal presence, of critical reflexivity in groups during

[30] Allahyari, *Visions of Charity*.

travel. Travelers who used a theme of radical transformation were not necessarily the ones with the most verifiable change in behaviors. Instead, they were the ones who had little connection to undocumented immigration to begin with and, crucially, traveled with group leaders that created a trip environment of critical reflexivity. Critical reflexivity is an aspect of immersion travel that scholars and observers alike have *hoped* could be present during travel but have been skeptical of happening. As one observer of short-term mission travel has put it, the fear is that travelers will "see everything and understand nothing."[31] The evidence here demonstrates that critically reflexive engagement with new social reality *is* possible. This reflexivity, though, does not always happen. Influential group leaders and willing group members are key.[32] Notably, the immersion travel producer, BorderLinks, is *not* the proximate force for achieving critical reflexivity. BorderLinks provided the experience and set a context, but the critical experience was made by travelers together, not passively received.

Supporters of immersion travel hope for something more to come of it. Overall, the immersion travel produced by BorderLinks influenced travelers to something more. This is not to say that most, or even many, BorderLinks travelers became involved in collective efforts to address the injustices of undocumented immigration that they discovered at the border. The mechanisms of change during travel were not determinative. Travelers had different interest levels and were at different biographical moments. And many returned to environments that appeared to lack organizational opportunities to do much beyond sharing the story. We could say that the hope for transformation that precedes the beginning of immersion travel was met, months after immersion travel, by the hope that returned travelers would somehow help change the way that undocumented immigration was understood and addressed far away from the US-Mexico border. As with much related to immersion travel, it is a hope with just enough evidence to be possible.

[31] Priest and Priest, "'They See Everything, and Understand Nothing' Short-Term Mission and Service Learning."
[32] Ganz, *Why David Sometimes Wins.*

8

The Possibilities and Problems of Immersion Travel

Perhaps helping others is a form of ritual passage for global citizenship in a global age . . . These stints, or shocks, in extreme circumstances, put the lives of the privileged in relief.

Erica Bornstein[1]

We didn't have the defense of shovels, or books, or any equipment of doing good that Northerners like to arm themselves with. All we had were our ears, which are not really a very good defense."

John, after a BorderLinks trip

In the last four decades, immersion travel has been embraced by a wide array of colleges, congregations, and nonprofit organizations as the ideal vehicle for nurturing transnational civic engagement. As a result, millions of people from the United States travel abroad each year in small groups to personally engage "the globe." Built on the malleable cultural structure of international travel, immersion travel carries ideals about the ability of privileged people to bridge to distant suffering, to understand through personal contact, and to translate newfound concern into meaningful social action.

In this final chapter, like an immersion traveler returning home, I begin where I started, considering immersion travel as part of a history of transnational civic relations between geographically separated, unequal places of the globe. I then consider the implications of my analysis for

---

[1] Bornstein, *Disquieting Gifts*, pp. 17–8.

transnational civic engagement by thinking about the phenomenon of immersion travel at three levels: immersion *trip*, immersion-producing *organization*, and immersion *traveler*.

BEYOND DISTANCE TO AWARENESS

In her recent ethnography of volunteerism in India, Bornstein observed that we live in,

> a moment in history when charity has become urgent again ... We now find new forms emerging. Hybrid, transnational, cosmopolitan, and ad hoc, many of these forms are underground, undocumented, and discounted by those whose eyes focus solely on institutions.[2]

My argument has been that immersion travel is one of these new forms of transnational engagement. It is a hybrid practice, using the material structure and cultural form of travel to produce a new species of awareness and to facilitate a variety of foreign-focused civic, religious, and political ends. It is not composed of big transnational institutions but of small groups from a range of domestic institutions playing out a new pattern of engagement. In an era of dense global connection, when distant suffering is continuously portrayed by the media and many means of response exist, immersion travel is based on the surprising assumption that direct, personal engagement is a more powerful way to become aware of and address global problems.

Despite this newness and uniqueness, I have argued that immersion travel needs to be understood in a history of attempts by (some) citizens of wealthy, powerful countries to aid (some) citizens of poorer, less powerful ones. According to Boltanski's account, historically, representations of suffering traveled in one direction, and humanitarian and philanthropic responses the other.[3] But this back and forth has always been filled with problems: the need to balance information with emotion; the looming danger of apathy for foreign others who were not directly seen or heard; and the limits of adequate humanitarian response. In the opening chapter of this book, I asked whether immersion travel might provide an answer to the problems that Boltanski identified. Could immersion travel prompt understanding while avoiding the dangers of representation? Could it increase empathy, connection, and commitment? Could it motivate new action?

---

[2] Ibid., p. 18.   [3] Boltanksi, *Distant Suffering*.

I am ready to say that the answer to these questions is an unequivocal "Yes, sort of." Immersion travel can help avoid the tendency to generalize suffering and produce pity for *a people* by localizing suffering and focusing on specific individual persons. Immersion travel can also remove the difficult balancing entailed in representation processes by decreasing physical, communicative, and cultural distance. When it makes suffering directly tangible, it can decrease doubt about the factuality or urgency of suffering. Immersion travel can connect empathic concern to judgment, widening the salient "circle of sympathy" that Adam Smith and latter-day cosmopolitans hoped might occur.[4] Finally, immersion travel can produce feelings and memories that encourage new action and renewed identity.

Immersion travel activates these possibilities through three mechanisms. First, it bridges the geographic distance between the removed audience and distant suffering, creating an embodied connection that can construct authoritative knowledge and emotions. Second, it does this through the cultural form of travel, a vehicle that is laden with possibility amid the creativity of unsettledness. Third, because immersion travel is promoted by feeder organizations and deployed by immersion travel producers, numerous organizational resources exist to interpret experience, stabilize expected change, and channel individual travelers' posttravel trajectories.

But to say that immersion travel can do these things is not to say that it produces a utopian antidote for global civil society. The mechanisms of immersion travel are potentials of practice, not guarantees. They might not emerge, or they might interact with other mechanisms of social life that constrain their effects. One of the strengths of Boltanski's analysis for framing this research was his assumption that the distance to suffering could be bridged without assuming that relations would become equitable or that the moral question of action would be easily reconcilable. So, while immersion travel *can* shift some of the problems of distance, other well-known problems in civil action and altruism arise. Just because immersion travel avoids media representations does not mean that it seamlessly constructs an object of suffering that carries clear meanings. Just because immersion travel introduces face-to-face interactions does not mean that these are easy, informative, or meaningful. And just because immersion travel heightens the authenticity of emotions and embodiment does not mean these necessarily lead to anything.

---

[4] Fonna Forman-Barzilai, *Adam Smith and the Circles of Sympathy: Cosmopolitanism and Moral Theory* (New York: Cambridge University Press, 2011).

To acknowledge these realities helps with evaluating this new transnational civic practice. Supporters assume its transformative potential; detractors assume its uselessness. Both positions misunderstand the nature of altruistic action, which is never straightforward but depends on choices for individuals set in an environment of altruistic practices, vocabularies, opportunities, and structures.[5] Both positions also misunderstand the complexity of distance. Boltanski's constant emphasis on the problematic condition of distance suggests that our evaluation criteria need to shift when thinking about civic action on the global stage. Unless we keep this in mind, we reproduce the mistake that Swidler and Watkins warned about at the end of their study on AIDS altruism in Africa: "Many of the problems with the altruistic enterprise are the inevitable result of having aspirations that far exceed our knowledge or capacity, of being forced … by the imaginations of distant publics, to promise more than can possibly be delivered."[6]

THE TRIP LEVEL: CULTURAL FORM, CONTENT, AND PROCESS

Beginning in the first chapter, I argued that understanding travel was crucial to understanding an immersion trip. This seems an obvious point, but the excitement around immersion travel usually clouds this recognition. To this end, immersion travel is a new type of global travel, and a new type of transnational civic practice, one that seeks out nontourist locales, builds on local-to-local connections, embeds ideals of personalism and partnership, and encourages civic action. The category of immersion travel includes a wide array of immersion types, from short-term missions, to study abroad, to volunteer tourism. Each of these styles differs from the case study of this book, but all share some processes in common.

A Cultural Form for Liminal Unsettledness

At the core of immersion travel is a cultural form: an intentionally produced liminal time and space that becomes filled with new relations, emotions, and knowledge and is laced with expectations of transformation. The cultural form of immersion travel allows the enactment of

---

[5] Alan Wolfe, "What Is Altruism?," in *Private Action and the Public Good*, ed. Walter W. Powell and Elisabeth S. Clemens (New Haven, CT: Yale University Press, 1998).

[6] Swidler and Watkins, *A Fraught Embrace*, p. 214.

personal transformation through a global civic experience such that the "truth" of immersion travel's transformative properties is omnipresent.

But there is also a predictability to this form. I introduced the concept of guided unsettledness to account for this predictability. Cultural sociologists have provided strong theoretical reasons to suspect that culture works differently in moments of unsettledness. However, research on unsettledness has often ignored periods of subjective unsettledness, which are used by organizations and individuals for creative identity projects. Immersion travel producers, feeder organizations, and travelers alike expect transformation; the cultural structure of immersion travel provides the experiential material for it. Yet immersion travelers are not thrown into chaos during their trips. Immersion travel pulls off an amazing cultural trick: it promises travelers that they will be changed in unpredictable ways, but at the same time keeps anything too unpredictable from occurring.

Content: Activities, Meanings, and Emotions

On this shared cultural form of immersion travel, different styles of immersion trips can be built. This *content* of immersion trips is crucial in three ways.

First, different meanings of transnational connection and engagement produce different immersion travel styles of practice. As scholars of tourism well know, international travel is a vehicle that makes new relations and new experience possible, but how this happens depends on the particular practices and meanings that get deployed. There is a broad and salient diversity that gets buried beneath the concepts of "global cosmopolitanism" or "transnational engagement" in immersion travel. By focusing on variations in the content of different styles, we can understand how they anchor different visions of transnational civil society, different models of relationship, and different preferred actions.[7] For example, short-term study-abroad trips emphasize the accrual of place-based knowledge, with travelers as knowers, while short-term mission trips emphasize partnering to provide aid and receive spiritual insight, with travelers as faithful doers.

Second, close attention to the activities of immersion travel exposes the sheer array of activities used in creating a "good" travel experience.

---

[7] Lawrence Hamilton, "'Civil Society': Critique and Alternative," in *Global Civil Society and Its Limits*, ed. Gordon Laxer and Sandra Halperin (New York: Palgrave Macmillan, 2003); Adler Jr. and Offutt, "The Gift Economy of Direct Transnational Civic Action."

Immersion trips draw from a set range of activities, including visits, talks, and simulations, to create objects of moral concern. These are all "bridging activities," formal activities devised to bridge the cultural distance between travelers and foreign hosts.[8] In doing this, activities navigate between the realms of heart knowledge and head knowledge, connecting emotions to information through stories and interaction. This experiential richness is unlikely to be accomplished by less-intensive or shorter awareness-raising strategies. Immersion travel is not a simple occasion of intercultural contact, no matter what travelers' accounts and their pictures show.[9]

Third, by looking more closely at what travelers did during a trip, what they liked to do, and what they felt while doing it, I argued that the content of immersion travel could help us to understand the emotional outcomes of trips. The "innards" of immersion travel at BorderLinks revealed the presence of mechanisms, like framing, emotional tutoring, and role modeling, that scholars of collective action have identified as potentially powerful for generating motivation and commitment.[10] Some activities, like talks by local activists, were especially crucial for producing anger. Other activities, like talks with state agents, were used for increasing knowledge while providing a sense of discovery. And still others, like viewing sites of suffering and meeting immigrants face to face, produced feelings of sorrow. Of significant note, many of these activities were outside the direct control of the immersion trip producer, dependent on outsiders interacting with travelers.

This collection of activities makes evident that immersion travel overdetermines emotional and moral experience. The panoply of content is difficult to disentangle but reveals that one reason immersion travel is viewed as successful is that it contains so many activities that travelers can respond to. Activities may even create an empathic "interaction effect," increasing the feel of authenticity and connection in a way that a single activity would not. For example, it is doubtful that travelers would abide the absence of face-to-face interaction during foreign travel, but other

---

[8] Kelner, *Tours That Bind.*

[9] Marshall Sahlins, *Islands of History* (Chicago: University of Chicago Press, 1985); Probasco, "Prayer, Patronage, and Personal Agency in Nicaraguan Accounts of Receiving International Aid."; Hutnyk, *The Rumour of Calcutta.*

[10] Benford and Snow, "Framing Processes."; Jasper, *The Art of Moral Protest*; Jeff Goodwin, James M. Jasper, and Francesca Polletta, *Passionate Politics: Emotions and Social Movements* (Chicago: University of Chicago Press, 2001).

activities likely heighten the meaning of that interaction. Cleary, an immersion trip is a complicated package in more ways than one.

THE ORGANIZATIONAL LEVEL: PRODUCING EMPATHY AND IMMERSION COSMOPOLITANISM THROUGH RELIGION

Until recently, the mundane organizational work of transnational civic engagement had gone missing in sociology.[11] For a social scientific understanding of transnational civic action, organizational processes are central.[12]

The organization presented here, BorderLinks, provided an ideal case for understanding the organizational work of an immersion travel producer. Here, I highlight what this case reveals about how organizations produce transnational engagement, how they elicit transnational empathy, and how the progressive religion that some sustain contributes to transnational civic life.

Organizational Work and Unintended Consequences

Drawing from research on organizations and social movements, I suggested that immersion travel producers are similar to movement halfway houses.[13] Travelers come from somewhere and are moving to somewhere, but cannot get there through their feeder organizations alone. This metaphor reminds us that immersion travel is a practice that "moves" participants but needs an organizational structure to do so. Immersion travel producers bridge geographic distance, institutional boundaries, and meanings.

But organizations face many challenges in doing this work month after month, for traveler after traveler. The bridging is not straightforward

---

[11] Krause, *The Good Project*; Mostafanezhad, *Volunteer Tourism*; Bornstein, "Child Sponsorship, Evangelism, and Belonging in the World of World Vision Zimbabwe."; Susan Cotts Watkins, Ann Swidler, and Thomas Hannan, "Outsourcing Social Transformation: Development NGOs as Organizations," *Annual Review of Sociology* 38, 1 (2012).

[12] Wolfe, "What Is Altruism?"; Lichterman and Eliasoph, "Civic Action."

[13] Morris, *Origins of the Civil Rights Movement*.

because of real organizational pressures related to institutional and resource hybridity. BorderLinks tacked between direct contact with the suffering "other" and a "balanced" representation of numerous voices that might sway or confuse travelers. Its clientele of feeder organizations expected both. But to present both, BorderLinks was formally neutral, promoting conversational rules that constrained engagement, avoided the discussion of politics, and tended to focus on the emotions of future action. These outcomes should attune us to the way that immersion travel producers can get caught in the middle. For supporters that see civic engagement as a way to social or political change, this organizational muddling is an important reality to understand. It suggests that immersion travel producers are adept at getting "halfway," but that *other* civic or social movement organizations are important for going further.

Empathy Production

In Chapter 5, I introduced the concept of empathy strategies. This concept arose from a perplexing observation: the much-hyped face-to-face interactions of immersion travel did not live up to the hype when observed in the natural flow of interaction. I used this, frankly, surprising discovery as a chance to understand what travel producers were trying to achieve and how they went about achieving it. Empathy strategies are the interactive templates that organizations use to establish a relationship with suffering persons by producing an emotional sense of suffering and the perspective taking of those who suffer. A relational empathy strategy, like face-to-face interaction, involved communicative interaction, while a mimetic empathy strategy simulated the conditions of suffering.

One advantage of conceptualizing organizational work this way was that it made sense of the real problems of face-to-face contact. Travelers expect such interactions and usually value them months later, but their emotional meaning is not immediately solidified due to the many fractures that arise in interaction. The meaning of these interactions comes from organizational framing and small group interpretation, not just the interactions themselves. The interactions end up being symbolically important, evidence that personal engagement occurred, which provided a memory for travelers of individuated social suffering. If we were to expect deep understanding or close bonding to come out of temporary interactions across economic inequality and cultural difference, we would seem to stretch the ideals of cosmopolitanism too far in actual practice.

Another advantage of observing the organizational work of empathy formation was showing the surprising efficacy of a mimetic strategy, like a hike in the desert, to produce a robust and long-lived sense of empathy. This strategy was especially adept at eliciting untroubled emotions, heart knowledge, and moral conclusions. To the best of my knowledge, this is the first theorization of simulation in the work of transnational awareness raising, despite the presence of simulation activity in other organizational settings. Part of the power of immersion travel is its ability to include simulations of distant suffering near to the actual contexts of suffering. If future research supports this conclusion, it should provoke a theorization of simulation activity in awareness raising, contrasting it with the relational and informational activities that are most well known. Mimetic strategies could even come to displace or at least buttress relational strategies in immersion travel as transnational civic organizations invest in and promote technology that simulates others' living conditions.

Progressive Religious Action on the Transnational Stage

A distinctive feature of the case in this book was its progressive, religious identity. BorderLinks exemplified the paradox that progressive, religious organizations often must resolve in American civic life, which is dominated by images of dogmatic, conservative religion. The organization had to articulate a distinct religious identity of "us," while displaying spiritual inclusivity about the breadth of the "us."[14] BorderLinks' way of being religious by *also being progressive* showed the distinctive role that progressive religion can have in transnational civic action, bridging to many types of organizations and people.

Religion was present through the history of the organization; the organization's connections to progressive, religious individuals and organizations; its "deep story" of social transformation tied to personal transformation; and its pedagogical practices of emphasizing the truth power of visible suffering heard from "real people." BorderLinks' embrace of the See-Judge-Act model was not overtly religious, despite the model's connection to a history of religious, political action. This model has resonated with the trend of experiential education among religious and nonreligious higher education institutions alike. Border-Links' use of a testimonial economy that prioritized suffering persons

---

[14] Edles, "Contemporary Progressive Christianity and Its Symbolic Ramifications."

provided an implicit way of focusing travelers on the preferred authority of "real" people. And while the organization's focus on personal transformation was religious in origin, it could be engaged by a religiously diverse set of travelers.

Overall, what the organization did was produce action that was religious and moral without being exclusive. Travelers could – and some did – pick up the religious roots and meanings of authoritative suffering and transformative story, but they did not have to consider them as religious. These aspects of BorderLinks' organizational identity suggest the distinct mechanisms that progressive religion can contribute to transnational engagement. Progressive, religious organizations in the transnational sphere try to avoid the mistake, clearly articulated in Rick's story, of seeking change in the other. We might think of them as producing an "immersion cosmopolitanism" that aims to boomerang back to influence the United States, an intended consequence like the unintended effects of some missionaries a century ago.[15]

TRAVELERS: GROUP PROCESSES AND CULTURE
IN TRANSFORMATION

To understand individual immersion travelers requires understanding an array of forces that make enacting immersion travel possible and shape its outcomes. The organizational nexus that pushes travelers into immersion travel means that invisible processes of self-selection have occurred long before the moment of travel.

Institutional Origins and Group Styles

During travel, small group processes are crucial. Group styles were an obvious way that travelers were embedded in group processes. The groups that I traveled with from religious feeder organizations enacted a story-building style that foregrounded emotional knowledge, trusted immigrant stories, and allowed individual immigrant accounts to stand in for the whole of immigration complexity. Meanwhile, secular college groups employed a sleuthing style that downplayed emotions, questioned the authenticity of all testimonies, and sought out numerous voices from

---

[15] Hollinger, *Protestants Abroad*; Keck and Sikkink, *Activists beyond Borders*.

"both sides" of the immigration debate. The variance in group styles made clear that the organizational roots of travelers mattered for travelers' understandings and feelings. During immersion travel, a transformation is in the offing, but its tenor is shaped by the feeder organizations that encourage the experience to begin with.

Critical Reflexivity in Transnational Engagement

Traveling groups were also crucial for developing critical reflexivity, the intensive questioning routines that were modeled by group leaders and drew on ideological resources connected to feeder organizations. This condition appeared necessary for the radical change articulated by some travelers. This evidence may raise hopes about the transformative potential of immersion travel, though two realities temper such hope. First, creative reflexivity was produced by groups – *not* the BorderLinks organization. Any group could not just go through the motions of immersion travel and expect to have such an experience. Second, even if travelers felt radically transformed, they were often confused about what, if anything, they could do to fulfill the moral obligation they felt. The world-questioning change that many immersion trip supporters desire appears as a possibility, but the connection between that existential state and action is often fuzzy in practice.[16]

Inspiring Action?

For many readers, the pragmatic question all along has been whether immersion travel works on individuals. Chapter 7 argued that immersion travel resides in a hazy space in which everyone expects that it *will* work *somehow*. Many studies of immersion travel overly focus on travelers' subjective accounts to demonstrate change. That is a mistake, as nearly all travelers use subjective accounts that emphasize the usefulness of travel experience.[17]

Through a longitudinal survey design, I showed that travelers at BorderLinks evidenced some new knowledge about the policy causes of

---

[16] Richard Kiely, "A Chameleon with a Complex: Searching for Transformation in International Service-Learning," *Michigan Journal of Community Service Learning* 10, 2 (2004).

[17] Kelner, *Tours That Bind*; Smelser, *The Odyssey Experience*.

immigration, stronger emotions related to immigrants and state agents, shifts in proimmigrant attitudes, and even new consumption and political behaviors. While other immersion travel research has shown generalized effects of immersion travel, my evidence suggests how it can be connected to particular, distant social problems. BorderLinks was focused on undocumented immigration; this specific focus appears to have "worked."

Should we be underwhelmed or impressed by these outcomes? This is the rub for transnational civic engagement that is trying to get privileged people from the Global North to act on behalf of less powerful people in the Global South. Beyond questions of power and authenticity in interaction is the fundamental question of what specific actions people could take from afar that would be helpful to change distant suffering. Here, it is helpful to contrast immersion travel to other modes of transnational civic engagement. One way to understand INGOs and humanitarian organizations, despite all their faults, is as well-institutionalized bodies of resources, motivations, and practices that accomplish clear actions in specific places to address distant suffering.[18] By contrast, immersion travel producers occupy a different niche in the world of transnational civic engagement. Organizations like BorderLinks appear adept at producing awareness, but much weaker at mobilizing transnational engagement that outlasts the travel experience itself. For an immersion travel producer like BorderLinks, the traveler's question of, "What should I do?" is difficult to answer. But if we think of immersion travel producers as similar to movement halfway houses, which work to deepen the motivation of persons who one day might support social action in some way, then BorderLinks appears more successful as an organization.

Even if BorderLinks' former travelers had little or no connection to organized efforts to address undocumented immigration, they had become more "aware." If we see immersion travelers as filling out the social role that Boltanski calls "spectator," then relaying their awareness is a crucial responsibility connected to that role. Having seen distant suffering, at the very least, a traveler should "maintain an orientation towards action, a disposition to act, even if this is only by speaking out in support of the unfortunate."[19] For Boltanski, responsible action is

---

[18] Krause, *The Good Project.*   [19] Boltankski, *Distant Suffering,* p. 153.

authentic if it is vocal, has some emotional or personal cost, and if it could conceivably be seen as prompting other action in the future. The storytelling that nearly all travelers do *is* a form of action; not a perfect solution, but a pragmatic step on a scale of increasingly powerful options. In the words of Lilie Chouliaraki, we might see this result as an example of "agonistic solidarity," a condition in which the concerns and voices of actual distant others are made present alongside the attempts – successful or not – of acting on their behalf.[20]

Can BorderLinks, its travelers, and the rest of us hope for something even more? Research based on the retrospective recollections of immersion travelers suggests that long-term effects of immersion travel are possible.[21] I suggest that these potential long-term effects be seen as occurring at a distinct register, one that is slow, generalized toward "the globe," and disconnected from close relations with distant people.

The effect of immersion travel could be similar to how the Freedom Summer experience became a prism through which participants peered as they made a host of decisions in the ensuing decades of their lives.[22] For such results, we must wait, but it is possible that some BorderLinks travelers may continue to embrace "new images of the world and of themselves ... [moving] towards an alternative vision of America and themselves."[23] Along the way, we should expect that some travelers will develop immersion travel "careers."[24] Trip participation is itself a behavior that signals transnational civic commitment; more trip participation might signal more awareness, more engagement. However, we should be suspicious of immersion travel participation as *prima facie* evidence of global commitment or knowledge. Travel experience may just be experience at the cost of global others.[25] As Judith Lasker, echoing the critique of Ivan Illich from decades earlier, writes,

[20] Chouliaraki, *The Ironic Spectator*, p. 194.
[21] Probasco, "Giving Time, Not Money."; Nepstad and Smith, "Rethinking Recruitment to High-Risk/Cost Activism: The Case of Nicaragua Exchange."; Wearing, *Volunteer Tourism*.
[22] McAdam, *Freedom Summer*; McAdam, "The Biographical Consequences of Activism."
[23] McAdam, *Freedom Summer*, p. 132.
[24] Howard S Becker, *Outsiders* (Simon and Schuster, 2008).
[25] Bornstein, "Volunteer Experience."; Smith, "International Volunteer Tourism as (De) Commodified Moral Consumption."

Those who defend [immersion] trips as transformative in positive ways for the volunteers and as therefore creating future advocates for the poor, even if they do not contribute anything to the host community in the short run, bear a responsibility to show that this is truly the case.[26]

NOTES ON PRODUCING EMPATHY AND ENGAGEMENT BEYOND US BORDERS

How might immersion travel become better at meeting its ideals of transnational empathy and engagement? Here, I offer some synthetic suggestions for those engaged in immersion travel based on my observations and interpretations at BorderLinks.

Doing "nothing" can be good. The navigation of material inequality and reciprocity in transnational interaction is incredibly complicated. By doing nothing, travelers within an organization like BorderLinks are forced to listen to foreign perspectives and see local processes they might otherwise ignore. Doing nothing requires a suspension of immediate response, opening discursive space to hear local needs and observe local initiatives. At the very least, travelers should understand that their presence alone does *something*. The work that foreign communities and persons do to host them and produce a good experience is costly and deserves compensation.[27] This economic relation is often invisible to travelers who see one week of a testimonial economy and have romantic visions of equitable, freely given relationships. Exposing and discussing this material basis of transnational interaction reveals that, even when "nothing" is occurring, something is.

But giving can be good, too. Most immersion travel groups won't "do nothing." In this case, giving should proceed, lest relationships transform into the "sustainability mantra ... [that] turns out to rest on a powerful moral ethic that embraces self-reliance and abhors dependency."[28] The various types of resource giving – donations, volunteer labor, medical services, teaching – should occur at the group level to avoid the dependencies that can arise in unequal gift exchanges. Group leaders are able to devise and enforce rules and rituals that help prevent

---

[26] Lasker, *Hoping to Help*, p. 113.
[27] Smith, "International Volunteer Tourism as (De) Commodified Moral Consumption."
[28] Swidler and Watkins, *A Fraught Embrace*, pp. 202–3.

individual coercion or shame.[29] To encourage partnerships, new frames for transnational giving might be introduced; for example, thinking of gifts as civic remittances.[30] Finally, travelers should be aware that during their travel not all foreign persons are involved or invested in immersion travelers' presence. From people outside the transnational relationship, "impulsive philanthropy" is likely to be elicited.[31] Organizations will differ in their opinions about this, but such giving can provide useful, immediate resources and an opportunity to query the social relations of transnational inequality.

Brokers are crucial. Travelers might be drawn to foreign locales by personal connections and avoid using brokers, but that approach has the possibility of overwhelming the staff of local organizations and displacing local goals. Binational, locally rooted brokering organizations are the best option for creating immersion travel that produces durable connections, promotes local voices, and provides sustainable resources for local communities. Immersion travel producers should be more transparent about the political economy of producing good travel experiences and authentic interactions over and over again, for wave after wave of traveling groups.[32] This transparency can encourage a better sense of the tenuous structures that undergird transnational civic engagement.

Articulate identity connections. Immersion travel producers, especially those like BorderLinks, should provide an account of the roots and motivations that animated their founding and their current work. The "deep stories" that producers tell travelers are not primarily about relaying historical accuracy, but initiating travelers into new narratives and meanings that make transformation possible. There are sociological reasons that progressive, religious organizations are "quiet," but it seems a public good at this point in American life to vocalize an alternative history of connection between religion and transnational civic engagement.[33]

Beware of face-to-face interaction. It is helpful to recall that face-to-face interactions fulfill ideals of personalism but are less important for relaying clear information and coherent frames. Random, foreign "others" should not be relied upon or expected to represent their

[29] Adler Jr. and Offutt, "The Gift Economy of Direct Transnational Civic Action."
[30] Adler Jr. and Ruiz, "The Immigrant Effect."
[31] Bornstein, "The Impulse of Philanthropy."
[32] Smith, "International Volunteer Tourism as (De) Commodified Moral Consumption."
[33] Philip Gorski, *American Covenant: A History of Civil Religion from the Puritans to the Present* (Princeton University Press, 2017).

positions of suffering in a way that meets standards of factuality and clarity. The powerful ideal of contact must be seen as related to specific conditions and abilities.[34] Face-to-face interaction that occurs at the group level (e.g., one teller to many listeners) is likely the best way to proceed, since it minimizes individual coercion and multiple misunderstandings. To increase the impact of such testimonies beyond sorrow, well-organized representation of suffering is needed. This does not mean that distant sufferers should lose their voice in communicating their reality to immersion travelers. It does mean, though, that some people might be better at narrating and that some stories may be better than others for articulating social structural realities. Brokers should consider employing voices that are cohesive, comprehensive, and motivational. For generating moral anger, activists are especially crucial.

Try simulation. Educators in many disciplines and settings are well aware of the power of simulation. Though simulations run the risk of simplifying reality and obscuring individuality, they are sometimes able to achieve empathic goals, part of what I have called mimetic empathy strategies. The affective side of motivation and learning has often been subsumed under educators' and activists' focus on effective discourse and accurate information.[35] Simulation provides a way to prompt embodied learning and, if it fails, is less costly to foreign partners or foreign individuals.

Generate criticism. If immersion travel supporters hope to problematize the causes of distant suffering, they must nurture critical reflexivity during travel. This does not come naturally and is not equivalent to having a seminar conversation where everyone shares their ideas or feelings. Criticism entails the assumption of a different future that can be achieved through constant questioning and the use of moral language or ideological discourse. Travelers, particularly young travelers, need an invitation into the sort of ongoing social analysis that has been key to democratic reformers and transnational activists alike.[36] Group leaders are especially important for displaying and encouraging this process.

[34] Katerina Manevska, Peter Achterberg, and Dick Houtman, "Why There Is Less Supportive Evidence for Contact Theory Than They Say There Is: A Quantitative Cultural-Sociological Critique," *American Journal of Cultural Sociology* (2017).

[35] Kiely, "A Transformative Learning Model for Service-Learning."

[36] Eliasoph, *The Politics of Volunteering*; Smith, "Transnational Processes and Movements"; Isaac Reed and Jeffrey Alexander, *Culture, Society, and Democracy: The Interpretive Approach* (Boulder, CO: Paradigm Publishers, 2007).

See global processes through places. Feeder organizations, such as colleges that send lots of immersion trips all over the globe, need to consider the weakness of such a generic approach. It is tailored to the interests of travelers but can make the world into a treasure hunt of different cultures. "Scatter-shot" travel may promote humanistic commonality without interrogating the structural processes of global financial policy, migration, national debt, or systemic violence that can influence any place. To push against this, feeder organizations – or a network of feeder organizations – should consider developing an educational framework that all their travelers could use to understand immersion travel. This would go behind "cultural sensitivity" training, moving travelers away from the social homogeneity and individual particularism that often get used for explaining social problems in distant places. For example, travelers could learn about global political or economic processes rooted in US policy, around which travelers might wield real power. It is useful to note that some high-profile voices in the arena of global civic engagement, exemplified by Paul Farmer's recent embrace of liberation theology, have begun to piece together frames of understanding that can make critical sense of broad pieces of globalization.[37]

Force travelers beyond transformation talk and good stories. Vocabularies of transformation ("My eyes were opened," "I'm more aware") are important and can be meaningful for future action, but they should not be the end point of posttravel life. Travelers need to have transformation talk queried, not in order to produce guilt but to clarify the inherent inequalities of transnational relations. They should be encouraged to tell stories of failure and doubt, while also displaying their commitment borne of experience. Feeder organizations need to provide travelers with opportunities to tell personal stories to a public and to practice confronting the conflict they encounter. They need to practice sharing both "heart" and "head/book" knowledge in ways that provide clear conclusions for others to hear so that they do not retreat to the safety of "my experience" and "my opinion" when challenged.

Lower expectations of what can be accomplished. The expectations placed on immersion travel are symptomatic of the pressures currently placed on higher education, with big goals that must be evaluated by

---

[37] Michael Griffin and Jennie Weiss Block, *In the Company of the Poor: Conversations with Dr. Paul Farmer and Fr. Gustavo Gutiérrez* (Maryknoll, NY: Orbis Books, 2013).

metrics that show the accomplishment of clear outcomes. By contrast, travelers and feeder organizations should not expect radical personal or social change. The "development" history of the Global South is full of the unrealistic, inappropriate, quick-fix visions of outsiders. There are dangers to the romanticization of localism, but working with transnational partners to meet basic needs is more immediately relevant than dreaming up big goals and new solutions.

Raise local possibilities. The phrases "global cosmopolitanism" and "global citizenship" surely catch an important ideal, but the average immersion traveler is likely most politically effective at the local and national levels.[38] The weakest link in the posttrip action sequence will always be the opportunities for collective action beyond the trip. Feeder organizations need to do much more to produce clear guidance to travelers about how to "be like Rick" and focus on domestic action that can influence transnational life.

A FINAL STOP

In drawing attention to immersion travel, my goal has been to understand the ideals, practices, and realities of a hugely popular transnational civic practice. Immersion travel occurs in many styles with some, like the type observed here, showing real possibilities for generating awareness, concern, and motivation to address distant suffering. By using a best-case-scenario immersion travel producer, I have made the case that immersion travel, like other civic engagement practices, sets a strong context for the enactment of ideals but, given basic cultural processes, inequalities, and sources of variation, will necessarily fall short of meeting those ideals. This pragmatic criticism is not given from an assumption that perfected civic action is possible. To the contrary, and as the history of transnational civic engagement shows, such action is always indeterminate and imperfect due to the real challenges of distant representation and coordination, not to mention the power of social forces that create and sustain obdurate social suffering.

The species of awareness that immersion travel can produce is a half step toward grander civic hopes of what might come of new commitment.

[38] Laxer and Halperin, *Global Civil Society and Its Limits.*

While we continue to have important scholarly arguments about historical changes in global empathy, and to investigate the sociological conditions that make transnational engagement more or less useful, immersion travelers will continue to return from their global encounters with stories to tell about the suffering they have seen. And, in the case of the US-Mexico border, while they tell those stories, humans will be crossing the desert, creating new transnational connections themselves. The question of this book has been whether and how privileged immersion travelers might have something to do with such people and their sufferings. They do, even if they don't know what to do about it.

Methodological Appendix

Immersion travel can be a difficult social phenomenon to study. Travelers share membership in their home organizations, but their traveling group is not usually long-lasting before or after the trip. The travel experience itself is all-encompassing, but only for a week. While short of being a total institution, immersion trips entail barriers and processes that constrain travelers and homogenize experience.[1] Once a group gets to the airport of their hometown, they are together for days, with limited personal space, on a schedule outside of their control. Albeit temporary and voluntary, this can produce a powerful feeling of transformation. It can also make it difficult to study.

To address this complexity, I used a number of methods, including pretrip surveys, evaluation surveys on the last day of travel, posttrip surveys months after travel, participant observation, organizational records review, and in-depth interviews with travelers, staff members, and other organizations. In this appendix, I review these methods, with special attention given to their intersection and their weaknesses. All research methods were approved by the Institutional Research Board at the University of Arizona.

ONE CASE WITH MANY CASES

BorderLinks had dozens of traveling groups that traveled through it each year. The groups could be roughly categorized into four types of feeder

[1] Erving Goffman, *Asylums: Essays on the Social Situation of Mental Patients and Other Inmates* (New York: Anchor Books, 1961).

TABLE A1 *Description of groups with weeklong ethnographic observation*

Group Name	Feeder Organization	Salient Social Characteristics
Southern Seminary	Mainline Protestant Seminary	Racial and age diversity Little Spanish ability Mixed travel experience
Sojourner University	Secular College	Racial and international diversity Mixed Spanish ability Extensive travel experience
Central College	Mainline Protestant College	Age diversity Mixed Spanish ability Mixed travel experience
Eastern College	Secular College	Racial and age diversity Low racial diversity Spanish proficiency
St. Michael's Church	Mainline Protestant Congregation	Middle-aged, white Little Spanish ability Extensive travel experience
Midwest Theological Seminary	Mainline Protestant Seminary	Low race and age diversity Little Spanish ability Mixed travel experience

organizations: religious colleges, secular colleges, seminaries or religious professional associations, and congregations. In effect, BorderLinks had many cases within a case. By observing different groups through a nearly identical trip experience, I was able to examine how group processes produced divergent understandings of the same experience. I participated in six BorderLinks trips.[2] The six groups I traveled with were selected to represent feeder organization diversity. Table A1 shows the breakdown of the groups I traveled with, comprising forty-four participants. (All the group names have been changed.)

[2] The names of all groups and most individuals are aliases. A few persons representing organizations (BorderLinks, Sierra Club) and one traveler requested that their names be used. In a few instances, personal descriptions of occupation or gender have been altered to prevent a breach of anonymity.

Between six and ten months after each trip, I attempted to interview every traveler. I was able to interview thirty-six of the forty-four people I traveled with. During the interviews, I asked travelers to describe their experience of returning home after the BorderLinks trip, to discuss the activities they remembered from the trip, to comment on whose "voice" they trusted in immigration debates, to reflect on difficulties during the trip, and to explain how, if at all, this affected them.

I also interviewed nine BorderLinks staff members from both sides of the border. During these semistructured interviews that lasted forty-five to ninety minutes, I asked about staff members' backgrounds, the experience of trip guiding, organizational processes, and their personal civic and political activities. I conducted in-depth interviews with six community partners, the various activists, government officials, and other interlocutors whom travelers listened to during their travel. In these interviews, I sought to understand what *they* thought of BorderLinks, why they spent their time and energy speaking with groups, what sorts of messages they hoped to leave with travelers, and what they thought of this form of transnational civic action. Included in these six interviews were two federal government employees (a federal defense attorney representing immigrants in Operation Streamline and an Immigration and Customs Enforcement agent) and four local leaders representing nonprofit organizations or humanitarian aid groups. I also conducted three interviews with the leaders of groups that planned a BorderLinks trip, then canceled.

EPISODIC ETHNOGRAPHY

Before participating in an immersion trip, a BorderLinks staff member first approached the group's leader about my participation. I then communicated with the group leader about the project, who, in turn, briefed travelers. Travelers were able to opt out of participation in the research, as a group or individually. One group opted out; no individual travelers did.

I met travelers on the first day of their trip and said goodbye on the last. As a consequence, I had to enter the field site each time I traveled with a group. I would travel to the airport with the BorderLinks staff member in the organization's van to be present at the very first moment of the group's arrival in Arizona. I would also see them off at the airport at the end of the trip. In between, I tried as much as possible to be a part of the group. This meant downplaying my knowledge about the border and moderate Spanish language ability to avoid being seen as a source of information or a BorderLinks staff member. Travelers were usually as curious about me as I was about them. When groups asked what I was studying, I tried to explain without using sociological terms and without saying what my theoretical expectations were of what would happen during the trip or after. A few groups were especially interested in knowing how *other* types of groups I traveled with encountered the experience. To their exasperation, I usually tried to turn the question around, asking what *they* thought the differences would be. This proved quite fruitful.

Unlike other ethnographic settings, there was not much break or downtime during a trip to exit the field to write down observations and thoughts. It was up to seven straight days with about seven hours of sleep a night in an open-air setting. This meant I had to write observations as quickly as possible during each day. With some groups, this was easy, since they brought pens and notebooks to record their own experience. As they brought out their notebooks, so did I. With other groups, notebooks were not present. On these trips, my sense was that my notebook would cue interest, so I would go to the bathroom or disappear into side rooms. There, I removed the small pen and notebook from my jeans pocket and wrote down as much as possible. I used a numbering system to disguise who the notes were about, just in case someone took a peek. Only twice was I asked a version of, "What are you writing in the notebook?" And both times, I replied, "What I see and hear." Which was true. At night, I would fill out my observations and observe emerging patterns by cellphone light or flashlight, often buried under a sleeping bag in a room full of bunks. Throughout the book, quotations from ethnographic settings are either written transcripts of what people said or reconstructions from notes taken soon afterward.

At times it was difficult to be just a participant, particularly when the educator and activist in me wanted to urge a group along or clarify crucial political points. Other times, this role was morally challenging. For example, Southern Seminary had a difficult desert hike that involved a panic attack for Kate. She was walking slowly at the far rear of the group in the minutes prior to the attack. Unlike the other group members who had plowed up the trail while ignoring this person's obvious difficulty, I was the only group member walking alongside Kate. A Mexican Border-Links staff member was behind us, so I was able to tell her, in Spanish, what was happening with Kate, who was speaking in English. The hike was paused, then cut short. This approach surfaced the issue to the group without appearing to judge the other members. The group eventually recovered from this breach and even used the incident to deepen dangerous meanings of the desert. I experienced a less dangerous but more emotionally painful moment with Central College. That group had intragroup tension that worsened during the week. By the final evening, as I sat in BorderLinks' kitchen area, a few group members shared with me their distaste for other members of the group. I did not elicit these comments, but just listened. Both of these experiences, and others, reaffirmed my focus on group processes.

There were two aspects of my own identity that I attempted to hide from public knowledge: my vegetarianism and my Catholicism.[3] Vegetarianism is not only an unfamiliar practice for some, but is also difficult to accommodate at many places along the US-Mexico border. With some groups, this hiding was not necessary if they included vocal vegetarian members who sought food accommodations. With other groups that had no vegetarians, my dietary preferences would have brought undue attention. On these trips, I ate whatever was served. Apparently, my ethical reasons for vegetarianism were not absolute. This was a helpful reminder, to me, of the situational conditions that can produce loose connections between morally salient ideals and behaviors.

Identifying a Catholic by looks or speech alone is hard. Omar McRoberts has argued that the religious backgrounds of ethnographers should not be turned off since, like other commitments of sociologists, they can inform the understanding of religious organizations and persons.[4] However, I did quiet mine. Since none of the groups I traveled with were from Catholic institutions, I wanted to allow any symbolic differentiation activity by groups to emerge *sui generis*. It did on a number of occasions, some of which became part of my analysis. I may have missed one of the most enjoyable and enlightening moments of my research if the St. Michael's Church group had known I was Catholic. During our trip, we were to spend an evening sleeping on the hard linoleum floor of a Mexican Catholic school. When we entered the room to set up our bedding, the only other object in the room was a four-foot-tall painting of a serious-looking Pope John Paul II that leaned against the wall. After some funny comments about the Pope watching over us while we slept, one group member jokingly placed it right next to their pastor's pillow

---

[3] Technically, I am a pescatarian and a cradle Catholic with a progressive orientation.

[4] "Beyond *Mysterium Tremendum*: Thoughts toward an Aesthetic Study of Religious Experience," *The Annals of the American Academy of Political and Social Science* 595, 1 (2004).

while he was out brushing his teeth. When he returned, with a playful look of mock shock on his face, we had an enormous round of laughter. The pastor declared his respect for ecumenical relations, then suggested the best resolution was to let the Pope alone. He then turned the picture toward the wall and propped it up gently. The group laughed again, and I smiled since, even for a Catholic, the Pope sometimes needs to be spun around and pointed in a new direction. This vignette reaffirmed my observation that the progressive religious space of BorderLinks did not lead to public sharing of religious difference, but instead a quiet tolerance of religious difference.

My presence appeared to be accepted by most groups. By the end of Sojourner University's trip, a member declared me the group's "mascot," a Durkheimian verification of my inclusion in their social group. Another group referred to me as "Almost Dr. Gary," suggesting the level of interest they had taken in understanding me. Another graciously invited me to visit and present the initial results of my research. The travelers from St. Michael's Church urged me to "stop by" when I was in their neck of the woods – roughly a few thousand miles from my home at the time.

I had three tests for noting whether I was included in a group. One test was whether the group presented me as a member. As part of their attempt to delegate expertise, BorderLinks staff members asked a group member to introduce the group to speakers at each stop during the immersion trip. Two groups introduced me with a distinct identity while still being part of their group ("and Gary from the University of Arizona"); two groups simply lumped me in as a nondescript group member; three of the groups asked me to present *them* to the people we met. Which I gladly did.

Another test was whether I was included in the various reflection and sharing activities during the week. On one occasion near the beginning of a trip I was excluded from a reflection; however, a group member noticed this, mentioned it to the group immediately, and a wave of ensuing apologies and laughs ensued. At no other time was I excluded from such an activity.

A final test was during picture taking near the end of a week. As a group gathered to have their picture taken, I always volunteered to be the picture taker. All groups except one promptly asked someone else to take a picture – with me included! Now, like it or not, the group pictures from five BorderLinks trips include a sociologist.

I do have reason to believe that some travelers were disappointed in me in some way. I was, after all, a friendly part of an indelible experience in which normative status relations were reconfigured and emotional connections made. I received a request from two Central College students to be Facebook friends after the trip. I declined, noting that it would compromise their anonymity to be publicly linked with me. Subsequently, neither of them filled out a posttrip survey or returned my calls to be interviewed. With some groups, I was also indirectly a pawn in the enforcement of status differences between travelers, particularly between students and professors. The professors of a group once asked me to walk with them so that "the kids" could be left alone to do their own thing for a few hours.

The leaders of groups were particularly patient with me. Part of my research was to expose the assumptions, motivations, and ideals behind immersion travel as a tactic aimed at some ill-defined end. This meant asking a lot of questions, particularly in posttrip interviews, about something that was taken for granted in their lives. *Of course*, immersion travel was important, they would say. *Of course*, it could change people. In the spirit of other cultural sociologists that walk a line between support and criticism, between providing reflexive insight and demanding purity, I hope they find something useful in this research for their important work.

Finally, most readers will have noticed the absence of specific identities from immigrants and some others interlocutors, instead replaced by intentionally vague reconstructions that lack pseudonyms. The design of this research primarily focused on travelers, their reactions to the events of travel, and their understandings of those they briefly encountered. This design could especially have consequences for the misrepresentation of immigrants, via traveler's reactions, or the loss of a crucial piece of understanding about how immigrants understand the interactions they have with others as they migrate. There were two reasons for this research design, though. First, to focus on particular immigrants and their stories would have required fulfilling additional research protections, which require a degree of stability in field research that was difficult to achieve in this research. Second, the constant breaching required to go between a travel group and the immigrants they interacted with would have prevented the sort of continuous, ethnographic flow my research depended on. I eagerly await more research about the experiences and understandings of "foreign" people that interact with immersion travelers.

TRAVELER SURVEYS

I surveyed BorderLinks' travelers during a ten-month period, covering both the high and low seasons of immersion travel. The survey covered travelers' demographic backgrounds, group affiliations, political attitudes, religious beliefs and behaviors, attitudes toward immigration, emotions toward immigration actors, and intragroup connections with their travel group. BorderLinks provided rosters of traveler names and email contact information for the survey. Travelers from each group were contacted up to three weeks before their travel, with two follow-up reminder emails. Of the twenty-four groups that were eligible to participate in the survey during this survey period, twenty-one received the survey. For two youth groups, I received contact information only a couple of days before the trip, which prevented recruitment for the survey. The presence of these groups in the sample would have undoubtedly lowered the age, as well as the pretrip civic and political activity levels of the full sample. The other group, a seminary, did not receive the survey due to my inability to make contact with the group leader far enough in advance. To compensate, I enrolled the next participating seminary group for replacement. In total, 217 persons were eligible to participate in the pretrip survey, and 180 responded, yielding a response rate of 82.9 percent. From what I learned about feeder organizations at BorderLinks, this sample is representative of traveling groups and travelers to Border-Links from about 2007 until at least 2012.

Travelers were also briefly surveyed at the immediate end of the trip. On the final day of any trip, BorderLinks had a history of providing an evaluation form for travelers. In coordination with the organization, I systematized the form and added more questions. These evaluation surveys listed the main activities of the week, asking the travelers to report how important the event was for them and whether it provoked emotions of sorrow or anger. Overall, 210 of 217 travelers responded to this evaluation survey for a response rate of 96.7 percent.

Beginning four months after each trip, I recontacted each of the 180 travelers that had completed the pretrip survey. Overall, sixty-eight travelers responded. This represented 37.8 percent of those who had completed the pretrip survey. The total response rate for the posttrip survey, given nonresponse in the pretrip survey, was 31.3 percent. In next section, I provide a brief overview of BorderLinks travelers based on surveys, focusing on their relative distinctiveness from "average" Americans and travelers in other immersion trip research.

TABLE A2 *Demographics for BorderLinks adult participants and comparison groups*

	BorderLinks Adults	American Adults (1,4)	Witness for Peace Adults (2)	BorderLinks Adult Church Members w/Monthly Worship Attendance	Global Issues Survey Adults (3)
White	86%	78%	96%	84%	79%
Some college education	98%[a]	55%***	90%	98%	60%
Female	63%	53%*	52%	59%	45%
Median household income[b]	$82,500	$50,233	$58,873		
Age (mean)***	32	46***	45	38	
Age: 30–59 years	29%	57%		43%	64%
Married[c]***	31%	57%***	51%	45%	69%

Data sources: 1. General Social Survey, 2008; 2. Smith, 1996; 3. Wuthnow, 2009; 4. Statistical Abstract of the United States, 2009. Global Issues Survey data are from American adult church members that attended worship services at least once a month ($n = 2231$). Data reported here are from subset that participated in a mission trip in the previous year (2.1% of active church members = 47). Not enough information was provided in either source 2 or 3 for tests of statistical difference.
[a] Completed college level for BorderLinks' adult participants was 44%. An additional 54% of participants were enrolled in college.
[b] Median annual household income reported for BorderLinks is the midpoint of range for the median income question category. Witness for Peace amount is inflation-adjusted from 1987 to 2009. Statistical test between BorderLinks adults and American adults not possible due to question differences.
[c] Married amount includes "committed, partnered relationship" for BorderLinks participants.
*$p < 0.05$, **$p < 0.01$, ***$p < 0.001$.

The Travelers

Table A2 provides a profile of BorderLinks travelers. The average Border-Links traveler was a white, well-educated female from a middle-class household. Very few BorderLinks travelers were Hispanic (7 percent). The second column in the table compares travelers to Americans in the General Social Survey. BorderLinks travelers were a very self-selected group. They were significantly different in education and sex than the general American adult population.

While it is useful to note differences between BorderLinks travelers and American adults, this tells us little about BorderLinks travelers in comparison to persons that participate in similar immersion travel activity. Two well-known studies provide comparison groups that may help to contextualize BorderLinks travelers. The first comparison group was composed of travelers from Witness for Peace delegations that traveled to Central America during the 1980s[5]. As Chapter 2 describes, Border-Links traced its roots to a similar era and religious milieu. The second comparison group was composed of travelers in short-term mission trips drawn from a nationally representative sample of adult American church-goers.[6] The Global Issues Survey (GIS) asked respondents whether they had participated in an international mission trip during the previous year.[7] Since some congregations refer to their participation in Border-Links as a version of a mission trip, this provided a useful comparison group. To help the comparison with this national sample of churchgoers, the second-to-last column in the table shows a subsample of those Border-Links travelers that reported attending worship services monthly or more before travel.

BorderLinks travelers had similar levels of education as Witness for Peace participants, but were more racially diverse, more likely to be female, and more likely to come from households with substantially higher median incomes. Compared to the GIS churchgoers who had gone on international mission trips, BorderLinks travelers were more likely to be white, have more education, and be female. The substantial difference in education level was likely due to BorderLinks' supply of young adults (eighteen to twenty-five) from colleges and universities.

The profile here suggests, not surprisingly, that travelers in a Border-Links trip were different from the American adult population at large. In common with both Witness for Peace and GIS mission trip participants, BorderLinks travelers had the financial resources to put toward such a resource-intensive form of transnational civic engagement. Like participants from both the comparison groups, the educational levels of BorderLinks travelers may have oriented them toward internationally cosmopolitan activities that emphasized learning and encountering diversity. The relatively high level of female participation in BorderLinks,

[5] Smith, *Resisting Reagan*.   [6] Wuthnow, *Boundless Faith*.   [7] Ibid., p. 294, note 35.

compared to other groups, was striking. Since BorderLinks travelers were younger than the comparison groups, female travelers in BorderLinks may have had fewer relationship obligations compared to those of older, female travelers that participated in church-based mission trips.[8]

The distribution of worship attendance was significantly different than among American adults, with higher rates of both frequent attenders and nonattenders. In comparison to Witness for Peace and GIS congregational mission trip delegations, BorderLinks travelers attended religious services less often. This may suggest the impact of educational feeder organizations that caught young people at the low point in a typical lifetime religious attendance cycle. It may also be due to liberal religious backgrounds, for which regular worship attendance is not the dominant form of religiosity.[9] Either way, BorderLinks, a publicly faith-affiliated religious organization, was attractive to those not actively engaged in traditional religious activity.

How did travelers get to BorderLinks to begin with? The survey shows clear evidence of "repeat travelers": in the twenty-one travel groups represented in the sample, six contained a current participant that had been on a BorderLinks trip before. Of those six trips, five were *led* by a repeat traveler. This familiarity with BorderLinks may have been a useful tool for organizing the participation of others since it allowed for personal testimonials about the importance and impact of this type of activity.[10] It was common in the course of my research to hear travelers refer to travel testimonials they had heard from previous BorderLinks travelers in their feeder organizations. When travelers mentioned this, they overwhelmingly recounted the way these former travelers had encouraged participation, noting how the trip had influenced their lives.

Familiarity with international travel may distinguish the initial willingness of immersion travel travelers, acting as an informal, primary-stage screening mechanism. Was familiarity with international travel an important factor among people who took part in BorderLinks? Simply put, BorderLinks travelers were a well-traveled group, as Table A3 shows. Fully 97 percent of participants had traveled outside of the United States at some point in their lives. A sizeable minority (21 percent) reported living overseas for six months or more as a member of Peace Corps, for an

---

[8] Wuthnow, *Boundless Faith.*   [9] Ammerman, "Golden Rule."
[10] David A. Snow, Louis A. Zurcher, Jr., and Sheldon Ekland-Olson, "Social Networks and Social Movements: A Microstructural Approach to Differential Recruitment," *American Sociological Review* 45, 5 (1980).

TABLE A3 *BorderLinks' travelers' travel experience*

	% of BorderLinks Participants
Traveled outside the United States	97
Involved in Peace Corps, nonprofit work or internship, or religious missionary outside the United States	21
Traveled to Mexico, Central America, or South America	69
Traveled on a short-term mission, immersion, or delegation trip outside of the United States	49
Traveled on a short-term mission, immersion, or delegation trip to Mexico, Central America, or South America	35

n = 180

internship, or as a missionary.[11] Over two-thirds (69 percent) of participants had already traveled to Mexico, Central America, or South America before participating in BorderLinks.

As I argued throughout, the practice and meaning of immersion travel are distinct from other types of travel, particularly tourism. Since Border-Links overtly distinguished its activity from tourism, it may not be surprising that many BorderLinks travelers could list a travel biography that did the same. Almost half (49 percent) of travelers had traveled aboard as part of an immersion trip, suggesting a familiarity with nontourist modes of travel. The median number of such trips among BorderLinks travelers was two, with one-quarter of travelers reporting three or more such trips. Participation in a BorderLinks trip for many travelers was a continuation of an already-established practice of transnational relationship building.[12] A BorderLinks trip was also a continuation of a type of relationship with a particular international region: more than one-third (36 percent) of participants had previously traveled to Mexico, Central America, or South America on an immersion trip.

---

[11] The survey items about long-term international experience did not include study abroad or living in foreign locations as a child. Given these exclusions, we could reasonably assume that the long-term familiarity with international locations was higher than the percentage reported here.

[12] An additional 14 percent of travelers were familiar with this form of immersion travel, having traveled this way to domestic locations. Overall, 37 percent of travelers had participated in a domestic immersion trip.

It would be an understatement to say this was a politically liberal group. About 85 percent of travelers had liberal leanings, with 48 percent considered "very liberal."[13] This distribution of political identity was significantly different from the American adult public. The survey of BorderLinks travelers also included a section on types of political activity, similar to the questions from the 2004 edition of the General Social Survey. These questions, shown in Table A4, asked whether travelers had done a particular activity in the previous twelve months, had done it in the more distant past, had not done the activity but might, and whether they had not done the activity and would not. For comparison purposes, this section only reports statistics for BorderLinks travelers eighteen years or older. On all items for which comparative General Social Survey data were available, BorderLinks adults were more engaged.

The most common political activity among BorderLinks travelers was signing a petition or letter. Over three-quarters of BorderLinks travelers (82 percent) had signed a petition at some point in their lives, with 63 percent having done so in the previous year. This was almost twice the 35 percent of American adults that reported doing so in the previous year. For other forms of low-risk political activity, 39 percent of Border-Links travelers reported attending a community meeting in the previous year, 40 percent reported contacting elected officials in the previous year, and 16 percent reported contacting the media in the previous year. On each of these measures of political activity, BorderLinks travelers were more active than American adults. Concerning more high-risk political activity, 62 percent of BorderLinks travelers reported participating in a protest or march at some point in their lives, with 31 percent having done so in the previous year. Again, BorderLinks travelers were more politically active than the general adult population, with only 6 percent of American adults having participated in a protest or march in the previous year.

While these travelers were clearly civically engaged before the trip, the survey also included a way to determine whether this engagement was already directed at immigration. Two of the questions from Table A4 were asked again, specifically about immigration. While 63 percent of travelers reported signing a petition in the previous year, only 24 percent of travelers reported signing a petition that was immigration related.

---

[13] Unless otherwise noted, the statistics reported here only apply to BorderLinks travelers over the age of 18, for comparative purposes.

TABLE A4 *Comparison of BorderLinks travelers civic and political activity to American adults*

	Done it in the past 12 months		Done it in the more distant past		Not done it, but might		Have not done it and will not	
	BorderLinks Adults (%)	US Adults (%)	BorderLinks Adults (%)	US Adults (%)	BorderLinks Adults (%)	US Adults (%)	BorderLinks Adults (%)	US Adults (%)
Attended community meetings to support or oppose local issues***	39	13	24	19	35	41	2	27
Signed petitions for some *other* social, environmental, or political cause***	63	35	19	32	18	23	1	10
Contacted or appeared in the media to express your views***	16	6	19	9	51	47	15	39
Contacted elected officials to express your social/political views on *other* issues***	40	22	19	21	36	38	4	19
Participated in public demonstrations, protests, or marches***	31	6	31	13	31	43	7	38

Data source for "US Adults": General Social Survey, 2004

Note: Actual questions from the General Social Survey: "Attended a political meeting or rally," "Signed a petition," "Contacted or appeared in the media to express your views," "Contacted, or attempted to contact, a politician or a civil servant to express your views," "Took part in a demonstration"

*p < 0.05 **p < 0.01 ***p < 0.001.

Similarly, while 40 percent reported contacting a politician in the past year, only 13 percent reported contacting a politician in the last year about immigration issues. This suggests there was room to change among BorderLinks travelers, a theme encountered in Chapter 7.

SURVEY NONRESPONSE TEST FOR THREE POINTS IN TIME

Table A5 shows characteristics of survey respondents at three times (t1, t2, and t3) to determine nonresponse bias at any point. The table shows only those variables that were significantly different at their mean when comparing respondents that completed one survey to another group that did not. These were the only variables, out of over 200 variables from the pretrip survey, that were significantly different among respondents in the t2 or t3 waves.

The first set of columns compares those who did the pretrip survey without doing the immediate posttrip evaluation survey to those who did both. Only a few characteristics distinguish these groups, suggesting they are quite similar. Those who did *not* respond to the evaluation survey were less familiar with their group before the trip, were less likely to be vegetarian, were more religious/spiritual, and were likely to have done an evangelical-style immersion trip in the past. Nonresponders at t2 appear to have come from a couple of religious congregations. It is not apparent how this nonresponse would have influenced information on the t2 evaluation survey. Given subgroup differences discussed in Chapter 7, this nonresponse may have depressed the reported emotional means of trip activities.

The second set of columns compares those who did the pretrip survey without doing the posttrip survey (*n* = 112) to those who did both (*n* = 68). Again, only a handful of questions out of more than 200 appear to distinguish those who did not do the posttrip survey. The nonrespondents at t3 were younger, had less pretrip international experience, had less personal intragroup connection, met more resistance from a close friend or family member prior to the trip, had less experience with immersion travel, had higher authoritarian personality scores, and had less experience with immersion trips outside the United States. Only one-third of travelers under the age of twenty-three responded to the posttrip survey, but 44 percent of respondents twenty-three or older responded. From these variables and examination of traveler records, it appears that posttrip survey nonrespondents were mostly young people, with travel, group, and developmental characteristics related to their age.

TABLE A5 *Comparison of sample at three time points*

	Respondents who did t1 survey vs. those who did t1 + t2			Respondents who did t1 survey vs. those who did t1 + t3		
	Means			Means		
	t1	t1 + t2	*p*	t1	t1 + t3	*p*
Percentage of R's group that R knew before BorderLinks trip	0.35	0.56	0.05			
R is a vegetarian	0.00	0.21	0.04			
R has never felt called by God	0.12	0.52	0.00			
R had religious or spiritual experience in last 12 months	0.71	0.40	0.02			
R has never had a religious or spiritual experience	0.06	0.35	0.02			
R has not felt one with the universe in the last 12 months	0.06	0.41	0.00			
R has done evangelization on an international immersion trip before	0.20	0.03	0.00			
R's age				27.04	34.43	0.00
R has done an internship or nonprofit work outside the US for 6 months or more				0.10	0.25	0.01
R tried to get someone to come on the BorderLinks trip and they are not coming				0.17	0.31	0.02
R has a friend who decided not to come on the BorderLinks trip				0.18	0.39	0.00
R knows a local business that employs undocumented immigrants				0.67	0.47	0.01
R knows a person who is not close whom expressed disapproval about the trip				0.22	0.10	0.04

	Respondents who did t1 survey vs. those who did t1 + t2			Respondents who did t1 survey vs. those who did t1 + t3		
	Means			Means		
	t1	t1 + t2	p	t1	t1 + t3	p
Number of immersion trips to Mexico, South, or Central America (mean)				0.55	0.94	0.05
R's score on authority personality scale				3.59	3.31	0.04
Number of immersion trips outside the US (mean)				0.91	1.51	0.02
N	17	163		112	68	

Statistical tests using two-group equality of proportions. Two-tailed tests.

To further understand the meaning of this nonresponse, I analyzed whether the lower responding youths that *did* respond were representative of the youths that *did not* respond. To do this, I dropped all travelers over the age of twenty-two and reexamined the remaining travelers with the same set of variables. Among these young people, nonrespondents were less civically engaged when compared to respondents. The nonrespondents had less experience attending a community meeting ($p = 0.03$), less experience contacting a politician about immigration ($p = 0.01$), were less likely to be part of an immigration advocacy group ($p = 0.04$), and less likely to be part of any advocacy group ($p = 0.01$). Nonrespondents were also more religious: they were less likely to be uncomfortable when politicians talked about their religious beliefs ($p = 0.02$), more likely to attend worship frequently ($p = 0.03$), and more likely to have recently read the Bible ($p = 0.05$).

These lower levels of engagement suggest nonrespondents may be the youngest in the sample. The lower levels of pretrip contact with the immigration issue alongside higher religiosity suggest that the nonrespondents belonged to congregational youth groups that traveled through BorderLinks. In fact, this interpretation is supported by other evidence. Nonrespondents were more likely to have less than college education (e.g., high schoolers) ($p = 0.04$) and were more likely to be from a congregation group ($p = 0.02$). From an analysis of trip records, congregational groups with high school students were the only groups in the study that came to BorderLinks from within a day's drive of the US border. The remaining characteristics that differentiate youth nonrespondents are all related to their groups coming from congregational feeder organizations, in some cases geographically proximate to the border. It appears these congregations used BorderLinks to produce an immersion trip *in general*, with the focus on immigration as a secondary characteristic. These nonrespondents were less likely to have read BorderLinks material (p = 0.01), less likely to be a vegetarian (p = 0.04), and more likely to have had disapproval from someone about going on the trip (p = 0.03). This last item, in particular, seems likely to relate to these nonrespondents still being under relatively close home supervision from parents.

My conclusion is that young people, particularly high schoolers, were tired of the research interventions and thus did not respond to the t3 survey. It is difficult to know how this nonresponse bias influenced the analysis of BorderLinks' trip outcomes. On the one hand, the absence of these persons from the posttrip analysis could inflate the positive outcomes. It is possible that they did not reply because the trip was an isolated experience without importance for them. These nonrespondents may have been turned off, or otherwise unaffected, by the experience. On the other hand, there is evidence that short-term mission trips can have a substantial impact on teenagers, which would mean the posttrip results reported are deflated.[14] The change-inducing effect of BorderLinks trips may be particularly salient for nonrespondents since they had lower levels of pretrip international experience. The youth who did not respond may have had much more room to change in their immigration-related behaviors.

It is difficult to know which of these scenarios is correct, whether this nonresponse bias positively or negatively influenced the reported results. The good news is that, compared to other research on immersion travel that does *not* report on respondent dropouts, my research can at least confront this hurdle that many survey researchers face. The best strategy of interpretation about BorderLinks' travel outcomes is to think of them as not pertaining to high school participants.

[14] Beyerlein et al., "The Effect of Religious Mission Trips."

Bibliography

Abend, Gabriel. "Thick Concepts and the Moral Brain." *European Journal of Sociology* 52, no. 1 (2011): 143–72.

Abramson, Corey M. *The End Game.* Cambridge, MA: Harvard University Press, 2015.

"From "Either-or" to "When and How": A Context-Dependent Model of Culture in Action." *Journal for the Theory of Social Behaviour* 42, no. 2 (2012): 155–80.

Adler, Jr., Gary J. "'Neutral' Talk, Conscience, and Political Legitimacy." In *Religion and Progressive Activism: New Stories about Faith and Politics,* edited by Todd N. Fuist, Ruth Braunstein, and Rhys H. Williams. New York: New York University Press, 2017.

Adler Jr., Gary J., and Andrea L. Ruiz. "The Immigrant Effect: Short-Term Mission Travel as Transnational Civic Remittance." *Sociology of Religion* 79, no. 3 (2018): srx060-srx60.

Adler Jr., Gary J., and Stephen Offutt. "The Gift Economy of Direct Transnational Civic Action: How Reciprocity and Inequality Are Managed in Religious 'Partnerships'." *Journal for the Scientific Study of Religion* 56, no. 3 (2017): 600–19.

Alexander, Jeffrey. *The Civil Sphere.* New York: Oxford University Press, 2006.

Alexander, Jeffrey, Bernhard Giesen, and Jason L. Mast. *Social Performance: Symbolic Action, Cultural Pragmatics, and Ritual.* New York: Cambridge University Press, 2006.

Allahyari, Rebecca Anne. *Visions of Charity: Volunteer Workers and Moral Community.* Berkeley: University of California Press, 2000.

Ammerman, Nancy T., 'Golden Rule Christianity: Lived Religion in the American Mainstream', In *Lived Religion in America,* edited by David D. Hall, 196–216. Princeton, NJ: Princeton University Press, 1997.

"Religious Identities and Religious Institutions." In *The Handbook of the Sociology of Religion,* edited by Michele Dillon, 207–24. New York: Cambridge University Press, 2003.

Pillars of Faith: American Congregations and Their Partners. Berkeley: University of California Press, 2005.

Anderson, Benedict. *Imagined Communities: Reflections on the Origin and Spread of Nationalism.* Revised edn. New York: Verso, 2006.

Andrews, Kenneth T., and Bob Edwards. "Advocacy Organizations in the U.S. Political Process." *Annual Review of Sociology* 30 (2004): 479–506.

Anheier, Helmut K. "Reflections on the Concept and Measurement of Global Civil Society." *Voluntas* 18, no. 1 (2007): 1–15.

Appiah, Kwame Anthony. *Cosmopolitanism: Ethics in a World of Strangers.* New York: W.W. Norton & Company, 2006.

Baggett, Jerome P. *Building Private Homes, Building Public Religion: Habitat for Humanity.* Philadelphia: Temple University Press, 2005.

Bail, Christopher. *Terrified: How Anti-Muslim Organizations Became Mainstream.* Princeton, NJ: Princeton University Press, 2014.

Baker, David. *The Schooled Society: The Educational Transformation of Global Culture.* Redwood City, CA: Stanford University Press, 2014.

Bandy, Joe. "Paradoxes of Transnational Civil Societies under Neoliberalism: The Coalition for Justice in the Maquiladoras." *Social Problems* 51, no. 3 (2004): 410–31.

Barnett, Michael. *Empire of Humanity: A History of Humanitarianism.* Ithaca, NY: Cornell University Press, 2011.

Barnett, Michael, and Thomas G. Weiss. *Humanitarianism in Question: Politics, Power, Ethics.* Ithaca, NY: Cornell University Press, 2008.

Batson, Charles Daniel. *Altruism in Humans.* New York: Oxford University Press, 2011.

Batson, C. Daniel, and Adam A. Powell. "Altruism and Prosocial Behavior." In *Handbook of Psychology*, edited by Theodore Millon and Melvin J. Lerner. Hoboken, NJ: John Wiley & Sons, Inc., 2003.

Bearman, Peter S., and Katherine Stovel. "Becoming a Nazi: A Model for Narrative Networks." *Poetics* 27, no. 2–3 (2000): 69–90.

Becker, Howard S. *Outsiders.* New York: The Free Press, 2008.

Becker, Penny Edgell. "Making Inclusive Communities: Congregations and the "Problem" of Race." *Social Problems* 45, no. 4 (1998): 451–72.

Belhassen, Yaniv, Kellee Caton, and William P. Stewart. "The Search for Authenticity in the Pilgrim Experience." *Annals of Tourism Research* 35, no. 3 (2008): 668–89.

Bell, Brenda, John Gaventa, and John Peters, *Myles Horton and Paulo Freire: We Make the Road by Walking: Conversations on Education and Social Change.* Philadelphia: Temple University Press, 1990.

Bellah, Robert N., Richard Madsen, William M. Sullivan, Ann Swidler, and Steven M. Tipton. *Habits of the Heart.* Berkeley: University of California Press, 1985.

Bender, Courtney. *Heaven's Kitchen: Living Religion at God's Love We Deliver.* Chicago: University of Chicago Press, 2003.

Benford, Robert D., and David A. Snow. "Framing Processes and Social Movements: An Overview and Assessment." *Annual Review of Sociology* 26 (2000): 611–39.

Berger, Bennett M. *The Survival of a Counterculture: Ideological Work and Everyday Life among Rural Communards.* New York: Transaction Publishers, 2004 [1981].

Berry, Jeffrey M., and David F. Arons. *A Voice for Nonprofits.* Washington, DC: Brookings Institute Press, 2003.

Beyerlein, Kraig, and David Sikkink. "Sorrow and Solidarity: Why Americans Volunteered for 9/11 Relief Efforts." *Social Problems*, no. 55, no. 2 (2008): 190–215.

Beyerlein, Kraig, Gary Adler, and Jennifer Trinitapoli. "The Effect of Religious Mission Trips on Youth Civic Participation." *Journal for the Scientific Study of Religion* 50, no. 4 (2011): 780–95.

Beyerlein, Kraig, and Mark Chaves. "The Political Activities of Religious Congregations in the United States." *Journal for the Scientific Study of Religion* 42, no. 3 (2003): 229–46.

Bloom, Paul. *Against Empathy: The Case for Rational Compassion.* New York: Random House, 2017.

Boli, John, and George M. Thomas, *Constructing World Culture: International Non-Governmental Organizations since 1875.* Palo Alto, CA: Stanford University Press, 1999.

Boltanksi, Luc. *Distant Suffering: Morality, Media, and Politics.* Translated by Graham Burchell. New York: Cambridge University Press, 1999 [1993].

Boltanksi, Luc, and Laurent Thevenot. "The Sociology of Critical Capacity." *European Journal of Social Theory* 2, no. 3 (1999): 359–77.

Bornstein, Erica. "Child Sponsorship, Evangelism, and Belonging in the World of World Vision Zimbabwe." *American Ethnologist* 28, no. 3 (2001): 595–622.

Disquieting Gifts: Humanitarianism in New Delhi. Stanford, CA: Stanford University Press, 2012.

"The Impulse of Philanthropy." *Cultural Anthropology* 24, no. 4 (2009): 622–51.

"Volunteer Experience." In *What Matters? Ethnographies of Value in a Not So Secular Age*, edited by Courtney Bender and Ann Taves, 119–43. New York: Columbia University Press, 2012.

Bourdieu, Pierre. *The Logic of Practice.* Translated by Richard Nice. Redwood City, CA: Stanford University Press, 1990 [1980].

Pascalian Meditations. Stanford, CA: Stanford University Press, 2000.

Bourdieu, Pierre, and Loic J. D. Wacquant. *An Invitation to Reflexive Sociology.* Chicago: University of Chicago Press, 1992.

Braunstein, Ruth. "Storytelling in Liberal Religious Advocacy." *Journal for the Scientific Study of Religion* 51, no. 1 (2012): 110–27.

Breunig, Mary. "Critical Praxis and Experiential Education." In *Sourcebook of Experiential Education: Key Thinkers and Their Contributions*, edited by Thomas E. Smith and Clifford E. Knapp, 56–63. New York: Routledge, 2011.

Briscoe, Forrest, Abhinav Gupta, and Mark S. Anner. "Social Activism and Practice Diffusion: How Activist Tactics Affect Non-Targeted Organizations." *Administrative Science Quarterly* 60, no. 2 (2015): 300–32.

Brown, Sally, and Alastair M. Morrison. "Expanding Volunteer Vacation Participation: An Exploratory Study on the Mini-Mission Concept." *Tourism Recreation Research* 28, no. 3 (2003): 73–82.

Bruner, Edward M. *Culture on Tour: Ethnographies of Travel.* Chicago: University of Chicago Press, 2005.

"Transformation of Self in Tourism." *Annals of Tourism Research* 18, no. 2 (1991): 238–50.

Bush, Evelyn L. "Measuring Religion in Global Civil Society." *Social Forces* 85, no. 4 (2007): 1645–65.

Cameron, C. Daryl, and B. Keith Payne. "Escaping Affect: How Motivated Emotion Regulation Creates Insensitivity to Mass Suffering." *Journal of Personality and Social Psychology* 100, no. 1 (2011): 1–15.

Cameron, C. Daryl, Victoria L. Spring, and Andrew R. Todd. "The Empathy Impulse: A Multinomial Model of Intentional and Unintentional Empathy for Pain." *Emotion* 17, no. 3 (2017): 395–411.

Campus Compact. "2015 Annual Member Survey." Campus Compact, 2016.

Castells, Manuel. "The New Public Sphere: Global Civil Society, Communication Networks, and Global Governance." *The Annals of the American Academy of Political and Social Science* 616, no. 1 (2008): 78–93.

Chouliaraki, Lilie. *The Ironic Spectator: Solidarity in the Age of Post-Humanitarianism.* Malden, MA, Polity Press, 2013.

Patricia Chow and Rajika Bhandari, "Open Doors 2011 Report on International Educational Change," (New York: Institute of International Education, 2011).

Clark, Candace. *Misery and Company: Sympathy in Everyday Life.* Chicago: University of Chicago Press, 1997.

"Sympathy Biography and Sympathy Margin." *The American Journal of Sociology* 93, no. 2 (1987): 290–321.

Cleary, Edward L. "The Brazilian Catholic Church and Church-State Relations: Nation-Building." *Journal of Church and State* 39, no. 2 (1997): 253–72.

Clifford, Bob. "The Market for Human Rights." In *Advocacy Organizations and Collective Action*, edited by A. Prakash and M. K. Gugerty, 133–54. New York: Cambridge University Press, 2010.

Cohen, Erik. "The Changing Faces of Contemporary Tourism." *Society* 45, no. 4 (2008): 330–3.

"The Sociology of Tourism: Approaches, Issues, and Findings." *Annual Review of Sociology* 10 (1984): 373–92.

"The Tourist Guide: The Origins, Structure, and Dynamics of a Role." *Annals of Tourism Research* 12 (1985): 5–29.

Collins, Randall. "Social Movements and the Focus of Emotional Attention." In *Passionate Politics*, edited by Jeff Goodwin, James M. Jasper, and Francesca Polletta. Chicago: University of Chicago Press, 2001.

Crane, Ken, Lachelle Norris, and Kevin Barry. "Mobilizing Communities through International Study Tours: Project Mexico Immersion and New Immigrants in the Midwest." *Human Organization* 69, no. 4 (2010): 362–74.

Cunningham, Hilary. "Transnational Politics at the Edges of Sovereignty: Social Movements, Crossings and the State at the U.S.-Mexico Border." *Global Networks* 1, no. 4 (2001): 369–87.

"Transnational Social Movements and Sovereignties in Transition: Charting New Interfaces of Power at the U.S.-Mexico Border." *Anthropologica* 44, no. 2 (2002): 185–96.

Curry-Stevens, Ann. "New Forms of Transformative Education Pedagogy for the Privileged." *Journal of transformative education* 5, no. 1 (2007): 33–58.

Davis, Mark H. "Empathy." In *Handbook of the Sociology of Emotions,* edited by Jan E. Stets and Jonathan H. Turner, 443–66. New York: Springer, 2006.

Davis, Mike. *Planet of Slums.* New York: Verso, 2006.

De Waal, Frans B.M. "Putting the Altruism Back into Altruism: The Evolution of Empathy." *Annual Review of Psychology* 59 (2008): 279–300.

DeGloma, Thomas. *Seeing the Light: The Social Logic of Personal Discovery.* Chicago: The University of Chicago Press, 2014.

Dekker, Paul. "Civicness: From Civil Society to Civic Services?." *Voluntas: International Journal of Voluntary and Nonprofit Organizations* 20, no. 3 (2009): 220–38.

Delgado-Wise, Raúl, and Humberto Márquez Covarrubias. "The Reshaping of Mexican Labor Exports under NAFTA: Paradoxes and Challenges." *International Migration Review* 41, no. 3 (2007): 656–79.

Della Porta, Donatella, and Sidney Tarrow. "Transnational Processes and Social Activism: An Introduction." In *Transnational Protest and Global Activism: People, Passions, and Power,* edited by Donatella Della Porta and Sidney Tarrow, 1–20. Lanham, MD: Rowman & Littlefield, 2005.

Dill, Jeffrey S. *The Longings and Limits of Global Citizenship Education: The Moral Pedagogy of Schooling in a Cosmopolitan Age.* New York: Routledge, 2013.

Dimaggio, Paul. "Culture and Cognition." *Annual Review of Sociology* 23, no. 1 (1997): 263–87.

Dove, April Lee. "Framing Illegal Immigration at the U.S.-Mexican Border: Anti-Illegal Immigration Groups and the Importance of Place in Framing." *Research in Social Movements, Conflicts and Change* 30 (2010): 199–237.

Dryzek, John S, and Simon Niemeyer. "Discursive Representation." *American Political Science Review* 102, no. 4 (2008): 481–93.

Dunch, Ryan. "Beyond Cultural Imperialism: Cultural Theory, Christian Missions, and Global Modernity." *History and Theory* 41 (2002): 301–25.

Eade, John. "Introduction to the Illinois Paperback." In *Contesting the Sacred: The Anthropology of Pilgrimage,* edited by John Eade and Michael Sallnow, ix–xxvii. Urbana: University of Illinois Press, 2000.

Eagleton, Terry. *The Trouble with Strangers: A Study of Ethics.* Malden, MA: Wiley-Blackwell, 2009.

Edles, Laura Desfor. "Contemporary Progressive Christianity and Its Symbolic Ramifications." *Cultural Sociology* 7, no. 1 (2013): 3–22.

Education, Institute of International. "Detailed Duration of U.S. Study Abroad, 2005/6–2015/16." In *Open Doors Report on International Education Exchange.* New York, 2017.

Edwards, Bob, and John D. McCarthy. "Social Movement Schools." *Sociological Forum* 7, no. 3 (1992): 541–50.

Einolf, Christopher J. "Empathic Concern and Prosocial Behaviors: A Test of Experimental Results Using Survey Data." *Social Science Research* 37, no. 4 (2008): 1267–79.

Elias, Norbert. *On the Process of Civilisation*. University College Dublin Press, 2012.

Eliasoph, Nina. *Avoiding Politics: How Americans Produce Apathy in Everyday Life*. New York: Cambridge University Press, 1998.

——. "Beyond the Politics of Denunciation: Cultural Sociology as the 'Sociology for the Meantime'." In *Culture, Society, and Democracy: The Interpretive Approach*, edited by Isaac Reed and Jeffrey Alexander, 55–100. Boulder, CO: Paradigm Publishers, 2007.

——. "Making a Fragile Public: A Talk-Centered Study of Citizenship and Power." *Sociological Theory* 14, no. 3 (Nov. 1996): 262–89.

——. *Making Volunteers: Civic Life after Welfare's End*. Princeton, NJ: Princeton University Press, 2011.

——. *The Politics of Volunteering*. Malden, MA: Polity Press, 2013.

Eliasoph, Nina, and Paul Lichterman. "Culture in Interaction." *American Journal of Sociology* 108, no. 4 (January 2003): 735–94.

Emirbayer, Mustafa, and Victoria Johnson. "Bourdieu and Organizational Analysis." *Theory and Society* 37 (2008): 1–44.

Evans, Sara M., and Harry C. Boyte. *Free Spaces: The Sources of Democratic Change in America*. Chicago: University of Chicago Press, 1992.

Farrell, Justin. "Moral Outpouring: Shock and Generosity in the Aftermath of the Bp Oil Spill." *Social Problems* 61, no. 3 (2014): 482–506.

Fernandes, Luiza Beth. "Basic Ecclesiastic Communities in Brazil." *Harvard Educational Review* 55, no. 1 (1985): 76–86.

Fetner, Tina. *How the Religious Right Shaped Lesbian and Gay Activism*. Minneapolis: University of Minnesota Press, 2008.

Fitting, Elizabeth. *The Struggle for Maize: Campesinos, Workers, and Transgenic Corn in the Mexican Countryside*. Durham, NC: Duke University Press, 2010.

Fobes, Catherine, and Tera Hefferan. "Educating Students for the Twenty-First Century: Using Praxis Projects to Teach about Global Learning in Mid-Michigan." *Michigan Sociological Review* 23 (2009): 81–104.

Forman-Barzilai, Fonna. *Adam Smith and the Circles of Sympathy: Cosmopolitanism and Moral Theory*. New York: Cambridge University Press, 2011.

——. "And Thus Spoke the Spectator: Adam Smith for Humanitarians." *The Adam Smith Review* 1 (2004): 167–96.

——. "Sympathy in Space(S) Adam Smith on Proximity." *Political Theory* 33, no. 2 (2005): 189–217.

Freire, Paulo. "Cultural Action and Conscientization." *Harvard Educational Review* 40, no. 3 (1970): 452–77.

——. *Pedagogy of the Oppressed*. New York: Sebury Press, 1970.

Freire-Medeiros, Bianca. *Touring Poverty*. New York: Routledge, 2014.

Frenzel, Fabian, Ko Koens, and Malte Steinbrink. *Slum Tourism: Poverty, Power and Ethics*. New York: Routledge, 2012.

Friedland, Roger. "God, Love and Other Good Reasons for Practice: Thinking through Institutional Logics." *Institutional Logics in Action: Research in the Sociology of Organizations* 39 (2013): 25–50.

Fuist, Todd N., Ruth Braunstein, and Rhys H. Williams. "Religion and Progressive Activism–Introducing and Mapping the Field." In *Religion and Progresssive Activism: New Stories about Faith and Politics*, edited by Ruth Braunstein, Todd N. Fuist, and Rhys H. Williams, 2017.

Ganz, Marshall. *Why David Sometimes Wins: Leadership, Organization, and Strategy in the California Farmworkers Movement*. New York: Oxford University Press, 2010.

Gard McGehee, Nancy. "Alternative Tourism and Social Movements." *Annals of Tourism Research* 29, no. 1 (2002): 124–43.

Gehm, John. "Urban Plunge: An Intensive Experience in Criminal Justice Education." *Journal of Criminal Justice Education* 10, no. 1 (1999): 137–52.

Gill, Jerry H. *Borderlinks II: Still on the Road*. Tucson, AZ: BorderLinks, 2004.
Borderlinks: The Road Is Made by Walking. Tucson, AZ: BorderLinks, 1999.

Gladstone, David L. *From Pilgrimage to Package Tour: Travel and Tourism in the Third World*. New York: Routledge, 2013.

Goffman, Erving. *Asylums: Essays on the Social Situation of Mental Patients and Other Inmates*. New York: Anchor Books, 1961.
The Presentation of Self in Everyday Life. New York: Doubleday, 1959.

Goodwin, Jeff, James M. Jasper, and Francesca Polletta. "Introduction: Why Emotions Matter." Chap. Introduction In *Passionate Politics: Emotions and Social Movements*, edited by Jeff Goodwin, James M. Jasper, and Francesca Polletta, 1–26. Chicago: The University of Chicago Press, 2001.
Passionate Politics: Emotions and Social Movements. Chicago: University of Chicago Press, 2001.

Gorski, Philip. *American Covenant: A History of Civil Religion from the Puritans to the Present*. Princeton, NJ: Princeton University Press, 2017.

Gotham, Kevin Fox. "Tourism and Culture." In *Handbook of Cultural Sociology*, edited by John R. Hall, Laura Grindstaff, and Ming-Cheng Lo, 608–16. New York, NY: Routledge, 2010.

Greeley, Andrew. *Religion as Poetry*. New Brunswick, NJ: Transaction Publishers, 1995.

Griffin, Michael, and Jennie Weiss Block. *In the Company of the Poor: Conversations with Dr. Paul Farmer and Fr. Gustavo Gutiérrez*. Maryknoll, NY: Orbis Books, 2013.

Griffin-Nolan, Edward Patrick. *Witness for Peace: A Story of Resistance*. Louisville, KY: Westminster/John Knox Press, 1991.

Habermas, Jurgen. *The Theory of Communicative Action*. Translated by Thomas McCarthy. Vol. 1, Boston: Beacon Press, 1984 [1981].

Hallett, Tim, and Marc J. Ventresca. "Inhabited Institutions: Social Interactions and Organizational Forms in Gouldner's *Patterns of Industrial Bureaucracy*." *Theory & Society* 35 (2006): 213–36.

Hamilton, Lawrence. "'Civil Society': Critique and Alternative." In *Global Civil Society and Its Limits*, edited by Gordon Laxer and Sandra Halperin, 63–84. New York: Palgrave Macmillan, 2003.

Hannerz, Ulf. *Transnational Connections: Culture, People, Places*. New York: Routledge, 1996.

Harkness, Sarah K., and Steven Hitlin. "Morality and Emotions." In *Handbook of the Sociology of Emotions*, edited by Jan E. Stets and Jonathan H. Turner, 451–71. New York: Springer, 2014.

Hart, Stephen. *Cultural Dilemmas of Progressive Politics: Styles of Engagement among Grassroots Activists*. Chicago: Chicago University Press, 2001.

Hartmann, Eric, and Richard Kiely. "Pushing Boundaries: Introduction to the Global Service-Learning Special Section." *Michigan Journal of Community Service Learning* 21, no. 1 (2014): 55–63.

Harvey, Elizabeth. "Pilgrimages to the Bleeding Border: Gender and Rituals of Nationalist Protest in Germany, 1919–39." *Women's History Review* 9, no. 2 (2000): 201–29.

Haskell, Thomas L. "Capitalism and the Origins of the Humanitarian Sensibility, Part 1." *The American Historical Review* 90, no. 2 (1985): 339–61.

Hefferan, Tara. *Twinning Faith and Development: Catholic Parish Partnering in the U.S. and Haiti*. Bloomfield, CT: Kumarian Press, 2007.

Hochschild, Adam. *Bury the Chains: Prophets and Rebels in the Fight to Free an Empire's Slaves*. New York: Houghton Mifflin Harcourt, 2005.

Hochschild, Arlie Russell. *The Managed Heart: Commercialization of Human Feeling*. Berkeley: University of California Press, 1983.

———. *Strangers in Their Own Land: Anger and Mourning on the American Right*. New York: The New Press, 2016.

Hoffman, Martin L. "Empathy and Prosocial Behavior." In *Handbook of Emotions*, edited by Michael Lewis, Jeannette M. Haviland-Jones, and Lisa Feldman Barrett, 440–55. New York: The Guilford Press, 2008.

Hollinger, David A. *Protestants Abroad: How Missionaries Tried to Change the World but Changed America*. Princeton, NJ: Princeton University Press, 2017.

Howell, Brian. "Roots of the Short-Term Missionary, 1960–1985." *Building Church Leaders*, www.buildingchurchleaders.com/articles/2006/rootsmis sionary.html.

———. *Short-Term Mission: An Ethnography of Christian Travel Narrative and Experience*. Downers Grove, IL: IVP Academic, 2012.

Howell, Brian, and Rachel Dorr. "Evangelical Pilgrimage: The Language of Short-Term Missions." *Journal of Communication and Religion* 30 (November 2007): 236–65.

Hunt, Lynn Avery. *Inventing Human Rights: A History*. New York: W.W. Norton & Company, 2007.

Hutnyk, John. *The Rumour of Calcutta: Tourism, Charity and the Poverty of Representation*. London: Zed Books, 1996.

Ignatow, Gabriel. "Culture and Embodied Cognition: Moral Discourses in Internet Support Groups for Overeaters." *Social Forces* 88, no. 2 (2009): 643–69.

Illich, Ivan. "To Hell with Good Intentions." Paper presented at the *American Midwest Regional Meeting of the Conference on Interamerican Student Projects*, St. Mary's Lake of the Woods Seminary, Chicago, 1968. www .ciasp.ca/CIASPhistory/IllichCIASPspeech68.pdf

Immerwahr, Daniel. *Thinking Small: The United States and the Lure of Community Development.* Cambridge, MA: Harvard University Press, 2015.

Jasper, James M. *The Art of Moral Protest: Culture, Biography, and Creativity in Social Movements.* Chicago: University of Chicago Press, 1997.

———. "The Emotions of Protest: Affective and Reactive Emotions in and around Social Movements." *Sociological Forum* 13, no. 3 (September 1998): 397–424.

Jasper, James M., and Jane D. Poulsen. "Recruiting Strangers and Friends: Moral Shocks and Social Networks in Animal Rights and Anti-Nuclear Protests." *Social Problems* 42, no. 4 (November 1995): 493–512.

Jasper, James M., and Lynn Owens. "Social Movements and Emotions." In *Handbook of the Sociology of Emotions*, edited by Jan E. Stets and Jonathan H. Turner. New York: Springer, 2014.

Jerolmack, Colin, and Shamus Khan. "Talk Is Cheap: Ethnography and the Attitudinal Fallacy." *Sociological Methods & Research* 43, no. 2 (2014): 178–209.

Jindra, Ines. "How Religious Content Matters in Conversion Narratives to Various Religious Groups." *Sociology of Religion* 72, no. 3 (2011): 275–302.

Joas, Hans. *The Creativity of Action.* Translated by Jeremy Gaines and Paul Keast. Chicago: University of Chicago Press, 1997.

———. *The Genesis of Values.* Chicago: University of Chicago Press, 2000.

———. *The Sacredness of the Person: A New Genealogy of Human Rights.* Washington, DC: Georgetown University Press, 2013.

Kaldor, Mary, Sabine Selchow, and Henrietta L. Moore. *Global Civil Society 2012: Ten Years of Critical Reflection.* New York: Palgrave Macmillan, 2012.

Kanczula, Antonia. "Kony 2012 in Numbers." *The Guardian*, April 20 2012.

Keane, John. *Global Civil Society?* New York: Cambridge University Press, 2003.

Keck, Margaret E., and Kathryn Sikkink. *Activists beyond Borders: Advocacy Networks in International Politics.* Ithaca, NY: Cornell University Press, 1998.

Keen, Suzanne. *Empathy and the Novel.* New York: Oxford University Press, 2007.

Kelner, Shaul. *Tours That Bind: Diaspora, Pilgrimage, and Israeli Birthright Tourism.* New York: New York University Press, 2010.

Kiely, Richard. "A Chameleon with a Complex: Searching for Transformation in International Service-Learning." *Michigan Journal of Community Service Learning* 10, no. 2 (2004): 5–20.

———. "A Transformative Learning Model for Service-Learning: A Longitudinal Case Study." *Michigan Journal of Community Service Learning* 12, no. 1 (2005): 5–22.

Kinney, Nancy T. "Structure, Context, and Ideological Dissonance in Transnational Religious Networks." *Voluntas* 26, no. 1 (2015): 382–407.

Klandermans, Bert, and Dirk Oegema. "Potentials, Networks, Motivations, and Barriers: Steps towards Participation in Social Movements." *American Sociological Review* 52, no. 4 (1987): 519–31.

Kleinman, Arthur, and Joan Kleinman. "The Appeal of Experience; the Dismay of Images: Cultural Appropriations of Suffering in Our Times." *Daedalus* 125, no. 1 (1996): 1–23.

Koch, Bradley J., Joseph Galaskiewicz, and Alisha Pierson. "The Effect of Networks on Organizational Missions." *Nonprofit and Voluntary Sector Quarterly* 44, no. 3 (2015): 510–38.

Kolb, David A. *Experiential Learning: Experience as the Source of Learning and Development*. Upper Saddle River, NJ: Pearson Education, 2014 [1983].

Krause, Monika. *The Good Project: Humanitarian Relief NGOs and the Fragmentation of Reason*. Chicago: The University of Chicago Press, 2014.

Lamont, Michèle, and Virag Molnar. "The Study of Boundaries in the Social Sciences." *Annual Review of Sociology* 28 (2002): 167–95

Lamont, Michèle, and Ann Swidler. "Methodological Pluralism and the Possibilities and Limits of Interviewing." *Qualitative Sociology* 37, no. 2 (2014): 153–71.

Laquer, Thomas W. "Mourning, Pity, and the Work of Narrative in the Making of 'Humanity'." In *Humanitarianism and Suffering: The Mobilization of Empathy*, edited by Richard Ashby Wilson and Richard D. Brown, 31–57. New York: Cambridge University Press, 2009.

Lasker, Judith N. *Hoping to Help: The Promises and Pitfalls of Global Health Volunteering*. Ithaca, NY: Cornell University Press, 2016.

Laxer, Gordon, and Sandra Halperin. *Global Civil Society and Its Limits*. New York: Palgrave Macmillan, 2003.

Lee, Caroline W. *Do-It-Yourself Democracy: The Rise of the Public Engagement Industry*. New York: Oxford University Press, 2015.

Leschziner, Vanina, and Adam Isaiah Green. "Thinking about Food and Sex: Deliberate Cognition in the Routine Practices of a Field." *Sociological Theory* 31, no. 2 (June 1, 2013 2013): 116–44.

Levinas, Emmanuel. *Totality and Infinity: An Essay on Exteriority*. Pittsburgh, PA: Duquesne University Press, 1969 [1961].

Lichterman, Paul. "Beyond the Seesaw Model: Public Commitment in a Culture of Self-Fulfillment." *Sociological Theory* 13, no. 3 (November 1995): 275–300.

Elusive Togetherness: Church Groups Trying to Bridge America's Divisions. Princeton, NJ: Princeton University Press, 2005.

"Religion and the Construction of Civic Identity." *American Sociological Review* 73, no. 1 (February 2008): 83–104.

"Religion in Public Action: From Actors to Settings." *Sociological Theory* 30, no. 1 (2012): 15–36.

The Search for Political Community: American Activists Reinventing Community. New York: Cambridge University Press, 1996.

Lichterman, Paul, and Nina Eliasoph. "Civic Action." *American Journal of Sociology* 120, no. 3 (2014): 798–863.

Lichterman, Paul, and Rhys H. Williams. "Cultural Challenges for Mainline Protestant Political Progressives." In *Religion and Progressive Activism: New Stories about Faith and Politics*, edited by Ruth Braunstein, Todd N. Fuist, and Rhys H. Williams, 117–37. New York: New York University Press, 2017.

Lizardo, Omar. "Improving Cultural Analysis: Considering Personal Culture in Its Declarative and Nondeclarative Modes." *American Sociological Review* 82, no. 1 (2017): 88–115.

Lizardo, Omar, Robert Mowry, Brandon Sepulvado, Dustin S. Stoltz, Marshall A. Taylor, Justin Van Ness, and Michael Wood. "What Are Dual Process Models? Implications for Cultural Analysis in Sociology." *Sociological Theory* 34, no. 4 (2016): 287–310.

Lizardo, Omar, and Michael Strand. "Skills, Toolkits, Contexts and Institutions: Clarifying the Relationship between Different Approaches to Cognition in Cultural Sociology." *Poetics* 38, no. 2 (2010): 205–28.

Lofland, John. "Charting Degrees of Movement Culture: Tasks of the Cultural Cartographer." In *Social Movements and Culture*, edited by Hank Johnston and Bert Klandermans, 188–216. Minneapolis: University of Minnesota Press, 1995.

Lofland, John, and Norman Skonovd. "Conversion Motifs." *Journal for the Scientific Study of Religion* 20, no. 4 (1981): 373–85.

Lough, Benjamin J. "A Decade of International Volunteering from the United States, 2004 to 2014." Saint Louis, MO: Center for Social Development, Washington University, 2015.

Lough, Benjamin J., Margaret Sherrard Sherraden, Amanda Moore McBride, and Xiaoling Xiang. "The Impact of International Service on the Development of Volunteers' Intercultural Relations." *Social Science Research* 46, no. July (2014): 48–58.

Lowe, Brian M. *Emerging Moral Vocabularies: The Creation and Establishment of New Forms of Moral and Ethical Meanings.* Lanham, MD: Lexington Books, 2006.

Lydgate, Joanna Jacobbi. "Assembly-Line Justice: A Review of Operation Streamline." *California Law Review* 98, no. 2 (2010): 481–544.

MacCannell, Dean. *The Ethics of Sightseeing.* Berkeley: University of California Press, 2011.

—— *The Tourist: A New Theory of the Leisure Class.* New York: Schocken Books Inc, 1989.

Madsen, Richard. "The Archipelago of Faith: Religious Individualism and Faith Community in America Today." *American Journal of Sociology* 114, no. 5 (2009): 1263–301.

Manevska, Katerina, Peter Achterberg, and Dick Houtman. "Why There Is Less Supportive Evidence for Contact Theory Than They Say There Is: A Quantitative Cultural–Sociological Critique." *American Journal of Cultural Sociology* (2017): 1–26.

Mansbridge, Jane. "The Making of Oppositional Consciousness." In *Oppositional Consciousness: The Subjective Roots of Social Protest*, edited by Jane Mansbridge and Aldon Morris, 1–19. Chicago: University of Chicago Press, 2001.

Martin, John Levi. "Life's a Beach, but You're an Ant, and Other Unwelcome News for the Sociology of Culture." *Poetics* 38, no. 2 (2010): 228–43.

—— "What Is Field Theory?." *American Journal of Sociology* 109, no. 1 (2003): 1–49.

Martinez, Daniel E., Robin C. Reineke, Raquel Rubio-Goldsmith, and Bruce O. Parks. "Structural Violence and Migrant Deaths in Southern Arizona: Data from the Pima County Office of the Medical Examiner, 1990–2013." *Journal on Migration and Human Security* 2, no. 4 (2014): 257–86.

Martinez, Demetria. "Pressing for Justice along the Border; Borderlinks Activists Work with the Poor at the U.S.-Mexico Line." *National Catholic Reporter*, March 4 1994.

Marullo, Sam, and Bob Edwards. "Editors' Introduction: Service-Learning Pedagogy as Universities' Response to Troubled Times." *American Behavioral Scientist* 43, no. 5 (2000): 746–55.

Massey, Douglas S., Jorge Durand, and Nolan J. Malone. *Beyond Smoke and Mirrors: Mexican Immigration in an Era of Economic Integration*. New York: Russell Sage Publications, 2003.

McAdam, Doug. "The Biographical Consequences of Activism." *American Sociological Review* 54, no. 5 (1989): 744–60.

———. *Freedom Summer*. New York: Oxford University Press, 1988.

———. *Political Process and the Development of Black Insurgency, 1930–1970*. Chicago: University of Chicago Press, 1982.

———. "Recruitment to High-Risk Activism: The Case of Freedom Summer." *The American Journal of Sociology* 92, no. 1 (1986): 64–90.

McBride, Amanda Moore, Benjamin J. Lough, and Margaret Sherrard Sherraden. "International Service and the Perceived Impacts on Volunteers." *Nonprofit and Voluntary Sector Quarterly* 41, no. 6 (2012): 969–90.

McBride, Amanda Moore, Michael Sherraden, Carlos Benítez, and Elizabeth Johnson. "Civic Service Worldwide: Defining a Field, Building a Knowledge Base." *Nonprofit and Voluntary Sector Quarterly* 33, no. 4 Supplemental (December 1, 2004): 8S–21S.

McCarthy, John D. and Mayer N. Zald. "Resource Mobilization and Social Movements: A Partial Theory." *The American Journal of Sociology* 82, no. 6 (1977): 1212–41.

McCleary, Rachel M., and Robert J. Barro. "Private Voluntary Organizations Engaged in International Assistance, 1939–2004." *Nonprofit and Voluntary Sector Quarterly* 37, no. 3 (2008): 512–36.

McFarland, Daniel A., and Reuben J. Thomas. "Bowling Young: How Youth Voluntary Associations Influence Adult Political Participation." *American Sociological Review* 71, no. 3 (2006): 401–25.

McRoberts, Omar M. "Beyond *Mysterium Tremendum*: Thoughts toward an Aesthetic Study of Religious Experience." *The Annals of the American Academy of Political and Social Science* 595, no. 1 (2004): 190–203.

Meisel, Joshua S. "The Ethics of Observing: Confronting the Harm of Experiential Learning." *Teaching Sociology* 36, no. 3 (2008): 196–210.

Menjivar, Cecilia. "Serving Christ in the Borderlands: Faith Workers Respond to Border Violence." Chap. 8 In *Religion and Social Justice for Immigrants*, edited by Pierrette Hondagneu-Sotelo, 104–22. New Brunswick, NJ: Rutgers University Press, 2007.

Meyer, David S., and Suzanne Staggenborg. "Movements, Countermovements, and the Structure of Political Opportunity." *The American Journal of Sociology* 101, no. 6 (1996): 1628–60.

Mezirow, Jack. "Understanding Transformation Theory." *Adult Education Quarterly* 44, no. 4 (1994): 222–32.

Mills, C. Wright. *The Sociological Imagination*. New York: Oxford University Press, 2000 [1959].

Minkoff, Debra C. "The Emergence of Hybrid Organizational Forms: Combining Identity-Based Service Provision and Political Action." *Nonprofit and Voluntary Sector Quarterly* 31, no. 3 (September 1, 2002 2002): 377–401.

Mische, Ann. *Partisan Publics: Communication and Contention across Brazilian Youth Activist Networks*. Princeton, NJ: Princeton University Press, 2007.

Morris, Aldon D. *Origins of the Civil Rights Movement: Black Communities Organizing for Change*. New York: The Free Press, 1986.

Morris, Aldon, and Naomi Braine. "Social Movements and Oppositional Consciousness." In *Oppositional Consciousness: The Subjective Roots of Social Protest*, edited by Jane Mansbridge and Aldon Morris, 20–37. Chicago: University of Chicago Press, 2001.

Mostafanezhad, Mary. *Volunteer Tourism: Popular Humanitarianism in Neoliberal Times*. New York: Routledge, 2016.

Munson, Ziad W. *The Making of Pro-Life Activists: How Social Movement Mobilization Works*. Chicago: University of Chicago Press, 2009.

Mutz, Diana C. *Hearing the Other Side: Deliberative versus Participatory Democracy*. New York: Cambridge University Press, 2006.

Nepstad, Sharon Erickson. *Convictions of the Soul: Religion, Culture, and Agency in the Central America Solidarity Movement*. New York: Oxford University Press, 2004.

———. "Creating Transnational Solidarity: The Use of Narrative in the U.S.-Central America Peace Movement." *Mobilization* 6, no. 1 (2001): 21–36.

———. "Oppositional Consciousness among the Privileged: Remaking Religion in the Central America Solidarity Movement." *Critical Sociology* 33, no. 4 (2007): 661–88.

———. "The Process of Cognitive Liberation: Cultural Synapses, Links, and Frame Contradictions in the U.S.-Central America Peace Movement." *Sociological Inquiry* 67, no. 4 (1997): 470–87.

Nepstad, Sharon Erickson, and Christian Smith. "Rethinking Recruitment to High-Risk/Cost Activism: The Case of Nicaragua Exchange." *Mobilization: An International Quarterly* 41, no. 1 (1999): 25–40.

———. "The Social Structure of Moral Outrage in Recruitment to the U.S. Central America Peace Movement." In *Passionate Politics: Emotions and Social Movements*, edited by Jeff Goodwin, James M. Jasper, and Francesca Polletta, 158–74. Chicago: The University of Chicago Press 2001.

Nevins, Joseph. *Operation Gatekeeper and Beyond: The War on "Illegals" and the Remaking of the U.S.-Mexico Boundary*. New York: Routledge, 2010.

Noy, Chaim. "This Trip Really Changed Me: Backpackers' Narratives of Self-Change." *Annals of Tourism Research* 31, no. 1 (2004): 78–102.

Offutt, Stephen. *New Centers of Global Evangelicalism in Latin America and Africa*. New York: Cambridge University Press, 2015.

———. "The Role of Short-Term Mission Teams in the New Centers of Global Christianity." *Journal for the Scientific Study of Religion* 50, no. 4 (2011): 796–811.

Oliver, Pamela E., and Hank Johnston. "What a Good Idea! Ideologies and Frames in Social Movement Research." *Mobilization* 5, no. 1 (2000): 37–54.

Oxfam America. "Our Signature Event: The Oxfam America Hunger Banquet." actfast.oxfamamerica.org/.

Paluck, Elizabeth Levy, Seth Green, and Donald P. Green. "The Contact Hypothesis Reevaluated." *Social Science Research Network (SSRN)* (2017).

Passy, Florence. "Political Altruism and the Solidarity Movement." In *Political Altruism? Solidarity Movements in International Perspective*, edited by Marco Giugni and Florence Passy, 3–25. New York: Rowman & Littlefield, Inc., 2001.

Perin, Jodi Rae. "Educational Travel for Societal Change: An Exploration of Popular Education along the Mexico-U.S. Border." MA Thesis, University of Arizona, Tucson (2003).

Perrin, Andrew J. *Citizen Speak: The Democratic Imagination in American Life.* Chicago: University of Chicago Press, 2006.

Perla Jr., Héctor. "Si Nicaragua Venció, El Salvador Vencerá: Central American Agency in the Creation of the US–Central American Peace and Solidarity Movement." *Latin American Research Review* 43, no. 2 (2008): 136–58.

Pettigrew, Thomas F., and Linda R. Tropp. "Does Intergroup Contact Reduce Prejudice? Recent Meta-Analytic Findings." In *Reducing Prejudice and Discrimination*, edited by Stuart Oskamp, 93–114. Mahwah, NJ: Lawrence Erlbaum Associates, 2000.

Piacitelli, Jill, Molly Barwick, Elizabeth Doerr, Melody Porter, and Shoshanna Sumka. "Alternative Break Programs: From Isolated Enthusiasm to Best Practices: The Haiti Compact." *Journal of Higher Education Outreach and Engagement* 17, no. 2 (2013): 24.

Piekielek, Jessica. "Visiting Views of the U.S.-Mexico Border: Reflections of Participants in Experiential Travel Seminars." MA Thesis, University of Arizona, Tucson (2003).

Pogorelc, Anthony J. "Movement to Movement Transmission and the Role of Place: The Relationship between Catholic Action and Call to Action." *Sociology of Religion* 72, no. 1 (2011): 415–34.

Polletta, Francesca. "Culture in and Outside Institutions." *Research in Social Movements, Conflicts and Change* 25 (2004): 161–83.

———. *Freedom Is an Endless Meeting: Democracy in American Social Movements.* Chicago: University of Chicago Press, 2002.

———. "How Participatory Democracy Became White: Culture and Organizational Choice." *Mobilization: An International Quarterly* 10, no. 2 (June 2005): 271–88.

———. *It Was Like a Fever: Storytelling in Protest and Politics.* Chicago: The University of Chicago Press, 2006.

Polletta, Francesca, and Pang Ching Bobby Chen. "Narrative and Social Movements." In *The Oxford Handbook of Cultural Sociology*, edited by Jeffrey Alexander, Ronald N. Jacobs, and Philip Smith, 487–506. New York: Oxford University press, 2012.

Polletta, Francesca, Pang Ching Bobby Chen, Beth Gharrity Gardner, and Alice Motes. "The Sociology of Storytelling." *Annual Review of Sociology* 37 (2011): 109–30.

Preston, Stephanie D., and Frans B.M. De Waal. "Empathy: Its Ultimate and Proximate Bases." *Behavioral and Brain Sciences* 25, no. 1 (2002): 1–20.

Priest, Robert J. *Effective Engagement in Short-Term Missions: Doing It Right!* Pasadena, CA: William Carey Library Publishers, 2008.

Priest, Robert J., Terry Dischinger, Steve Rasmussen, and C.M. Brown. "Researching the Short-Term Mission Movement." *Missiology: An International Review* 34, no. 4 (2006): 431–51.

Priest, Robert J., and Joseph Paul Priest. "'They See Everything, and Understand Nothing' Short-Term Mission and Service Learning." *Missiology: An International Review* 36, no. 1 (2008): 53–73.

Probasco, LiErin. "Giving Time, Not Money: Long-Term Impacts of Short-Term Mission Trips." *Missiology: An International Review* 41, no. 2 (April 1, 2013 2013): 202–24.

——— "Prayer, Patronage, and Personal Agency in Nicaraguan Accounts of Receiving International Aid." *Journal for the Scientific Study of Religion* 55, no. 2 (2016): 233–49.

Putnam, Robert D. *Bowling Alone: The Collapse and Revival of American Community*. New York: Simon & Schuster, 2001.

Reed, Isaac, and Jeffrey Alexander. *Culture, Society, and Democracy: The Interpretive Approach*. Boulder, CO: Paradigm Publishers, 2007.

Regan, Margaret. *The Death of Josseline: Immigration Stories from the Arizona Borderlands*. Boston: Beacon Press, 2010.

Reger, Jo. "Organizational 'Emotion Work' through Consciousness-Raising: An Analysis of a Feminist Organization." *Qualitative Sociology* 27, no. 2 (2004): 205–22.

Reynolds, Amy. *Free Trade and Faithful Globalization: Saving the Market*. New York: Cambridge University Press, 2014.

Rifkin, Jeremy. *The Empathic Civilization: The Race to Global Consciousness in a World in Crisis*. New York: Penguin, 2009.

Sahlins, Marshall. *Islands of History*. Chicago: University of Chicago Press, 1985.

Said, Edward W. *Orientalism*. Pantheon Books, 1978.

Schnable, Allison. "New American Relief and Development Organizations: Voluntarizing Global Aid." *Social Problems* 62, no. 2 (2015): 309–29.

——— "What Religion Affords Grassroots NGOs: Frames, Networks, Modes of Action." *Journal for the Scientific Study of Religion* 55, no. 2 (2016): 216–32.

Schudson, Michael. *The Good Citizen: A History of American Civic Life*. New York: Free Press, 1998.

Schwittay, Anke, and Kate Boocock. "Experiential and Empathetic Engagements with Global Poverty: 'Live Below the Line So That Others Can Rise above It'." *Third World Quarterly* 36, no. 2 (2015): 291–305.

Sewell, William H. "The Concept(s) of Culture." In *Beyond the Cultural Turn*, edited by Victoria E. Bonnell and Lynn Hunt, 35–71. Berkeley: University of California Press, 1999.

Shapira, Harel. *Waiting for Jose: The Minuteman's Pursuit of America*. Princeton, NJ: Princeton University Press, 2013.

Waiting for José: The Minutemen's Pursuit of America. Princeton, NJ: Princeton University Press, 2017.

Sherkat, Darren E., and T. Jean Blocker. "Explaining the Political and Personal Consequences of Protest." *Social Forces* 75, no. 3 (1997): 1049–76.

Sherraden, Margaret Sherrard, John Stringham, Simona Costanzo Sow, and Amanda Moore McBride. "The Forms and Structure of International Voluntary Service." *Voluntas: International Journal of Voluntary and Nonprofit Organizations* 17, no. 2 (2006): 156–73.

Simmel, Georg. *On Individuality and Social Forms*. Chicago: University of Chicago Press, 1971.

"The Alpine Journey." *Theory, Culture & Society* 8 (1991): 95–8.

"The Number of Members as Determining the Sociological Form of the Group." *American Journal of Sociology* 8, no. 2 (1902): 158–96.

"The Stranger." In *The Sociology of Georg Simmel*, edited by Kurt H. Wolff, 402–8. New York: The Free Press, 1950.

Singh, Vikash. *Uprising of the Fools: Pilgrimage as Moral Protest in Contemporary India*. Stanford, CA: Stanford University Press, 2017.

Smelser, Neil J. *The Odyssey Experience: Physical, Social, Psychological, and Spiritual Journeys*. Berkeley: University of California Press, 2009.

Smilde, David. *Reason to Believe: Cultural Agency in Latin American Evangelism*. Berkeley: University of California Press, 2007.

Smith, Adam. *The Theory of Moral Sentiments*. New York: Cambridge University Press, 2002 [1759].

Smith, Christian. *The Emergence of Liberation Theology: Radical Religion and Social Movement Theory*. Chicago: University of Chicago Press, 1991.

Resisting Reagan: The U.S. Central America Peace Movement. Chicago: University of Chicago, 1996.

Smith, Jackie. "Bridging Global Divides? Strategic Framing and Solidarity in Transnational Social Movement Organizations." *International Sociology* 17, no. 4 (2002): 505–28.

"Transnational Processes and Movements." In *The Blackwell Companion to Social Movements*, edited by David A. Snow, Sarah A. Soule, and Hanspeter Kriesi, 311–36. Malden, MA: Blackwell Publishing Ltd., 2004.

Smith, Peter. "International Volunteer Tourism as (De) Commodified Moral Consumption." In *Moral Encounters in Tourism*, 45–59. New York, Routledge, 2016.

Smith, Steven Rathgeb. "Hybridity and Nonprofit Organizations: The Research Agenda." *American Behavioral Scientist* 58, no. 11 (October 1, 2014 2014): 1494–508.

Smith, Thomas E., and Clifford E. Knapp. *Sourcebook of Experiential Education: Key Thinkers and Their Contributions*. New York: Routledge, 2011.

Snee, Helene. "Framing the Other: Cosmopolitanism and the Representation of Difference in Overseas Gap Year Narratives." *The British Journal of Sociology* 64, no. 1 (2013): 142–62.

Snow, David A., E. Burke Rochford, Jr., Steven K. Worden, and Robert D. Benford. "Frame Alignment Processes, Micromobilization, and Movement Participation." *American Sociological Review* 51, no. 4 (1986): 464–81.

Snow, David A., Louis A. Zurcher, Jr., and Ekland-Olson Sheldon. "Social Networks and Social Movements: A Microstructural Approach to Differential Recruitment." *American Sociological Review* 45, no. 5 (1980): 787–801.

Soule, Sarah A. "Situational Effects on Political Altruism: The Student Divestment Movement in the United States." In *Political Altruism? Solidarity Movements in International Perspective*, edited by Marco Giugni and Florence Passy, 161–76. New York: Rowman & Littlefield Publishers Inc., 2001.

"The Student Divestment Movement in the United States and Tactical Diffusion: The Shantytown Protest." *Social Forces* 75 (1997): 855–82.

Soule, Sarah A., and Brayden G. King. "Competition and Resource Partitioning in Three Social Movement Industries." *American Journal of Sociology* 113, no. 6 (2008): 1568–610.

Stamatov, Peter. "Activist Religion, Empire, and the Emergence of Modern Long-Distance Advocacy Networks." *American Sociological Review* 75, no. 4 (2010): 607–28.

The Origins of Global Humanitarianism: Religion, Empires, and Advocacy. New York: Cambridge University Press, 2013.

Stein, Karen. "Time Off: The Social Experience of Time on Vacation." *Qualitative Sociology* 35, no. 3 (2012): 335–53.

Stone, Matthew J, and James F. Petrick. "The Educational Benefits of Travel Experiences: A Literature Review." *Journal of Travel Research* 52, no. 6 (2013): 731–44.

Summers-Effler, Erika. *Laughing Saints and Righteous Heroes: Emotional Rhythms in Social Movement Groups.* Chicago: University of Chicago Press, 2010.

"The Micro Potential for Social Change: Emotion, Consciousness, and Social Movement Formation." *Sociological Theory* 20, no. 1 (2002): 41–60.

Swidler, Ann. "Cultural Power and Social Movements." In *Social Movements and Culture*, edited by Hank Johnston and Bert Klandermans. Social Movements, Protest, and Contention, 25–40. Minneapolis: University of Minnesota Press, 1995.

"Culture in Action: Symbols and Strategies." *American Sociological Review* 51, no. 2 (1986): 273–86.

Talk of Love: How Culture Matters. Chicago: University of Chicago Press, 2001.

Swidler, Ann, and Susan Cotts Watkins. *A Fraught Embrace: The Romance and Reality of AIDS Altruism in Africa.* Princeton, NJ: Princeton University Press, 2017.

Sykes, Kevin J. "Short-Term Medical Service Trips: A Systematic Review of the Evidence." *American Journal of Public Health* 104, no. 7 (2014/07/01 2014): e38–e48.

Tavory, Iddo, and Daniel Winchester. "Experiential Careers: The Routinization and De-Routinization of Religious Life." *Theory & Society* 41, no. 4 (2012): 351–73.

Taylor, Verta. "Social Movement Continuity: The Women's Movement in Abeyance." *American Sociological Review* 54, no. 5 (1989): 761–75.

Taylor, Verta, and Lisa Leitz. "From Infanticide to Activism: Emotions and Identity in Self-Help Movements." In *Social Movements and the Transformation of American Health Care*, edited by Jane C. Banaszak-Holl, Sandra R. Levitsky, and Mayer N. Zald, 266–83. New York: Oxford University Press, 2010.

Taylor, Verta, and Nancy E. Whittier. "Collective Identity in Social Movement Communities: Lesbian Feminist Mobilization." In *Frontiers in Social Movement Theory*, edited by Aldon D. Morris and Carol M. Mueller, 104–29. New Haven, CT: Yale University Press, 1992.

Thomas, Emma F., Craig McGarty, and Kenneth I. Mavor. "Transforming 'Apathy into Movement': The Role of Prosocial Emotions in Motivating Action for Social Change." *Personality and Social Psychology Review* 13, no. 4 (2009): 310–33.

Thornton, Patricia H, William Ocasio, and Michael Lounsbury. *The Institutional Logics Perspective: A New Approach to Culture, Structure, and Process.* New York: Oxford University Press, 2012.

Tilly, Charles. *From Mobilization to Revolution.* Reading, MA: Addison Wesley, 1978.

Trinitapoli, Jenny, and Stephen Vaisey. "The Transformative Role of Religious Experience: The Case of Short-Term Missions." *Social Forces* 88, no. 1 (2009): 121–46.

Tufekci, Zeynep. ""Not This One": Social Movements, the Attention Economy, and Microcelebrity Networked Activism." *American Behavioral Scientist* 57, no. 7 (2013): 848–70.

Turner, Stephen. "The Strength of Weak Empathy." *Science in Context* 25, no. 3 (2012): 383–99.

Turner, Victor. *The Forest of Symbols: Aspects of Ndembu Ritual.* Ithaca, NY: Cornell University Press, 1967.

   The Ritual Process: Structure and Anti-Structure. Piscataway, NJ: Aldine Transaction, 1995.

Turner, Victor, and Edith Turner. *Image and Pilgrimage in Christian Culture: Anthropological Perspectives.* New York: Columbia University Press, 1978.

Ufford-Chase, Rick. "Rick Ufford-Chase: Elder, Mission Co-Worker, Peacemaker." www.rickuffordchase.com/index.html.

Urry, John, and Jonas Larsen. *The Tourist Gaze 3.0.* 3rd edn. Thousand Oaks, CA: Sage Publications, Ltd., 2011.

Vaisey, Stephen. "Motivation and Justification: A Dual-Process Model of Culture in Action." *American Journal of Sociology* 114, no. 6 (2009): 1675–715.

Vannini, Phillip, and Alexis Franzese. "The Authenticity of Self: Conceptualization, Personal Experience, and Practice." *Sociology Compass* 2, no. 5 (2008): 1621–37.

Vásquez, Manuel A. "Structural Obstacles to Grassroots Pastoral Practice: The Case of a Base Community in Urban Brazil*." *Sociology of Religion* 58, no. 1 (1997): 53–68.

Ver Beek, Kurt Alan. "Lessing from the Sapling: Review of Quantitative Research on Short-Term Missions." In *Effective Engagement in Short-Term Missions: Doing It Right!*, edited by Robert J. Priest, 474–502. Pasadena, CA: William Carey Library Publishers, 2008.

Vertovec, Steven, and Robin Cohen. "Introduction: Conceiving Cosmopolitanism." In *Conceiving Cosmopolitanism: Theory, Context, and Practice*, edited by Steven Vertovec and Robin Cohen. New York: Oxford University Press, 2002.

Vetlesen, Arne Johan. *Perception, Empathy, and Judgement: An Inquiry into the Preconditions of Moral Performance*. University Park, PA: The Pennsylvania State University Press, 1994.

Viterna, Jocelyn S. "Pulled, Pushed, and Persuaded: Explaining Women's Mobilization into the Salvadoran Guerrilla Army." *American Journal of Sociology* 112, no. 1 (07 2006): 1–45.

Vrasti, Wanda. *Volunteer Tourism in the Global South: Giving Back in Neoliberal Times*. New York: Routledge, 2012.

Wagner-Pacifici, Robin. "Pity and a Politics of the Present." *Theory & Event* 5, no. 4 (2001).

Watkins, Susan Cotts, Ann Swidler, and Thomas Hannan. "Outsourcing Social Transformation: Development NGOs as Organizations." *Annual Review of Sociology* 38, no. 1 (2012): 285–315.

Wearing, Stephen. *Volunteer Tourism: Experiences that Make a Difference*. New York: CABI Publishing, 2001.

Wilkinson, Iain. *Suffering: A Sociological Introduction*. Maldin, MA: Polity Press, 2005.

Wilkinson, Iain, and Arthur Kleinman. *A Passion for Society: How We Think about Human Suffering*. Berkeley: University of California Press, 2016.

Williams, Rhys H. "What Progressive Efforts Tell Us about Faith and Politics." In *Religion and Progressive Activism: New Stories about Faith and Politics*, edited by Ruth Braunstein, Todd N. Fuist, and Rhys H. Williams, 348–64. New York: New York University Press, 2017.

Williams, Rhys H. "The Cultural Contexts of Collective Action: Constraints, Opportunities, and the Symbolic Life of Social Movements." Chap. Five In *The Blackwell Companion to Social Movements*, edited by David A. Snow, Sarah A. Soule, and Hanspeter Kriesi, 91–115. Malden, MA: Blackwell Publishing Ltd., 2004.

"Religion and Political Resource: Culture or Ideology?" *Journal for the Scientific Study of Religion* 35, no. 4 (1996): 368–78.

Williams, Rhys H., and Susan M. Alexander. "Religious Rhetoric in American Populism: Civil Religion as Movement Ideology." *Journal for the Scientific Study of Religion* 33, no. 1 (1994): 1–15.

Willis, Paul. *Learning to Labor: How Working Class Kids Get Working Class Jobs*. New York: Columbia University Press, 1977.

Wilson, Erin K. "From Apathy to Action: Promoting Active Citizenship and Global Responsibility amongst Populations in the Global North." *Global Society* 24, no. 2 (2010): 275–96.

Winchester, Daniel. "A Hunger for God: Embodied Metaphor as Cultural Cognition in Action." *Social Forces* 95, no. 2 (2016): 585–606.

Wise, Timothy. "Agricultural Dumping under NAFTA: Estimating the Costs of U.S. Agricultural Policies to Mexican Producers." In *Mexican Rural Development Report*. Washington, DC: Woodrow Wilson International Center for Scholars, 2010.

Wolfe, Alan. "What Is Altruism?" In *Private Action and the Public Good*, Edited by Walter W. Powell and Elisabeth S. Clemens. New Haven, CT: Yale University Press, 1998.

Wood, Richard L. *Faith in Action: Religion, Race, and Democratic Organizing in America*. Chicago: University of Chicago Press, 2002.

Wuthnow, Robert. *Acts of Compassion: Caring for Others and Helping Ourselves*. Princeton, NJ: Princeton University Press, 1991.

"Beyond Quiet Influence?: Possibilities for the Protestant Mainline." In *The Quiet Hand of God: Faith-Based Activism and the Public Role of Mainline Protestantism*, edited by Robert Wuthnow and John H. Evans, 381–404. Berkeley: University of California Press, 2002.

Boundless Faith: The Global Outreach of American Churches. Berkeley: University of California Press, 2009.

Communities of Discourse: Ideology and Social Structure in the Reformation, the Enlightenment, and European Socialism. Cambridge, MA: Harvard University Press, 1989.

Sharing the Journey: Support Groups and America's New Quest for Community. New York: Free Press, 1994.

"Taking Talk Seriously: Religious Discourse as Social Practice." *Journal for the Scientific Study of Religion* 50, no. 1 (2011): 1–21.

Young, Michael. "A Revolution of the Soul: Transformative Experiences and Immediate Abolition." In *Passionate Politics: Emotions and Social Movements*, edited by Jeff Goodwin, James M. Jasper, and Francesca Polletta, 99–114. Chicago: The University of Chicago Press, 2001.

Young, Michael P. *Bearing Witness against Sin: The Evangelical Birth of the American Social Movement*. Chicago: The University of Chicago Press, 2006.

Young, Michael P., and Stephen M. Cherry. "The Secularization of Confessional Protests: The Role of Religious Processes of Rationalization and Differentiation." *Journal for the Scientific Study of Religion* 44, no. 4 (2005): 373–95.

Yukich, Grace. "Constructing the Model Immigrant: Movement Strategy and Immigrant Deservingness in the New Sanctuary Movement." *Social Problems* 60, no. 3 (2013): 302–20.

One Family under God: Immigration Politics and Progressive Religion in America. New York: Oxford University Press, 2013.

Zald, Mayer N. "Theological Crucibles: Social Movements in and of Religion." *Review of Religious Research* 23, no. 4 (1982): 317–36.

Zelizer, Viviana A. "The Social Meaning of Money: 'Special Monies'." *American Journal of Sociology* 95, no. 2 (1989): 342–77.

Index

Continued from page ii..,

Ahmet T. Kuru, *Secularism and State Policies toward Religion: The United States, France, and Turkey*

Andrew R. Lewis, *The Rights Turn in Conservative Christian Politics: How Abortion Transformed the Culture Wars*

Damon Maryl, *Secular Conversions: Political Institutions and Religious Education in the United States and Australia, 1800–2000*

Jeremy Menchik, *Islam and Democracy in Indonesia: Tolerance without Liberalism*

Pippa Norris and Ronald Inglehart, *Sacred and Secular: Religion and Politics Worldwide*

Amy Reynolds, *Free Trade and Faithful Globalization: Saving the Market*

Sadia Saeed, *Politics of Desecularization: Law and the Minority Question in Pakistan*

David T. Smith, *Religious Persecution and Political Order in the United States*

Peter Stamatov, *The Origins of Global Humanitarianism: Religion, Empires, and Advocacy*